THE OFFICIAL  SPORT GUIDE

GRAND PRIX 2006》》

THIS IS A CARLTON BOOK

This edition published in 2006 by
Carlton Books Limited
20 Mortimer Street
London W1T 3JW

10 9 8 7 6 5 4 3 2 1

A CIP catalogue record for this book is available
from the British Library.

The publisher has taken reasonable steps to
check the accuracy of the facts contained herein
at the time of going to press but can take no
responsibility for any errors.

ISBN 13: 978-1-84442-341-5
ISBN 10: 1-84442-341-7

Editor: Nigel Matheson
Art Direction: Darren Jordan
Designer: Ben Ruocco
Production: Lisa French
Picture Research: Tom Wright

Printed in the UK

In 2005, Schumacher and Ferrari were put in the shade by Alonso and Renault. Can they fight back

THE OFFICIAL  GUIDE

GRAND PRIX 2006》》

BRUCE JONES

CARLTON
BOOKS

CONTENTS

Fernando Alonso propelled Renault to new heights last year and will be looking for a repeat

Bridgestone will go all out to recapture lost ground, but for 2007 they'll have a monopoly

ANALYSIS OF THE 2006 SEASON

Last year was one of the best in Formula One history, not only because Michael Schumacher's domination was broken and more drivers grabbed the opportunity to win races, but also because the calibre of racing improved. The rules have changed again for 2006, so will Fernando Alonso be able to triumph once more?

Formula One could be on the cusp of a golden age, although Michael Schumacher fans will say that occurred during 2000–04. Indeed it was undoubtedly a time in which a master craftsman weaved his magic but, in terms of entertainment, it didn't always make for compulsive viewing. This year could be a belter.

The rule changes last year that banned tyre changes in races and specified that engines should last for two grands prix weren't universally popular, but the quality of racing, often with faster drivers having to make up places from mid-grid or worse, was spectacular. There was no finer example than the Japanese Grand Prix, when Kimi Raikkonen and Fernando Alonso tigered their way through the field to the front.

With five different drivers winning races, the season matched 2004, fortunately without the domination of one driver, but it was the fact that 13 drivers visited the podium – up four on 2004

– that made it the best World Championship for a very long time and we can only hope that this year will build on that.

The sport's governing body, the FIA, conducted a massive survey among Formula One fans last summer and the overwhelming repsonse from the 93,018 respondents was that fans wanted to see more overtaking. That came as no surprise, but the sport's governing body clearly listened and is attempting to push through rule changes for 2007 with the sole intention of cleaning up the airflow over cars. This is so that the car behind isn't stuck in turbulent air and can thus get close enough to attempt a passing move. Slick tyres are sure to be reintroduced, much to the delight of the drivers, and the tyre war will be brought to a close with the implementation of a single tyre supplier. A whole raft of further changes are due for 2008.

For 2006, though, the main change is to qualifying, with the

format altered to make the excitement build right the way to the end of the one-hour session at Saturday lunchtime. Those one-at-a-time sessions, in which the cars ran in the order of their finishing position of the previous race, have been scratched. This will be hugely popular among drivers who found that the misfortune of being the first to retire from the previous round turned into a double punishment as they had to go out to qualify when the track was at its worst.

For 2006, everyone will go out to qualify from the very start, with an unlimited number of laps. Their aim is to ensure that they are not among the slowest five cars at the quarter-hour mark, for these will be eliminated and will fill the final five positions on the starting grid. This guarantees track action from everybody and will keep the TV directors on their toes. After a five-minute break, the same format will apply to the next quarter of an hour, with a further five cars being eliminated.

So, half the field will be out and the remaining half of the field will have a further five minutes for set-up adjustments before heading out for a 20-minute burst of activity to decide the top ten of the grid. It will be just as it was at the tail-end of the 1990s when the final few minutes of the hour were a blur, with one driver claiming pole, only to be demoted and perhaps claiming it back next time around. Traffic might be a problem, but this will all be part of the mix. It should make for a fascinating spectacle.

The other main change for this season is the introduction of V8 engines in place of last year's V10s, with a reduction in capacity to 2400cc. Teams who can't afford a V8 will be allowed to keep their V10s, to be run at reduced revs (see feature on page 52–53).

There had been moves by the FIA to expand the World Championship by one race to 20 grands prix, but teams baulked at this, saying that it would lead to the burn-out of their personnel. As a result, the calendar will stick with the same ingredients, albeit juggled so that the action kicks off in Bahrain rather than Australia. If there is one race among these that must run smoothly, though, it's the United States GP, as Formula One cannot afford another farce like last year's, which rudely slammed the door in the face of American fans.

This season looks set to be a cracker. You can be sure that Michael Schumacher will be giving his all to fight back against the new stars, Fernando Alonso will be out to make it two in a row, Kimi Raikkonen will be flying in his attempt to become champion, while Juan Pablo Montoya, Jenson Button, Rubens Barrichello and perhaps a new face or two will be looking to put their names up in lights. Toyota may even score its first win. It's great to have so many variables going into a new season. Enjoy it.

RENAULT

Renault made the early running last year by winning the first four grands prix and Fernando Alonso broke clear of the pack to become the French manufacturer's first world champion. Will this year see a repeat of this feat?

Fisichella will be giving his all to move out from Alonso's shadow

Renault enjoyed their double success last year. To gauge just how much they enjoyed it, don't just look at the faces of drivers Fernando Alonso and Giancarlo Fisichella or managing director Falvio Briatore as they celebrated on the podium. Look at the mechanics and engineers as they saluted the winning car and driver at the end of the race. They acted like a happy family, something that isn't always the case in Formula One.

Indeed, few things rankle with the folk at Renault, but one thing that is sure to upset them is to suggest that they won the 2005 drivers' and constructors' titles through reliability rather than speed. The reason that many stuck to this line is that McLaren, and Kimi Raikkonen in particular, were the pace-setters through the summer months and the early autumn.

That particular argument falls down, however, as Renault were their equal for the final two grands prix in Japan and China, emphasizing how Renault developed their car right to the very end and reaped the dividends. That, of course, coupled with some appalling luck for McLaren, particularly with a series of engine failures.

It's safe to say that Renault had a dream start with those four straight wins, one for Giancarlo Fisichella and then three for Alonso. It was revealed

THE GOLDEN YEAR: 1983

Renault were radical from the moment they hit Formula One midway through 1977, as they introduced turbocharged engines. By 1979, they had developed the reliability to match their speed and Jean-Pierre Jabouille gave the French manufacturer their maiden win. However, it was in 1983 that they took their first serious tilt at either the drivers' or constructors' titles. Their Michel Tetu-designed RE30C chassis was sufficiently sorted to harness the towering surge of horsepower from their turbocharged V6 and Alain Prost was more than capable of handling both. He started winning at the third round, fittingly in France, then again in Belgium, Britain and Austria. Having backed up these successes with a string of podium places, the French ace looked set for his first title, going to the final round in South Africa with a two-point lead over Brabham's Nelson Piquet. But there it all went wrong, as his turbo failed and Piquet claimed the crown. Renault quit at the end of 1985 and it would be 22 years until this wrong was put right by Fernando Alonso.

after the third round in Bahrain that the engine had been run at less than full power to ensure reliability, and yet it had still won. This would undoubtedly have been seen as ominous by many as chairman Patrick Faure had said in the lead-up to the opening race that the team would be pushing not just for race wins, but for the title. With some 940bhp at their disposal, the second healthiest figure of all the teams – behind only Honda – Renault had clearly made great gains to haul in and pass rivals such as BMW, Ferrari and Toyota.

To maintain their lead in the points table, executive director of engineering Pat Symonds, in particular, helped the drivers extract the maximum from the Tim Densham-designed R25 as the season advanced and the car was a step forward from the R24 that proved so tricky to drive the year before.

If there was a dark spot in Renault's season, it was when both drivers retired while leading in Canada. That coupled with the fact that neither of the blue and yellow cars would win again until the final round in China. Fisichella had found the Japanese GP a few miles too short, as he was passed by Raikkonen on the final lap. However, the decision to disregard the new V8 engine regulations for 2006 and to keep developing its engine right to the end of the season to ensure that they kept McLaren at bay paid dividends. They offered extra revs both for qualifying (allegedly 19,200rpm) and the race and it paid off handsomely, leaving McLaren unable to pass them in China.

Not only was there unbridled joy at the winning of first the drivers' crown and then the constructors' title, but also a modicum of relief as company CEO Carlos Ghosn is famously not a man fond of racing as he reckons that "it's an investment if you're winning and an expense if you're not." This success might just encourage him to keep paying the team's bills beyond the end of its contract which lasts until the end of 2007.

Renault fans should be much encouraged, as Symonds says that he has high hopes for 2006, as he reckons that Renault always adapt well to regulation changes. Perhaps the introduction of the smaller and lighter 2.4-litre V8 engine offers just the range of options that he feels will extract the best from the design team. Renault are confident that their V8 will be reliable, so that's a good start. Yet, like their rivals, they have little idea what the best power output figures might be, save for the fact that they'll probably be as much as 200bhp down on 2005's 3.0-litre V10s.

Renault will be strong again, but will McLaren be stronger?

FOR THE RECORD

Country of origin:	England
Team base:	Enstone, England
Telephone:	(44) 01608 678000
Website:	www.renaultf1.com
Active in Formula One:	From 1977-85 and from 2002
Grands Prix contested:	193*
Wins:	25
Pole positions:	43
Fastest laps:	22

* NOTE THAT THESE FIGURES DO NOT INCLUDE THE 238 RACES THE TEAM RAN AS BENETTON

2005 DRIVERS & RESULTS

Driver	Nationality	Races	Wins	Pts	Pos
Fernando Alonso	Spanish	19	7	133	1st
Giancarlo Fisichella	Italian	19	1	58	5th

THE TEAM

Chairman:	Patrick Faure
Managing director:	Flavio Briatore
Technical director:	Bob Bell
Engineering director:	Pat Symonds
Engine director:	Denis Chevrier
Chief designer:	Tim Densham
Sporting manager:	Steve Nielsen
Test driver:	Heikki Kovalainen
Chassis:	Renault R26
Engine:	Renault V8
Tyres:	Michelin

Alain Prost celebrates winning the 1883 French GP for Renault

FERNANDO ALONSO

For Fernando, 2003 marked him out as a star, 2004 toughened him up through disappointment, but 2005 put him on a pedestal as a driver who was not only blindingly fast but who didn't make mistakes. In short, he is a worthy world champion.

Many people keep asking who will be "the next Michael Schumacher". Juan Pablo Montoya was picked out as one candidate, Kimi Raikkonen as another and, from 2003, Fernando Alonso as a third. There never will be another Michael, so here instead is Fernando, the first of a new generation of world champions.

The signs were there from his days in karting, but it was his transition to cars under the guidance of former Formula One racer Adrian Campos that made people take notice. His momentum was unstoppable, which is why he was on the grid for the Australian GP in a Minardi in 2001 four months before his 20th birthday.

He didn't disappoint then and hasn't disappointed since, turning not only into a model professional thanks to Flavio Briatore's grooming, but also into perhaps the most complete driver on the grid after Schumacher. Better still, he's got a style of his own out of the car and is certainly no one's man. And, best of all, he has dragged a nation previously interested

Alonso set new standards in 2005 and he'll hope his car will be as competitive again

only in motorbikes into the Formula One fold. That country, of course, is Spain, and in particular his less-than-fashionable region of Asturias. Judging by the flags in the grandstands for last year's races,

his supporters are booking their annual holidays to fit in with the grands prix.

Fernando finds that living at home in Oviedo is now impossible if he's to apply himself to Formula One, which is why he has now based himself in Oxford, to be near Renault's HQ and away from all distractions. Fernando's focus is 100 per cent.

TRACK NOTES

Nationality:	SPANISH
Born:	29 JULY 1981, OVIEDO, SPAIN
Website:	WWW.FERNANDOALONSO.COM
Teams:	MINARDI 2001, RENAULT 2003-06

CAREER RECORD

First Grand Prix:	2001 AUSTRALIAN GP
Grand Prix starts:	70
Grand Prix wins:	8
	2003 Hungarian GP, 2005 Malaysian GP, Bahrain GP, San Marino GP, European GP, French GP, German GP, Chinese GP
Poles:	9
Fastest laps:	3
Points:	237
Honours:	
	2005 FORMULA ONE WORLD CHAMPION, 1999 FORMULA NISSAN CHAMPION, 1997 ITALIAN & SPANISH KART CHAMPION, 1996 WORLD & SPANISH KART CHAMPION, 1995 & 1994 SPANISH JUNIOR KART CHAMPION

CAREER HISTORY

Like most of the latest generation of Formula One drivers, Fernando was racing karts from childhood. In fact, his progress was so marked that he had to bide his time after becoming world kart champion until he could start racing cars in 1999. His first season was stunning, landing the title in the powerful Formula Nissan series. Stepping up to Formula 3000 in 2000, he was just one rung below Formula One and yet was still able to blow all of his opponents away at the toughest circuit they visited: Spa-Francorchamps. Small wonder, then, that Paul Stoddart snapped him up to race for Minardi in 2001. Flavio Briatore took over the management and turned Fernando into Renault's test driver for 2002 before he joined the team full time in 2003, with his first win coming in Hungary that year.

GIANCARLO FISICHELLA

Pole and victory in last year's opening round in Australia looked to be putting Giancarlo on the road to the glory that many people had thought his due for so long. However, that didn't take into account the speed of his own team-mate.

Whatever the vagaries of fortunes for the 2005 season opener in Australia, with rain strafing qualifying and wrecking the chances of most of the top runners, people the length of the pitlane were delighted that Giancarlo qualified on pole position in his first race back with the team for whom he had raced from 1998 to 2001 before being moved on to Jordan. That he turned that into victory was fine by everyone; it was just reward for one of the sport's most popular drivers.

The big problem was that he did not win again all season, despite moments in Canada and Japan when he probably should have done so. Worse still, if there was mechanical failure in the Renault team, or a malfunctioning fuelling rig, it was inevitably he who was afflicted and not his team-mate. Worst of all, though, was the fact that that team-mate, Fernando Alonso, was simply on fire and able to overshadow him more often than not.

With three wins in rounds two to four, compared to Giancarlo's three retirements, it

Fisichella ought to have won more than once in 2005 and will seek to make amends this year

was game, set and match to the Spaniard.

To his credit, Giancarlo always insisted that he was receiving equal equipment and didn't hide behind that age-old excuse offered by most drivers when they spend

race after race looking at their team-mate's car disappearing into the distance.

Having held onto his place at Renault for 2006, Giancarlo will have to show his true mettle this season. Indeed, it's safe to say that this is a make-or-break year for the likeable and talented Italian and one that will decide whether he will stay at the sharp end of the sport or not.

TRACK NOTES

Nationality:	ITALIAN
Born:	14 JANUARY 1973, ROME, ITALY
Website:	WWW.GIANCARLOFISICHELLA.IT
Teams:	MINARDI 1996, JORDAN 1997 & 2002-03,
	BENETTON 1998-2001, SAUBER 2004,
	RENAULT 2005-06

CAREER RECORD

First Grand Prix:	1996 AUSTRALIAN GP
Grand Prix starts:	161
Grand Prix wins:	2
(2003 Brazilian GP, 2005 Australian GP)	
Poles:	2
Fastest laps:	2
Points:	174
Honours:	
	1994 ITALIAN FORMULA THREE CHAMPION
	& MONACO FORMULA THREE WINNER, 1991
	EUROPEAN KART RUNNER-UP, 1990 WORLD KART
	RUNNER-UP, 1989 EUROPEAN KART RUNNER-UP

CAREER HISTORY

Second in the world karting championship in 1990, Giancarlo progressed to Formula Three in 1992 and was Italian champion in 1994, the year in which he also won the Monaco street race. He couldn't afford to step up to Formula 3000 in 1995, but Alfa Romeo placed him in touring cars instead. Impressed by his speed in this different discipline, famous talent spotters Minardi made him a Formula One driver in 1996. Progressing to Jordan in 1997, he ran second in Argentina, until he was taken off by team-mate Ralf Schumacher. He did finish second later that year, in Belgium, and became a Benetton driver in 1998. More second places followed, but it was only when he returned to Jordan in 2002 that he became winner, in the 2003 Brazilian GP. A year with Sauber was followed by his move back to his previous team – Benetton – now Renault.

McLAREN

Fired up by getting so close to both the constructors' and drivers' titles in 2005, McLaren will be determined to succeed this time around and they have all the ingredients to do so, including two excellent drivers, Raikkonen and Montoya.

Juan Pablo Montoya will be looking to continue his strong form in 2006

If you want to annoy team principal Ron Dennis, tell him that you think that second is the first of the losers. It's something that this arch-perfectionist knows only too well. Yet, the fact that they were edged out by Renault – and Kimi Raikkonen likewise to Fernando Alonso – will only harden the team's resolve to bag both titles. It also represented a major rediscovery of competitiveness after they had slumped to fifth in 2004.

As is the case with all the teams, the change to 2.4-litre V8 engines could be the major factor in their form this year, but the signs were that Mercedes were back to something approaching their best form in 2005, albeit producing an engine that could be infuriatingly fragile. Indeed, the engineers at Mercedes' racing engine arm - Ilmor in Northamptonshire - will be only too aware that a series of engine failures, often down to tuppeny-threepenny parts, could have cost them both titles.

The best news of all, though, is that Adrian Newey was back on song with his design for last year's car and there's no reason why this shouldn't continue with the MP4-21. If success breeds success, then Raikkonen and Juan Pablo Montoya have every reason to hold high hopes–for 2006. However, the Formula One paddock was shocked when it was revealed last November

THE GOLDEN YEAR: 1988

A team seldom manages to fill its two seats with the two best drivers of their time, but McLaren did just that when Ayrton Senna crossed over from Lotus to join Alain Prost. The Steve Nichols-designed MP4/4 was powered by Honda for the first time in the final year of turbocharged engines. These replaced the TAG Porsche units that had helped McLaren to constructors' titles in 1984 and 1985 and which gave drivers' titles for Niki Lauda in 1984 then Prost in 1986 and 1987. No team could come close in 1988 and McLaren cleaned up, with the Brazilian edging out the Frenchman and with all their rivals trailing far behind. In fact, the ultra-talented duo won every one of the 16 grands prix bar the Italian GP, when Ferrari raised its game on home ground for Gerhard Berger to win. Senna won eight times and Prost seven, but the points system was such that drivers only counted their best 11 results, meaning that Prost's 105 points were reduced to 87, three fewer than Senna's eventual tally that had to be reduced by only four points.

that Newey would quit to join Red Bull Racing. This won't wreck 2006, as the car's design is complete, but it will restrict its development. It's in 2007, though, that his departure will be felt most keenly. Paddy Lowe has been promoted from within to head the design programme.

General manager Martin Whitmarsh said last January that the MP4-20 would be a Ferrari beater and he was proved to be right. What impressed last year was the way in which the team sorted the early-season problem of the MP4-20 failing to get heat into its tyres quickly, thus hampering its hopes in qualifying. Not only that, but the developments left the car easy on its tyres, enabling the use of softer compounds and helping the cars find even more speed.

Raikkonen and Montoya are capable of adding many more wins, with the Colombian anxious to prove he is equal number one in the team after falling into Raikkonen's shadow when he missed races early last year after an injury to his shoulder.

For all this optimism, McLaren will lose one of its greatest advantages: the use of a third car on the Fridays of all grands prix, something permitted only to teams that ranked fifth and below in the previous year. Indeed, Alexander Wurz and Pedro de la Rosa worked wonders in this arena. Without a third car, Raikkonen, Montoya and the engineers will have to be all the clearer in their thinking to get their set-up right.

Charges had been levelled that the construction of its opulent McLaren Technology Centre on the outskirts of Woking and the pursuit of projects for other arms of McLaren – such as building the Mercedes-Benz SLR McLaren – had led to Dennis taking his eye off the ball. Furthermore, the endless battles for control in Formula One have certainly taken away some of Dennis' attention as the potential breakaway Grand Prix World Championship continues to be talked about as the teams seek to claim a larger slice of F1's revenue from Bernie Ecclestone. There is also talk of them setting up a second team run from McLaren's previous HQ in Woking for 2007, most likely with Japanese backing, and this could prove a further distraction. However, with expectations of claiming both titles for the first time since McLaren and Mika Hakkinen ruled the roost in 1998, you can be sure Dennis and co will leave no stone unturned in their pursuit of both titles.

FOR THE RECORD

Country of origin:	England
Team base:	Woking, England
Telephone:	(44) 01483 728211
Website:	www.mclaren.com
Active in Formula One:	From 1966
Grands Prix contested:	596
Wins:	148
Pole positions:	122
Fastest laps:	126

2005 DRIVERS & RESULTS

Driver	Nationality	Races	Wins	Pts	Pos
Pedro de la Rosa	Spanish	1	-	3	20th
Juan Pablo Montoya	Colombian	17	3	60	4th
Kimi Raikkonen	Finnish	19	7	112	2nd
Alexander Wurz	Austrian	1	-	6	17th

THE TEAM

Team principal:	Ron Dennis
Managing director:	Martin Whitmarsh
Technical director:	Paddy Lowe
Director of engineering:	Neil Oatley
Team manager:	Dave Ryan
Chief designer:	Mike Coughlan
Chief engineer:	Steve Hallam
Test driver:	Pedro de la Rosa
Chassis:	McLaren MP4-21
Engine:	Mercedes V8
Tyres:	Michelin

Senna leads lap 1 in Detroit in 1988. Prost was to end up second

KIMI RAIKKONEN

Don't mention mechanical reliability to this taciturn Finn, as a distinct lack of it prevented him from becoming world champion last year. The speed may well have been there, but not the results to match. Only the world title will do for 2006.

On the form he showed in the middle of last season, it seems peculiar that Kimi isn't heading into the 2006 season as world champion, for he had mated his pace-setting skills at the wheel with the undoubted speed of the McLaren-Mercedes MP4-20 and all seemed right with the world.

Except it wasn't and Fernando Alonso outpointed him to become world champion for Renault, a result that could easily have driven Kimi back to the wild antics in a London lap-dancing club that earned him all the wrong headlines early in 2005.

Sundry mechanical failures had cost him a ten-place grid demotion more times than were good for his sanity. So upset did Kimi become about setting the fastest lap in qualifying, then having to start the grand prix in the second half of the grid after the team had had to accept a penalty for replacing an engine, that he talked of quitting the team. It left Kimi having to fight his way up the order, with his recovery drives to second and third in France and Britain being particularly impressive.

Raikkonen was amazed seven wins in 2005 didn't yield the title. He wants it this year

However, none could match his drive to the front in Japan, when he was desperately attempting to keep McLaren's hopes of the constructors' title alive after his own hopes of the drivers's title had perished in the previous round. Even the most hardened hack stood and cheered his last-lap pass of Giancarlo Fisichella's Renault for the lead around the outside through the first corner.

So, McLaren must produce another car, Mercedes a potent V8 and then it's up to Kimi to apply himself all over again.

TRACK NOTES

Nationality:	FINNISH
Born:	17 OCTOBER 1979, ESPOO, FINLAND
Website:	WWW.KIMIRAIKKONEN.COM
Teams:	SAUBER 2001, McLAREN 2002-06

CAREER RECORD

First Grand Prix:	2001 AUSTRALIAN GP
Grand Prix starts:	87
Grand Prix wins:	9
	2003 Malaysian GP, 2004 Belgian GP, 2005 Spanish GP, Monaco GP, Canadian GP, Hungarian GP, Turkish GP, Belgian GP, Japanese GP
Poles:	8
Fastest laps:	16
Points:	281
Honours:	

2005 & 2003 FORMULA ONE RUNNER-UP, 2000 BRITISH FORMULA RENAULT CHAMPION, 1999 BRITISH FORMULA RENAULT WINTER SERIES CHAMPION, 1998 EUROPEAN SUPER A KART RUNNER-UP & FINNISH KART CHAMPION & NORDIC KART CHAMPION

CAREER HISTORY

If the norm for hotshots is karting, a junior single-seater formula, Formula Three, Formula 3000 GP2 and then Formula One, Kimi had no time for that. He did the karting and the junior fomula, but then bypassed the next two stages when his manager Steve Robertson talked Sauber into testing him at the end of 2000. He impressed, licence problems were sorted with the FIA – he had only 23 car races to his name – and so he appeared on the grid at the Australian GP for Sauber in 2001. Points first time out impressed everyone and Kimi was seen as the man most likely to succeed Michael Schumacher. This is yet to happen, but he joined McLaren in 2002 and scored his first win early in 2003. A changed points system kept him in touch with Schumi until the final round, but a lack of competitiveness in 2004 reduced his impact.

JUAN PABLO MONTOYA

Juan Pablo had fallen out of love with Williams and was looking forward to joining McLaren in 2005, but the year didn't pan out as he would have wished. The Colombian will be doubly fired up to be crowned world champion this time round.

Reputations are made and broken with startling frequency in racing. Many a driver has cruised into Formula One without so much as a hiccough. Their reputation looks to be cast in iron. But then, one bad season and all that work is undone.

One driver who looked as though he had too much momentum for such a thing to happen is this feisty Colombian. Yet a dip in form, or even in application, can hit even the best and here he is, a winner in his maiden season, lining up for his sixth season in Formula One and needing to build his name all over again.

What must be so galling for Juan Pablo is that he produced some beautiful drives last year for McLaren, but even the keenest fans will probably look back and say "that was the year when he injured his shoulder". Indeed it was, in a fall on a tennis court said the official release, although there was a whispering campaign that he had fallen off a motorbike. Either way, it forced Juan Pablo to miss the Bahrain and San Marino GPs and he wasn't back to full strength on

Montoya had the speed in 2005 but under-achieved. He will want more wins in 2006

his return for the Spanish GP. Team-mate Kimi Raikkonen was in a winning vein by then and it took Juan Pablo a further seven races to score a victory. Juan Pablo scored his first win for McLaren – the fifth win of

his career - at Silverstone, going on to add further wins in Italy and Brazil.

Juan Pablo's contribution to McLaren's tilt at the constructors' title was zero in the final two races, although it wasn't his fault that he was taken out on lap one of the Japanese GP and likewise when his car struck a raised drain cover in China.

What Juan Pablo needs is a consistent season in which he can attack without interruptions.

CAREER HISTORY

Kart racing in Colombia was followed by attending a racing school in the US when Juan Pablo was 17, before returning to race in Colombia. Back in the US in 1994, he was third in the Barber Saab Pro-Series. Britain was next and he scored two wins in the 1996 Formula Three championship. Advancing to Formula 3000 in 1997, Juan Pablo found his metier, finishing as runner-up to Ricardo Zonta before beating Nick Heidfeld to the title in 1998. He'd spent that year as a test driver for Williams but, as they had no vacancy in their race line-up, he raced in ChampCars for two seasons, winning the title in his first year and then the Indianopolis 500 in 2000. Williams gave him his Formula One break in 2001 and Juan Pablo won that year's Italian GP, adding two more wins in 2003 when ranking third and then one more in 2004.

FERRARI

By recent standards, Ferrari's 2005 campaign was a shocker. Their only victory came in a boycotted race, yet still Michael Schumacher and the team ranked third overall. You'd expect them to bounce back in 2006, but as yet nobody can really be sure.

Michael Schumacher will be anxious to get back to the front in 2006

After decades of appearing to have cash to burn, Ferrari apparently found supplies drying up in 2005 when its road car sales dipped as the US dollar weakened against the euro. This is said to have been the reason behind their early decision to sign up to the new Concorde Agreement that will bind in signatories to contest the Formula One World Championship from 2008 to 2012. A hefty financial sweetener is thought to have been offered to ensure that the sport's most famous team was the first to sign up.

Yes, cut off the inflow of cash and fans of Ferrari will be shocked to realize that the prancing horse is not so sure to prance at will. Spoiled by the team's stunning form between 1998 and 2004 that yielded five drivers' titles and six constructors' crowns, Ferrari's more recent fans won't be aware that Formula One has always proved cyclical, even after such a purple patch.

There was more to the team's dip in form in 2005, though, and many a finger was pointed at the fact that they were one of only three teams using Bridgestone tyres, and the only top team at that. This would have been bad enough if regulations had stayed as before, but the introduction of the rules stating that tyre changes were banned during a race, meaning that a set of tyres had to be nursed through close on 200

THE GOLDEN YEAR: 1952

Ferrari has a history unmatched in the sport, having been involved ever since Formula One's opening season, 1950. Sure, fans today will think of Michael Schumacher's clean sweep in the early years of the 21st century as its greatest period. They're probably right, but it was in 1952 that the team first grabbed the reins and suggested that it was the outfit to beat. Ferrari's first wins came in 1951, but its seven wins in 1952 propelled the Italian team to its first championship success, with Alberto Ascari taking six scalps to be crowned world champion. Five more wins brought him the title the following year, too. Small wonder then that the team's blood red cars adorned with a black prancing horse on its yellow badge became the ones to beat. Certainly, they have been beaten over the intervening decades as Mercedes, Cooper, Lotus, Brabham, Stewart, McLaren and Williams have all enjoyed spells in the driver's seat in years when Ferrari weren't good enough to set the pace, but Ferrari is undeniably the backbone of the sport.

miles, meant that considerable testing was needed to ensure the optimum outcome. So much did Ferrari dislike the one set of tyres rule, that team president Luca di Montezemolo said that it made the drivers little more than taxi drivers.

This wasn't the only sniping that emitted from Maranello, with team principal Jean Todt also calling the other teams "bad losers" and accusing them of simply being jealous of Ferrari's success. It must be said that this exposed the pressure both were under, as they hadn't been so vocal when the team was winning.

That said, though, there was a certain improvement of Ferrari's trenchant "them-and-us" attitude last autumn when the team was said to be ready to sign an agreement to limit testing, perhaps as Williams and Toyota will share Bridgestone development work with Ferrari,

albeit under the proviso that it can continue to run unlimited tests on its own Fiorano circuit...

With technical director Ross Brawn and chief designer Rory Byrne also staying on until 2007, personnel changes are few and far between, but the arrival of Gerald Brussoz from Michelin could be even more significant than that of Felipe Massa from Sauber to replace Rubens Barrichello, especially if he can sort their tyre woes and make them able to qualify as well as race.

Massa might be the breath of fresh air that Ferrari needs after running the same driver line-up for six years, but he's there principally because he is managed by Todt's son, Nicolas, and because he's not likely to be too much of a threat to Michael, while Ferrari waits to see if their seven-time world champion will retire at the end of the year or wish to carry on.

Looking to 2006, Ferrari announced last October that they would break with their recent tradition and launch its new car in January rather than after the first three or four races of the season. Then again, this isn't as radical as you might think, since updating its 2005 car for the interim wouldn't be such an option, as considerable changes will have to be made to mate it with the new V8 engines that

are being introduced this year.

Finally, keep a close eye on Ferrari's progress and decide whether this is a team that Kimi Raikkonen really ought to be joining from McLaren for 2007, whether or not Michael retires. Look, too, for signs that Michael will retire, as predicted, or remain in love with the sport sufficiently to carry on, especially if Ferrari have a second less-than-competitive season.

FOR THE RECORD

Country of origin:	Italy
Team base:	Maranello, Italy
Telephone:	(39) 0536 949111
Website:	www.ferrariworld.com
Active in Formula One:	From 1950
Grands Prix contested:	723
Wins:	183
Pole positions:	179
Fastest laps:	184

2005 DRIVERS & RESULTS

Driver	Nationality	Races	Wins	Pts	Pos
Rubens Barrichello	Brazilian	19	0	38	8th
Michael Schumacher	German	19	1	62	3rd

THE TEAM

Chairman & CEO:	Luca di Montezemolo
Team principal:	Jean Todt
Technical director:	Ross Brawn
Engine director:	Paolo Martinelli
Team manager:	Stefano Domenicali
Chief designer:	Rory Byrne
Chief engineer:	Luca Baldisserri
Test drivers:	Luca Badoer & Marc Gene
Chassis:	Ferrari F2006
Engine:	Ferrari V8
Tyres:	Bridgestone

Alberto Ascari found winning all seven races in 1952 thirsty work

MICHAEL SCHUMACHER

Michael Schumacher is a proud man and will want to put the weak end to his disappointing 2005 season behind him. If this year's Ferrari is good, there's no reason at all why the great German can't claim world title number eight.

Last year's rule changes appeared to count against Ferrari, as Bridgestone struggled to produce a tyre capable of performing competitively all the way through a grand prix. Yet the problem was at its most marked in qualifying and Michael was convinced that, if the team could sort this problem, then he and Rubens Barrichello would have a chance in the races.

Ferrari's engine was also eclipsed by many of the team's rivals as that too had to be detuned to last two grand prix meetings. And so it was that Michael found himself in the pack rather than stroking clear at the front. It wasn't surprising that the media began to question whether he might retire before his Ferrari contract comes to its conclusion at the end of this season. After all, isn't 36 a bit old? Michael responded by saying that he plans to race until he is 40.

Michael is still totally in love with racing, so he will have been delighted that the media were then distracted by rumours of him being linked to McLaren in a straight

Schumacher has seven titles to his name but so far has shown few signs of retiring

swap with Kimi Raikkonen for 2007.

Despite all the disappointment, Michael still managed to win a grand prix, albeit the much-boycotted US GP, and in the process extended his record tally of wins to 84.

TRACK NOTES

Nationality:	GERMAN
Born:	3 JANUARY 1969, KERPEN, GERMANY
Website:	WWW.MICHAEL-SCHUMACHER.DE
Teams:	JORDAN 1991, BENETTON 1991-95, FERRARI 1996-2006

CAREER RECORD

First Grand Prix:	1991 BELGIAN GP
Grand Prix starts:	232
Grand Prix wins:	84

1992 BELGIAN GP, 1993 PORTUGUESE GP, 1994 BRAZILIAN GP, PACIFIC GP, SAN MARINO GP, MONACO GP, CANADIAN GP, FRENCH GP, HUNGARIAN GP, EUROPEAN GP, 1995 BRAZILIAN GP, SPANISH GP, MONACO GP, FRENCH GP, GERMAN GP, BELGIAN GP, EUROPEAN GP, PACIFIC GP, JAPANESE GP, 1996 SPANISH GP, BELGIAN GP, ITALIAN GP, 1997 MONACO GP, CANADIAN GP, FRENCH GP, BELGIAN GP, JAPANESE GP, 1998 ARGENTINIAN GP, CANADIAN GP, FRENCH GP, BRITISH GP, HUNGARIAN GP, ITALIAN GP, 1999 SAN MARINO GP, MONACO GP, 2000 AUSTRALIAN GP, BRAZILIAN GP, SAN MARINO GP, EUROPEAN GP, CANADIAN GP, ITALIAN GP, US GP, JAPANESE GP, MALAYSIAN GP, 2001 AUSTRALIAN GP, MALAYSIAN GP, SPANISH GP, MONACO GP, EUROPEAN GP, FRENCH GP, HUNGARIAN GP, BELGIAN GP, JAPANESE GP, 2002 AUSTRALIAN GP, BRAZILIAN GP, SAN MARINO GP, SPANISH GP, AUSTRIAN GP, CANADIAN GP, BRITISH GP, FRENCH GP, GERMAN GP, BELGIAN GP, JAPANESE GP, 2003 SAN MARINO GP, SPANISH GP, AUSTRIAN GP, CANADIAN GP, ITALIAN GP, US GP, 2004 AUSTRALIAN GP, MALAYSIAN GP, BAHRAIN GP, SAN MARINO GP, SPANISH GP, EUROPEAN GP, CANADIAN GP, US GP, FRENCH GP, BRITISH GP, GERMAN GP, HUNGARIAN GP, JAPANESE GP, 2005 US GP

Poles:	64
Fastest laps:	68
Points:	1248
Honours:	

2004, 2003, 2002, 2001, 2000, 1995, & 1994 FORMULA ONE WORLD CHAMPION, 1998 FORMULA ONE RUNNER-UP, 1990 GERMAN FORMULA THREE CHAMPION & MACAU GP WINNER, 1988 GERMAN FORMULA KONIG CHAMPION

CAREER HISTORY

The greatest driver of his generation triumphed at every level in kart racing and then won so many races in his maiden season of car racing that he advanced from Formula Konig to Formula Ford and nearly won that title too, despite missing the early rounds. German Formula Three confirmed his talents, although he was edged out of the 1989 title. He cleaned up in 1990, then raced for Mercedes in sportscars in 1991 and had a one-off outing in Japanese Formula 3000, before getting his Formula One break when Jordan's Bertrand Gachot was jailed. Benetton poached him and he was a grand prix winner by 1992, winning the first of two world titles for the team in 1994 before joining Ferrari in 1996 and turning the team around to such an extent that his 2000 crown was the first of five he won for the team in consecutive years.

FELIPE MASSA

It's time to deliver as Felipe steps up from Sauber to Ferrari. In any other year, this might be a dream drive, but Felipe will be praying that Ferrari will become competitive again. Then there's the small matter of beating his team-mate...

It is said that, across the years, every aspiring driver dreams of racing for Ferrari. After the past few years, that ambition will only have increased as Michael Schumacher and Ferrari swept all before them. But it will be with mixed feelings that Felipe makes the leap from midfield Sauber to the most famous team in the world.

Mixed feelings because he'll be praying that the Italian team can bounce back from their weakest campaign since the late 1990s, when Schumacher and Rubens Barrichello had the embarrassment of both finishing out of the points in the team's home grand prix at Monza.

With Renault and McLaren on top of their game, Toyota gaining ground fast and Honda looking to catch them, it won't be as easy to hit the top as before, especially if Bridgestone again comes second best in the battle to produce the most competitive tyres.

However, Ferrari is Ferrari and the 25-year-old Brazilian will be anxious to see what he can do with one of the top teams, a team with an image unlike that of Sauber's,

Massa was a test driver for Ferrari in 2003, but this year is his shot at the real thing

which tends to be neither good enough to run at the front nor bad enough to feature in the coverage of races among the slowcoach teams who are so often lapped.

Then there's the not-inconsiderable matter of being number two to Michael. Felipe knows him moderately well from his year as Ferrari's test driver in 2003.

However, he is more than aware that Michael expects to dominate his team-mates and that the team is built around him. Should Felipe put one over the team leader, though, it will certainly be a feather in his cap and will help him in the years ahead.

TRACK NOTES

Nationality:	BRAZILIAN
Born:	25 APRIL 1981, SAO PAULO, BRAZIL
Website:	WWW.FELIPEMASSA.COM
Teams:	SAUBER 2002 & 2004-05, FERRARI 2006

CAREER RECORD	
First Grand Prix:	2001 AUSTRALIAN GP
Grand Prix starts:	53
Grand Prix wins:	0
	best result: fourth, 2004 Belgian GP, 2005 Canadian GP
Poles:	0
Fastest laps:	0
Points:	27
Honours:	
2001 EUROPEAN FORMULA 3000 CHAMPION, 2000 EUROPEAN & ITALIAN FORMULA RENAULT CHAMPION, 1999 BRAZILIAN FORMULA CHEVROLET CHAMPION	

CAREER HISTORY

Felipe was little known in Formula One circles when he was given his Formula One break by Sauber in 2002. Having starred in karting in Brazil, he moved up to single-seaters and won Brazil's Formula Chevrolet series at his second attempt. In 2000, he was an instant hit in Formula Renault, winning both the Italian and European titles. He progressed to Formula 3000 in 2001, not to the Formula One-supporting FIA Championship, but to the less-fancied Euro series, and duly won that. Sauber spotted his latent talent and offered him a test. Although they dropped him from their line-up for 2003 as they considered him too erratic, the rest is history. A year as test driver for Ferrari smoothed the rough edges and his first year back with Sauber produced a fourth place in the Belgian GP, a result he matched in Canada in 2005.

TOYOTA

Sages said from the outset of 2002 that Toyota would become winners. It might take time, but their financial clout would make sure that they did. With pole positions and a couple of second places in 2005, they are moving in the right direction.

Toyota made startling progress last year and are determined to win in 2006

Having ranked eighth at the end of their third season in Formula One, Toyota upped the ante in 2005 and worked their way forward to a competitive fourth overall, scoring nigh on ten times as many points. This year, third overall or even higher is possible.

The crucial key to Toyota's progress isn't just money but organization, with the fruits of technical director Mike Gascoyne's focus at the team's Cologne base being clear for all to see as a competitive and reliable car was delivered. Its V10 engine was one of the best, too, said to rank fourth in terms of horsepower, with 935bhp being quoted. This will be reduced for

2006, but if Luca Marmorini's Toyota engine department can come up with an efficient V8, then this may well be the boost that the Japanese constructor needs to turn strong runs into race wins.

Furthermore, team drivers Jarno Trulli and Ralf Schumacher - both of them grand prix winners - deserve accolades for the way that they settled into the team. Having both been impressed with the Gustav Brunner-designed TF105 chassis in pre-season testing, Trulli was particularly impressive in the first half of the season, with Ralf coming on strong when the TF105B was introduced with two grands prix to go. Both were helped

THE GOLDEN YEAR: 2005

With but four years from which to make the selection of Toyota's highest point in Formula One and the first few scarcely troubling the scorers, it's hardly surprising that last season, 2005, is the one chosen, as it was by far Toyota's most successful yet. Sure, Cristiano da Matta had led the British GP in 2004, even ahead of team-mate Olivier Panis for a while, but this was a race that had been jumbled by incident. No, it was the way that Toyota hit the ground running in 2005 that impressed, as well as the fact that their form didn't tail away from then on. Indeed, after Jarno Trulli's second-place finishes in Malaysia and then Bahrain followed by a third at Barcelona, he went on to qualify on pole position for the United States GP. Then Ralf Schumacher came good by finishing third at the Hungarian GP. The German seemed to find another gear with the arrival of the TF105B and claimed pole position in Japan before rounding off the season with third place at the Chinese GP.

by the spadework of test driver Ricardo Zonta, who proved fast and accurate, both as the team's test and third driver. Remember, however, that ranking fourth means that Toyota won't have a third driver asisting them in the Friday practice sessions at grands prix in 2006.

One of the keys that Gascoyne pointed out at the launch of last year's car was that it must preserve its tyres. It's not hard to understand that the signing of Michelin engineer Pascal Vasselon at the end of March was a help with this.

If there's a question mark over Toyota's progress, it hangs on whether their move from Michelin to Bridgestone is an inspired one. Certainly, the Japanese company's tyres were no match for Michelin's through 2005, when a set of tyres had to last a grand prix. But much was made of the fact that Ferrari were the only top team using them, thus hampering their development. With Williams also making the switch for 2006, the feedback from three top teams ought to signal an improvement.

Although Toyota claimed before its first season that it would be happy just to qualify, its ambition has always been naked. No sooner had Trulli given Toyota its first podium by finishing second in the Malaysian GP than Toyota's management, led by Tsutomo Tomita, applied pressure for wins. Trulli responded with second place next time out, but that final step wouldn't come, even though Ralf led during the early stages in Japan. This, though, was down to qualifying with a light fuel load, but had the safety car not scrapped his early lead, he might well have given Toyota its day of days.

What became clear with the introduction of the TF105B was that it has great promise, although Trulli in particular found it heavy to steer, something this real touch driver doesn't like. However, this may actually be no indication of comparative form, as all cars will handle differently with the smaller new-for-2006 V8s in their tails.

Gascoyne said midway through 2005 that he would drop his hands-on role to allow Dieter Gass to be promoted from chief race engineer and this may help the Englishman in the development of the team.

As a result of the team's considerable recent improvement, Panasonic have signed to continue its association, the electrical giant having agreed to pay £75 million to stay on board for another three years.

If there's one problem remaining with Toyota, other than its lack of wins, it's that it lacks an image.

Perhaps the white-and-red livery is a little dull. Perhaps there are not enough entertaining characters to snatch the headlines for them. Whatever it is, only race wins will help to propel Toyota into the forefront of fans' minds.

FOR THE RECORD

Country of origin:	Germany (Japan)
Team base:	Cologne, Germany
Telephone:	(49) 2234 18230
Website:	www.toyota-f1.com
Active in Formula One:	From 2002
Grands Prix contested:	70
Wins:	0
Pole positions:	2
Fastest laps:	1

2005 DRIVERS & RESULTS

Driver	Nationality	Races	Wins	Pts	Pos
Ralf Schumacher	German	18	-	45	6h
Jarno Trulli	Italian	19	-	43	7th
Ricardo Zonta	Brazilian	1	-	0	n/a

THE TEAM

Team principal:	Tsutomo Tomita
President:	John Howett
Technical director:	Mike Gascoyne
Engine director:	Luca Marmorini
Chief designer:	tba
Chief engineer:	Dieter Gass
Team manager:	Richard Cregan
Test drivers:	Ricardo Zonta and Oliver Panis
Chassis:	Toyota TF106
Engine:	Toyota V8
Tyres:	Bridgestone

Ralf Schumacher was king of qualifying for Toyota and took pole at Indy

RALF SCHUMACHER

Pole position and a podium finish for Toyota in the last two races of 2005 could well prove that Ralf is looking forward to his most promising season in Formula One since 2001, when he won three times for Williams. He's certainly ready for it.

Changing teams can often inject fresh life into a jaded driver. We saw it in 2005 with David Coulthard and, equally so, with Ralf. Life at Williams had become tough for him and the move to Toyota certainly did the trick of reviving him. Many had felt that it was just a very well-paid retirement scheme, but they were failing to take into account the ambition of the team, the budget it had available to pursue those dreams and the pride of a driver belittled.

Ralf responded well to his new environment and, whisper it, even appeared to be enjoying himself again. Racing for a team based in Germany with many German mechanics will also have helped.

Many had predicted that all wouldn't be rosy between the two Toyota drivers, though, as both have quite fragile temperaments. But civil war didn't break out, even when Trulli held the upper hand early on. Instead, the points flowed and Ralf collected 14 scores from his 18 starts – he missed the team's non-start at the US GP after having his second major clash with the walls at

Schumacher enjoyed a strong finish to 2005 and will be looking to pick up where he left off

Indianapolis in two years. Fortunately, he was more shaken than hurt and was back for the following race. Then, in Hungary, Ralf looked down from the podium for the first time since the Japanese GP in 2004.

The late-season introduction of the TF105B was a breakthrough for Ralf as he found that its revised front-suspension package suited his driving style and he promptly placed it on pole for Toyota's home race at Suzuka.

The momentum is with him, so what chance a Ralf win in 2006?

TRACK NOTES

Nationality:	GERMAN
Born:	30 JUNE 1975, KERPEN, GERMANY
Website:	WWW.RALF-SCHUMACHER.DE
Teams:	JORDAN 1997-98,
	WILLIAMS 1999-2004, TOYOTA 2005-06

CAREER RECORD

First Grand Prix:	1997 AUSTRALIAN GP
Grand Prix starts:	146
Grand Prix wins:	6
	2001 San Marino GP, Canadian GP,
	German GP, 2002 Malaysian GP,
	2003 European GP, French GP
Poles:	6
Fastest laps:	8
Points:	294
Honours:	
	1996 FORMULA NIPPON CHAMPION, 1995
	GERMAN FORMULA THREE RUNNER-UP &
	MACAU GP WINNER, 1993 GERMAN FORMEL
	JUNIOR RUNNER-UP

CAREER HISTORY

Ralf was almost born in a kart, as his parents ran a kart circuit and brother Michael was already a hotshot, Ralf inevitably went racing, and finished as runner-up in the German championship in 1992. Advancing to single-seaters in 1993, Ralf was runner-up in the Formel Junior series. Formula Three followed and he was runner-up to Norberto Fontana in his second year, but made his name by winning the invitation race around the streets of Macau. A year in Japan followed and Ralf made the most of it, winning the Formula Nippon crown, proving that he was more than just Michael's brother. Third place on his third outing for Jordan, in Argentina in 1997, was followed with second place in Belgium in 1998 before moving on to Williams in 1999. His first win came in 2001, followed by five more before he moved to Toyota for 2005.

JARNO TRULLI

Dropped by Renault at the end of 2004, Jarno showed that he was not finished by producing a series of stunning drives last year, propelling Toyota to their first podium results as he rebuilt his reputation as one of the quickest on the scene.

A cruel term was created last year. It was the 'Trulli train', something that happened when Jarno qualified well but, even with a similar fuel load, wasn't able to race at a commensurate pace throughout the race as his Toyota TF105 struggled increasingly as its tyres wore down, leaving a train of cars delayed in his wake. It made an appearance in the opening round in Australia, but he delayed no one en route to second-place finishes in Malaysia and Bahrain.

The San Marino GP was the Trulli train's second showing, with further outings at Magny-Cours and the Hungaroring. This was frustrating for those stuck behind him, but it wasn't Jarno's fault.

Team-mate Ralf Schumacher didn't have the same predicament, as he tended not to qualify as well as the Italian, who remains one of the ultimate practitioners of the flying lap, with his ultra-finely honed driving skills famous for being able to correct every nuance of a slide.

All in all, with a further podium visit at the Spanish GP and nine point-scoring

Trulli feels appreciated again and this could mean he'll deliver results to match his skills

drives in all, Jarno's move to Toyota was a triumph. Certainly, the team had never had it so good as it rocketed to fourth overall in the constructors' championship and Jarno and Ralf finished seventh and sixth overall

at season's end. If there's one regret, it's that he led the Michelin-shod cars into the pits at the end of the formation lap for the United States GP at Indianapolis after the wranglings about tyre safety, thus abandoning his hard-fought pole position.

What will encourage Jarno is the fact that he's enjoying a good working relationship with Ralf. Better still, Toyota has the largest budget in F1 and is determined to become the top team in the years ahead. Now that is a train that Jarno would like to be on.

TRACK NOTES

Nationality:	ITALIAN
Born:	13 JULY 1974, PESCARA, ITALY
Website:	WWW.JARNOTRULLI.COM
Teams:	MINARDI 1997, PROST 1997-99, JORDAN 2000-01, RENAULT 2002-04, TOYOTA 2004-06

CAREER RECORD

First Grand Prix:	1997 AUSTRALIAN GP
Grand Prix starts:	149
Grand Prix wins:	1 (2004 Monaco GP)
Poles:	3
Fastest laps:	0
Points:	160
Honours:	
1996 GERMAN FORMULA THREE CHAMPION, 1994 WORLD KART CHAMPION	

CAREER HISTORY

Jarno was world kart champion in 1994. Spotted and duly sponsored by the then-Benetton boss Flavio Briatore, he burst straight into Formula Three midway through 1995. He won the German Formula Three crown in 1996, with Nick Heidfeld ranked third. Such was his confidence that he said he'd graduate directly to Formula One, which he did with Minardi for 1997. He didn't stay there long, joining the Prost team midway through last season when Olivier Panis broke his legs. Jarno even had the audacity to lead the Austrian GP. However, even with second place in the 1999 European GP, he'd have done better to move on to another team sooner. He qualified his Jordan on the front row twice in 2000, but it was his move to Renault in 2002 that showed his skills to the full and he scored his only win to date, at Monaco in 2004.

WILLIAMS

This has all the hallmarks of a year of consolidation, but Williams and returning partners Cosworth could just ruffle a few feathers with Mark Webber and rookie Nico Rosberg. That's if their V8 engine proves to be one of the better ones.

This is a make-or-break year for Williams and Webber in the Cosworth

Williams parted company with BMW last year and also lost out on their chance to welcome Jenson Button back to its ranks. However, they were awarded a cash payment of £16 million from Button as he won his battle to change his mind and stay with BAR. And this will have softened the loss, especially as the vacancy left when he elected to stay at BAR Honda is being filled by a younger driver of great promise.

Sir Frank Williams was less than happy about Button's attempts to renege on his contract, but was human about it all the same: "I understand Jenson's concerns about his team's competitive position and our uncompetitive position at the moment. Teams go up and down. We shall be back, if not in the second half of 2005, certainly next year."

This new signing to partner Mark Webber is Nico Rosberg, son of 1982 world champion Keke Rosberg. By some bizarre coincidence, this means that their charge could be led by a Rosberg in a Cosworth-powered Williams, just as was the case in 1982. Coincidences aside, the 20-year-old German – GP2 champion in 2005 – ought to keep Webber on his toes through 2006. That is something that the team would appreciate as the Australian tends to withdraw into himself rather than tackling problems

THE GOLDEN YEAR: 1996

Williams first hit the highest note in 1979 and scored their first drivers' title in 1980 through Alan Jones, with the constructors' title to boot. Eight constructors' titles have followed since, with six drivers' titles for six different drivers. Nigel Mansell against Nelson Piquet was great in 1986, but the battle between second generation drivers Damon Hill and Jacques Villeneuve a decade later was quite something. Villeneuve came close to winning on his Formula One debut in the Adelaide opener, but it was Hill who set the early-season pace in his Renault-powered FW18. After the French GP, though, Villeneuve started to claw back his deficit from his team-mate to the extent that his victory in the penultimate round in Portugal meant that it was all to play for in the Japanese finale. This was a cracker of a race and it seemed to be going Hill's way: then the Englishman ultimately secured the title when Villeneuve crashed out after his car had shed a wheel. Closest rivals, Ferrari, ended the year with less than half of Williams' points tally.

head-on in the style they so liked from his compatriot Alan Jones in the early 1980s.

Knowing the identity of the driver in their second seat in October is also a great step forward from the shambles of only appointing Nick Heidfeld last year at the 11th hour after a showdown with test driver Antonio Pizzonia. This isn't to say that Heidfeld was a bad choice. Indeed, his second place at Monaco and pole position at the Nurburgring are clear proof that he wasn't, but it's better to have any incoming driver accustomed not only to the car but also to the team through a winter's testing.

The chief problem with last year's FW27 was that it failed to deliver the much-hoped-for aerodynamic performance. Indeed, a raft of modifications introduced at the French GP failed to work, so it comes as little suprise that long-standing designer Gavin Fisher has been replaced. The new head of the design team is Jorg Zander from BAR and formerly Toyota.

The second problem was that the BMW engine had lost its pre-eminence and was one of the worst at getting the car away from a standing start. Worse still, the collapse of the team's relationship with its engine supplier was painful to witness and it couldn't end soon enough for either party.

So, for 2006, Williams will be renewing a long-standing relationship with Cosworth, fittingly now that it will be supplying engines of the V8 format with which the pair scored their first joint successes as long ago as 1979. The deal is only for a year, before an expected move to Toyota power, but Sir Frank Williams is confident that they can win races together in 2006 and director of engineering Patrick Head will have demanded a chassis worthy of the V8. Heads will roll if he doesn't get it, as he rightly believes that Williams must raise its game if it's to remain as a contender.

One factor that is sure to boost the new car's performance is that Williams will be entitled – as a team that finished fifth or lower last year – to run a third car in the Friday practice sessions, with Narain Karthikeyan tipped to step down from racing to perform this role.

Money is always an issue in Formula One and the loss of a works engine deal will have hit hard, explaining why the team took the decision to "make space" at their Grove headquarters by selling off as many as 20 of their much-valued old cars. The collector who bought the lot will have left happy and the Williams bank account will have enjoyed the top-up.

Indeed as money seemed to be getting so tight, there was even talk midway through 2005 of former BAR boss David Richards looking to buy a stake in the team, perhaps even as much as 30 per cent, but in the end Sir Frank Williams rejected the deal.

FOR THE RECORD

Country of origin:	England
Team base:	Grove, England
Telephone:	(44) 01235 777700
Website:	www.williamsf1.com
Active in Formula One:	From 1973
Grands Prix contested:	515
Wins:	113
Pole positions:	125
Fastest laps:	128

2005 DRIVERS & RESULTS

Driver	Nationality	Races	Wins	Pts	Pos
Nick Heidfeld	German	14	-	28	11th
Antonio Pizzonia	Brazilian	5	-	2	22nd
Mark Webber	Australian	19	-	36	10th

THE TEAM

Team principal:	Sir Frank Williams
Director of engineering:	Patrick Head
Technical director:	Sam Michael
Chief designer:	Jorg Zander
Chief aerodynamicist:	Loic Bigois
Team manager:	Dickie Stanford
Third driver:	Alexander Wurz
Chassis:	Williams FW28
Engine:	Cosworth V8
Tyres:	Bridgestone

Mansell dominated for Williams in 1991. Here he gives Senna a lift home

MARK WEBBER

Politics between Williams and BMW and fluctuating form were the bane of Mark's 2005 campaign and he's sure to come out fighting to ensure that his second year with Williams is more successful than the first which left him in tenth place overall.

It's always a pleasure when a driver who has fought hard to advance their racing career makes it into Formula One. Mark is one such driver and many in the paddock were delighted that he'd been able first to step up from Minardi to Jaguar Racing for 2003 and then on another rung up the ladder to join Williams last year. Yet it was here that the story began to go wrong.

Perhaps the sport's insiders had expected too much, but the relationship between Mark and the team's hierarchy wasn't as strong as people had predicted. However, more than that, the bad atmosphere between Williams and engine supplier BMW helped no one. Indeed, Mark said that he thought the best solution was for Williams and BMW to part company, which they duly did.

BMW were still fans of Mark's talents, though, and discussed the possibility of him moving across to their new team for 2006. It wasn't an option he took.

In 2005, there were moments when all was great, such as when he raced to his first

Webber's reputation took a knock in 2005 but a stable atmosphere should help him now

podium, at Monaco, after showing world champion Fernando Alonso a clean pair of heels. Even that, though, was spoiled, as he lost out at the final round of pit stops to none other than his team-mate Nick Heidfeld.

Apart from fluctuating form, the chief bugbear was that the Williams-BMW FW27 was dreadful away from a standing start, regularly losing a place or two on the run to the first corner. Another key to Mark's hopes is the performance of the Bridgestone tyres to which Williams is switching, with many feeling that the Michelin-shod teams will hold the upper hand at least for the start of the season.

TRACK NOTES

Nationality:	AUSTRALIAN
Born:	27 AUGUST 1976, QUEANBEYAN, AUSTRALIA
Website:	WWW.MARKWEBBER.COM
Teams:	MINARDI 2002, JAGUAR 2003-04, WILLIAMS 2005-06

CAREER RECORD

First Grand Prix:	2002 AUSTRALIAN GP
Grand Prix starts:	69
Grand Prix wins:	0
	best result: third, 2005 Monaco GP
Poles:	0
Fastest laps:	0
Points:	62
Honours:	

2001 FORMULA 3000 RUNNER-UP, 1998 FIA GT RUNNER-UP, 1996 BRITISH FORMULA FORD RUNNER-UP & FORMULA FORD FESTIVAL WINNER

CAREER HISTORY

Formula Ford in his native Australia was followed by more of the same in Britain in 1996 and Mark made his move to Europe stick by winning the Formula Ford Festival at Brands Hatch. This eased him into Formula Three, with rugby legend David Campese trying to assist him. There was no money in the pot for Formula 3000 in 1998, so it was good that Mercedes recognised Mark's talent and signed him to race for their sportscar team. He ended the year as runner-up. Achieving his graduation to Formula 3000 in 2000, he ranked third, then was runner-up in 2001, while also acting as test driver for Benetton. His day of days came on his Formula One debut for Minardi in 2002, when he finished fifth at home in Australia, a result he failed even to equal in two years with Jaguar, despite some sterling qualifying performances.

NICO ROSBERG

This season, Nico Rosberg will be racing a Cosworth-powered Williams like his father before him. But dismiss him as just another son of a racing father at your peril. The 20-year-old German prodigy could be the most talented of all.

Squint in the direction of Nico Rosberg and he could almost be a young version of his father Keke, with the same wavy blond hair but minus the trademark bushy moustache and ever-present cigarette. This year, however, it could well be that Rosberg II is also a world champion in the making. Certainly, coming into Formula One with Williams is one heck of a way to start on the sport's biggest stage.

The drive came his way when Williams lost their battle to keep Jenson Button to a contract he had signed in 2004. With a cash payment from Button to release him, Williams may yet be the big-time winners if Nico advances as expected.

Teamed up alongside Mark Webber, Nico will be hoping for a solid first season. If all his dreams are answered, though, it would be astonishing if he could achieve the success of the Rosberg/Williams/Cosworth combination of 1982 when his father became world champion.

Don't count on this, though, as that would be something close to a miracle.

All eyes will be on Rosberg to see if he can emulate his father with Keke's old team

Not because Nico is a slouch behind the wheel - as his racing career CV shows, he certainly isn't - but because Williams and Cosworth don't have the budget to take on the likes of Renault, Honda and Toyota on an equal footing, to say nothing of Ferrari and McLaren-Mercedes.

No, the best that Nico - the inaugural GP2 champion - can hope for is that he can settle in with this famously tricky team, do a solid job and develop his skills.

However, perhaps the most positive signal is that Nico set a record score when he tried one of the team's cognitive tests recently, something that definitely impressed Sir Frank Williams. Technical director Sam Michael has also declared himself a fan, so the red carpet has very much been rolled out in welcome.

TRACK NOTES

Nationality:	GERMAN
Born: 27 JUNE, 1985, WIESBADEN, GERMANY	
Website:	WWW.NICOROSBERG.COM
Teams:	WILLIAMS 2006

CAREER RECORD

First Grand Prix:	2006 BAHRAIN GP
Grand Prix starts:	0
Grand Prix wins:	0
Poles:	0
Fastest laps:	0
Points:	0
Honours:	
	2005 GP2 CHAMPION,
	2002 FORMULA BMW CHAMPION

CAREER HISTORY

With a father as racing mad as Keke, the 1982 world champion, it's not surprising that Nico was racing karts from a young age. He started at 11 and stepped up to cars as soon as he could in 2002 when he was 16. Success was instant, as he started off with a pair of wins at the opening round of the Formula BMW Championship. Seven more wins followed and he was a runaway champion. European Formula Three was his home for the next two years, racing for Team Rosberg. Eighth overall and then fourth, with three wins in 2004, was sufficient to propel Nico into GP2 – Formula One's new feeder formula. Racing for the ART Grand Prix team, set up by Ferrari boss Jean Todt's son Nicolas, Nico won five times, with the last two at the final round helping him to outpoint pre-season favourite Heikki Kovalainen for the title.

HONDA RACING

In the first season since Honda completed its buy-out of BAR, established stars Jenson Button and new signing Rubens Barrichello are anxious to take the team to places it has never been before – such as the top step of the podium...

BAR suffered a fall from grace in 2005, but has been reborn as Honda

Dropping from second overall in the constructors' championship in 2004 to sixth overall last year will not have pleased those with ambition at the team formerly known as BAR. Nor will having both cars disqualified at the San Marino GP for being fitted with a secondary fuel tank inside their regulation tank and being banned from the next two grands prix. Nor will their drivers' failure to score a single point until the tenth round, the French GP. And nor will the distractions of whether lead driver Jenson Button would be forced to honour a contract he had signed to return to Williams for 2006. However, the team will have gained satisfaction from

the way that they upped their pace and Button scored in every race thereafter.

As Takuma Sato's points tally plummeted from 45 in 2004 to just one last year, it is not surprising that the team chose to drop him, even though he was popular with the Japanese fans and, ergo, with Honda's hierarchy. To think that Honda Racing Development would only back a Japanese driver is to sell them short, though, as they were perfectly happy to employ American drivers when they entered F1 in the mid-1960s. Honda were happy enough, too, when Ayrton Senna and Alain Prost dominated with Honda power for McLaren in the late

THE GOLDEN YEAR: 2004

Born with a bang in 1999, landed with a daft motto "a tradition of excellence" and tipped by one of its founders to win on its Formula One debut, BAR did nothing but disappoint in its early years. There were signs that Jenson Button would be able to achieve more in 2003 than founding driver Jacques Villeneuve had managed thus far, but it was in 2004 that the team showed its true colours. Ferrari and, in particular, Michael Schumacher were dominant, but Button was often the best of the rest. Podiums were soon expected rather than prayed for and that maiden win seemed to be just around the corner. This never quite materialized and he ended the year third overall, with team-mate Takuma Sato eighth, but this was enough to boost BAR from fifth overall in 2003 to second overall, outpointing Renault late in the season. So, no wins and no titles, but the string of results propelled BAR into the limelight and let them drop their tag of an over-financed yet underachieving team and that first win seemed possible.

1980s, so it comes as no surprise that they have gone for non-nationals again in Englishman Jenson Button and Brazilian Rubens Barrichello. Indeed, this is probably the strongest line-up they've had.

This duo could certainly work well as they are expected to get on well together, especially as Barrichello will surely be delighted to be coming to a team that will treat him other than as second best like he was at Ferrari, a team built around Michael Schumacher. Button too will benefit, by having a team-mate capable of helping to develop the car. And certainly, too, Barrichello ought to help the team to rank higher in the constructors' championship than Sato did in 2005. They will also be assisted by third driver Anthony Davidson on grand prix Fridays, as they ranked outside the top four last year.

Driver choice aside, the most important factor that ought to affect the team's chance of not only scoring its first grand prix win, but also of seeing one of their drivers become world champion, is Honda's money. At the start of last year, Honda bought a 45 per cent stake in BAR. Then, last October, it added the other 55 per cent for total control, so now it's Honda Racing.

Honda has always believed that motor racing is the best way to develop its engineers and so it has a closer relationship with the team than other manufacturers. Honda has had engineers and designers working with and alongside BAR's best for several seasons and so will be up to speed on the chassis side as well.

Certainly it is clear that their engine department is now as strong as it was in the late 1980s and early 1990s, when it powered McLaren and Williams to win after win, as theirs was the most powerful V10 of all. Pushing to achieve similar dominance with this year's V8, they were the first to start testing this new format of engine, doing so as early as May last year in an attempt to steal a march on the opposition.

Nick Fry will remain as team principal and will hope that he is not faced with the aerodynamic problems that afflicted the car in the first half of last season. He will be supported by former ChampCar champion Gil de Ferran, who brings a clear technical mind to the party.

One thing not to be under-estimated is that Honda wants to be the champion constructor and won't rest until it becomes so, knowing that the real kudos will come from doing so before Toyota can steal their thunder.

FOR THE RECORD

Country of origin:	England
Team base:	Brackley, England
Telephone:	(44) 01280 844000
Website:	www.BARf1.com
Active in Formula One:	From 1999
Grands Prix contested:	118
Wins:	0
Pole positions:	2
Fastest laps:	0

2005 DRIVERS & RESULTS

Driver	Nationality	Races	Wins	Pts	Pos
Jenson Button	British	17	-	37	9th
Anthony Davidson	British	1	-	0	n/a
Takuma Sato	Japanese	16	-	1	23rd

THE TEAM

Team principal:	Nick Fry
Technical director:	Geoff Willis
Sporting director:	Gil de Ferran
Team manager:	Ron Meadows
Chief designer:	Kevin Taylor
Chief engineer:	Craig Wilson
Third driver:	Anthony Davidson
Chassis:	RA106
Engine:	Honda V8
Tyres:	Michelin

You could say the only way is up as Honda takes control for 2006

RUBENS BARRICHELLO

It's bizarre that it might take Rubens leaving the most high-profile team in motorsport to put his talents back under the spotlight. Yet this is precisely what his move from Ferrari to Honda Racing – formerly BAR – just might achieve.

No one ever quite believed Rubens when he joined Ferrari from Stewart for 2000 and said that he was going to the Italian team as equal number one to Michael Schumacher. Six years and seven wins later, to the German's 49 wins and five world titles, Rubens has plumped for pastures new. This is a year before his contract with Ferrari expired, but the move probably came not a year too soon.

Honda ought to suit him, as the chemistry between himself and Jenson Button appears to be good. Furthermore, Rubens feels a special tie to the Japanese manufacturer as his mentor, Ayrton Senna, had enjoyed such a strong relationship with them in his Lotus and McLaren days.

The working relationship he strikes up with Button will be key, as the English driver will be keen to have a team-mate who can help propel the team forwards.

On a personal level, he also ought to benefit from an intra-team atmosphere that is less skewed than Ferrari's. He knows full well that Button is established there as he

Barrichello will be revitalised at leaving Ferrari and has points to prove to critics

starts his fourth campaign with the team, but the level of entrenchment is nowhere near as profound as Schumacher's had been at Ferrari. Put simply, the team knows that it needs two strong drivers rather than

just focusing on one and letting the other live off the scraps. Rubens said last year that there had been many a time when he had had to "bite his tongue" and leave unsaid what needed to be uttered simply in the name of team harmony. At Honda Racing, he ought to feel welcome enough to speak his mind.

TRACK NOTES

Nationality:	BRAZILIAN
Born:	23 MAY 1972, SAO PAULO, BRAZIL
Website:	WWW.BARRICHELLO.COM
Teams:	JORDAN 1993-96, STEWART 1997-99,
	FERRARI 2000-05, BAR 2006

CAREER RECORD

First Grand Prix:	1993 SOUTH AFRICAN GP
Grand Prix starts:	217
Grand Prix wins:	9
	2000 German GP, 2002 European GP,
	Hungarian GP, Italian GP, US GP, 2003 British
	GP, Japanese GP, 2004 Italian GP, Chinese GP
Poles:	13
Fastest laps:	15
Points:	589
Honours:	
	2002 FORMULA ONE RUNNER-UP, 1991
	BRITISH FORMULA THREE CHAMPION, 1990
	EUROPEAN FORMULA OPEL CHAMPION, 1988
	BRAZILIAN KART CHAMPION

CAREER HISTORY

Some drivers ascend the ranks like a rocket, others with less alacrity. Rubens was a rocket. National kart champion in his native Brazil, Rubens attracted backers who said they would pay for him to go to Europe and see if he could make it to Formula One. And he did, winning the European Formula Opel and British Formula Three titles in 1990 and 1991 respectively, beating David Coulthard to the honours in each. He then ranked third in Formula 3000 in 1992, but had done enough to be snapped up by Jordan for 1993, running second in the European GP at Donington Park behind his hero Ayrton Senna. Moving on to Stewart in 1997, Rubens continued to impress, but he craved a top car. He got this when he joined Ferrari in 2000, winning the German GP. More wins followed, but he was very much the number two to Michael Schumacher.

JENSON BUTTON

Jenson could have had a good 2005 season, but it fell off the rails at Imola and he was made to look bad as he wriggled his way out of a Williams contract. Now he must look ahead and turn both himself and Honda into winners.

It's safe to say that lawyers don't rank highly on most people's list of favourite people. Jenson may beg to differ, though, as one dug into the law books to extract him from a deal he had signed to return to Williams. It took a payment of £16 million to Williams for Button to extricate himself from the move that he once desired, but Jenson won few friends by reneging on the deal simply because he had decided that Williams would be less competitive than the team with which he wished to stay.

Jenson is now contracted to Honda Racing until the end of 2010 in a deal worth £55 million – meaning that his outgoings to Williams are more than covered.

Honda have, of course, been winners in Formula One before, back in its first crack at the big time in the 1960s when Richie Ginther won the Mexican GP in 1965 and John Surtees triumphed in the Italian GP in 1967. But what must happen over the next few years is that the team builds on the foundations provided by BAR and Jenson must help guide them forward to their first

Button showed fortitude in bouncing back in 2005 and desperately wants that first win

win in the modern era. Jenson is very aware that he has now passed the 100 grands prix mark and still has to record a win.

After such a strong 2004 campaign, in which he finished third behind the Ferrari

drivers, Jenson had high hopes for 2005. These were dashed early on with a less-than-competitive start, but the way he bounced back in the second half of the year – legal wrangling aside – will have re-established his reputation and given him momentum for the season ahead.

TRACK NOTES

Nationality:	BRITISH
Born:	19 JANUARY 1980, FROME, ENGLAND
Website:	WWW.JENSONBUTTON.COM
Teams:	WILLIAMS 2000, BENETTON/RENAULT 2001-02, BAR 2003-06

CAREER RECORD

First Grand Prix:	2000 AUSTRALIAN GP
Grand Prix starts:	101
Grand Prix wins:	0
best result: second, 2004 San Marino GP, Monaco GP, German GP, Chinese GP	
Poles:	2
Fastest laps:	0
Points:	167

Honours:
1999 MACAU FORMULA THREE RUNNER-UP,
1998 FORMULA FORD FESTIVAL WINNER,
BRITISH FORMULA FORD CHAMPION &
McLAREN AUTOSPORT BRDC YOUNG DRIVER,
1997 EUROPEAN SUPER A KART CHAMPION,
1991 BRITISH CADET KART CHAMPION

CAREER HISTORY

A hotshot in karts, winning his first title at the age of 11, before graduating to cars in 1998, he won the British Formula Ford title at his first attempt and graduated to Formula Three, starting his first race from pole. Ending up third overall in the British series against more experienced drivers, Jenson was considering a second season in Formula Three, or perhaps a move up to Formula 3000, but he was called in to test for the Prost Formula One team and impressed. This put him into the frame at Williams which was looking for someone to partner Ralf Schumacher and he ended up as an 11th-hour signing for the team. Despite strong form, he had to make way for Montoya in 2001 so moved on to Benetton – which became Renault – but was there in the team's development seasons and only shone when he joined BAR, with 2004 producing four second places and third overall in the drivers' standings.

RED BULL RACING

Jordan used to be the fun team in Formula One. As of last year, that mantle has been passed to Red Bull Racing – a team that came close to claiming a podium finish on its maiden outing. This year, they'll be propelled by Ferrari power.

Red Bull Racing began their first year in style but can they keep it up?

Dietrich Mateschitz is a man with considerable wealth from the runaway global success of his Red Bull energy drink. He's also a man who loves Formula One and who likes to surprise.

There were surprises aplenty last year, from the removal of team principal Tony Purnell and managing director David Pitchforth in the countdown to the opening race and their replacement by Christian Horner and Gunther Steiner, to David Coulthard coming close to giving them a podium finish first time out in Australia.

Then there was the small matter of their profile in the paddock, with no team even coming close to being so flash or so appealing. Their paddock base was the centre of fun, with a party or two at every grand prix and the team's very own paddock newspaper to keep it all rolling along. The other teams must have felt very staid in comparison. No other team could have carried off the joint promotion of the new *Star Wars* film that the team immersed itself in last May at Monaco with such aplomb. This is why Red Bull Racing's profile is so very good for Formula One: it has certainly dented its often staid and elitist image.

Impressively, the Cosworth-powered RB1s were good enough to ensure that there were on-track results to celebrate,

GOLDEN YEAR: 1999

This was when the team was in the first of its three incarnations, Stewart, before it morphed into Jaguar Racing in 2000 and finally Red Bull Racing last year. The year was 1999 and the white cars bedecked with tartan stripes had produced a pair of third-place finishes at Imola and Magny-Cours for Rubens Barrichello, but little of note from Johnny Herbert. Then came the 14th round at the Nurburgring. Autumn in the Eifel forest often means mixed weather and this is exactly what transpired, with Herbert keeping his head as others lost theirs. By all rights, the race should have been won by Ralf Schumacher for Williams, but a puncture slowed him and Herbert not only won for Stewart, but Barrichello finished third, giving Jackie Stewart one last hoorah before he sold the team to Ford, which duly re-entered it as Jaguar Racing. This podium double was worth its weight in gold as the 14 points it provided propelled the team up the charts to finish an eventual fourth overall, one point ahead of Williams.

too. It is safe to say that few expected a great deal from the team, but both cars were in the points in that season opener in Melbourne and Coulthard used both his experience and guile to score on eight more occasions.

If there was anything to be negative about, it was that the team could not make up their mind on who to run in the second car, starting the season with a plan to give Christian Klien a go in the first three races and then Formula 3000 champion Vitantonio Liuzzi in the next four, before deciding who would be awarded the drive for the remainder of the season. Both scored points, but still no decision was made, with neither driver benefitting from the chopping and changing. So Klien rejoined the battle for the Canadian GP and, despite being told repeatedly that this race would be his last, kept the seat for the remainder of the year.

Coulthard, on the other hand, enjoyed continuity. Perhaps his best drive came at the Nurburgring, where he used his experience to keep out of trouble at the opening corner and, but for a drive-through penalty, would have finished in third place.

With Red Bull dollars buying a second team for 2006, Scuderia Toro Rosso – formerly Minardi – the driver line-up has been kept as Coulthard and Klien and the chief difference is that the RB2s will be propelled by Ferrari power. There's more to this deal than simply a desire for Ferrari horsepower, as a fair deal of political play was involved: the two-year deal was tied up when the team signed the new Concorde Agreement that binds them from 2008 on, something that Ferrari had been first to do in the ongoing battle with the other manufacturers who remain on the side of the breakaway Grand Prix World Championship.

Red Bull Racing's management will have observed how Ferrari attempted to use the team it previously supplied with engines – Sauber – as a political pawn, but Mateschitz is a man who knows his own mind, so he will be no pushover if he doesn't agree. In sporting director Christian Horner, he has an old head on young shoulders and someone who offers welcome clarity in the oft-confusing world of the pit and paddock, thanks in no small part to his experience as a racer, having competed in Formula 3000 before turning to team management.

Red Bull can be assured that the new Ferrari V8 will be a good engine, as it was out testing as early as the start of last August and will have more development miles on the clock than the majority of its rivals.

Continuity on the technical side will be welcome too, with Mark Smith now settled as the team's technical director after his troubled transfer from Jordan last March. However, the signing of Formula One's leading designer – Adrian Newey – illustrates the team's intent.

FOR THE RECORD

Country of origin:	England
Team base:	Milton Keynes, England
Telephone:	(44) 01908 279700
Website:	WWW.REDBULLRACING.COM
Active in Formula One:	From 1997
	(as Stewart until 2000 then Jaguar until 2004)
Grands Prix contested:	153
Wins:	1
Pole positions:	1
Fastest laps:	0

2005 DRIVERS & RESULTS

Driver	Nationality	Races	Wins	Pts	Pos
David Coulthard	British	19	-	24	12th
Christian Klien	Austrian	15	-	9	15th
Vitantonio Liuzzi	Italian	4	-	1	24th

THE TEAM

Team principal:	Christian Horner
Chairman:	Dietrich Mateschitz
Technical operations director:	Gunther Steiner
Technical director:	Mark Smith
Director of engineering:	Anton Stipinovic
Chief aerodynamicist:	Ben Agathangelou
Chief engineer:	Stefano Sordo
Third driver:	Robert Doornbos
Chassis:	Red Bull RB2
Engine:	Ferrari V8
Tyres:	Michelin

It was all smiles in 1999 when Stewart scored their first win

DAVID COULTHARD

This popular Scot, one of the elder statesmen of Formula One, re-established his reputation last year as he got stuck into making Red Bull Racing a credible team, showing their young guns the way forward. For 2006, he says his target is race wins.

It was all change for David last season as he set about racing for a team other than McLaren for the first time since 1995. The team in question was Red Bull Racing, a metamorphosis of Jaguar Racing.

Little was expected of them and peversely, as he'd been put in the shade at McLaren by tyro Kimi Raikkonen, little was expected of him. So, to have run as high as second before finishing fourth in the opening race in Australia must have given David great delight and provided him with a position from which he could stick two fingers up at his critics.

That point-scoring drives followed in three of the next four races gave the team far more presence than it used to have in its guise as Jaguar. David scored in nine of the 19 races, including another fourth place at the Nurburgring that would have been third but for a pitlane speeding incident that forced him to lose time with a drive-through penalty.

Monaco ought to have yielded a strong result, too, but David's car was thumped

Coulthard reminded people of his skills in 2005, making up for his car's lack of speed

from behind by Michael Schumacher's Ferrari as they came upon Christijan Albers' Minardi broadside in the track.

Even so, the results were stronger than expected as the team did a solid job. However,

what made the biggest difference for David was that the team required more input from him. He was less of a small cog in a very large machine as he'd become at McLaren.

TRACK NOTES

Nationality:	SCOTTISH
Born:	27 MARCH 1971, TWYNHOLM, SCOTLAND
Website:	WWW.DAVIDCOULTHARD-F1.COM
Teams:	WILLIAMS 1994-95,
	McLAREN 1996-2004, RED BULL 2005-06

CAREER RECORD

First Grand Prix:	1994 SPANISH GP
Grand Prix starts:	194
Grand Prix wins:	13

1995 Portuguese GP, 1997 Australian GP, Italian GP, 1998 San Marino GP, 1999 British GP, Belgian GP, 2000 British GP, Monaco GP, French GP, 2001 Brazilian GP, Austrian GP, 2002 Monaco GP, 2003 Australian GP

Poles:	12
Fastest laps:	18
Points:	499

Honours:

2001 FORMULA ONE RUNNER-UP, 1991 BRITISH FORMULA THREE RUNNER-UP & MACAU GP WINNER, 1989 McLAREN AUTOSPORT YOUNG DRIVER OF THE YEAR & BRITISH JUNIOR FORMULA FORD CHAMPION, 1988 SCOTTISH KART CHAMPION

CAREER HISTORY

His biggest break didn't come when he won the Scottish kart title in 1998, but when he picked up the McLaren Autosport Young Driver award at the end of his first season in cars. Not only did this give him a run-out in a Formula One car, but it started a relationship with McLaren. David's passage through Formula Opel and Formula Three was filled with wins, his time in Formula 3000 less so. His break into Formula One came in 1994, when Ayrton Senna was killed in the San Marino GP and he stepped up from Williams' test team. A winner for Williams by the end of 1995, he then joined McLaren just as Williams turned into the team to watch and thus went his best chance of being champion, as Mika Hakkinen and then Kimi Raikkonen duly outperformed him at McLaren, even though he took 12 more wins over the nine seasons.

CHRISTIAN KLIEN

Christian will be delighted to embark on his third year with the team – the second since it was called Red Bull Racing – since this means that he has survived the constant trials set up against Vitantonio Liuzzi throughout last season.

At the start of 2004, when Christian broke into Formula One with the then Jaguar Racing, most insiders felt that this was down to the £8 million he was bringing from Red Bull. After all, the team needed the money and he was a 21-year-old with a meagre track record.

Still, he was able to claim a sixth place in that maiden season, equalling the best result from team-mate Mark Webber. However, that was only down to the fact that Red Bull bought the team that he stayed on for last year, albeit on a trial basis, driving in the first three grands prix before Vitantonio Liuzzi was given a similar run to try to prove he was the better prospect.

Christian's qualifying record against Webber had been poor in 2004, so it was interesting to observe that he was regularly a match for team leader David Coulthard in 2005, although his lack of racing experience was shown time and again during the grands prix as the Scotsman raced clear to superior results. But the signs were good, as Christian was

Klien came on strong in 2005 and having a full season ahead of him will be a boost

in the points six times from his 15 starts, benefiting from a timely safety-car period in the Chinese GP to end the season on a career high with a fifth place.

Christian will be delighted he's still with

the senior squad at Red Bull Racing. He will be fully aware that he will need to start delivering results that are worthy of, or which even flatter, the car. If the Ferrari V8 is good, though, the changing of the 2005 order is a distinct possibility and it's not beyond the realms of possibility that he or Coulthard could step on to the podium. If this happens, just imagine the partying at Red Bull Racing's paddock HQ.

TRACK NOTES

Nationality:	AUSTRIAN
Born:	7 FEBRUARY, 1983, HOHENEMS, AUSTRIA
Website:	WWW.CHRISTIAN-KLIEN.COM
Teams:	JAGUAR 2004, RED BULL RACING 2005-06

CAREER RECORD

First Grand Prix:	2004 AUSTRALIAN GP
Grand Prix starts:	33
Grand Prix wins:	0
	best result: fifth, 2005 Chinese GP
Poles:	0
Fastest laps:	0
Points:	12

Honours:
2003 EUROPEAN FORMULA THREE RUNNER-UP, 2003 MARLBORO MASTERS WINNER, 2002 GERMAN FORMULA RENAULT CHAMPION, 1996 SWISS KADET KART CHAMPION

CAREER HISTORY

As with all Formula One drivers, Christian was a junior karting champion who hoped to shine when moving up to the junior single-seater categories. Racing in the German Formula BMW Junior Cup in 1999, he ranked fourth and moved up the following year to Formula BMW, run by Keke Rosberg's team, placing third overall at his second attempt in 2001. Dominant form in the 2002 German Formula Renault series earned Christian a ride in the European Formula Three Championship with Mucke Motorsport in 2003. Then the 20-year-old Austrian was by far the best rookie in that year's series and notched up three wins, but had to settle for the role of runner-up behind former Toyota Formula One test driver Ryan Briscoe. However, he did gain the plaudits for winning the prestigious Marlboro Masters international invitation race at Zandvoort.

BMW SAUBER

BMW have flitted on and off the Formula One scene since the 1980s, but now, for the first time, it has a team of its own, having bought out Sauber to mould in its own fashion. Don't expect miracles, though: this will be a period of consolidation.

BMW Sauber will find out what it takes to run a team in Formula One

Little Sauber, in sleepy Hinwil, will have been reeling since it was taken over by BMW. Up to 100 new staff will have been recruited, money won't be on such a tight rein and Peter Sauber will no longer be the boss. In fact, he'll attend only four grands prix as an advisor for sponsor Credit Suisse. Also, the cars mayno longer appear in Sauber's dowdy blue, but BMW's favoured red, white and blue.

The new man at the helm will be Mario Theissen, who has spent six years in the Williams pit when BMW were engine suppliers. That partnership with Williams became uncomfortable for both parties, which is why Theissen pushed BMW to take over a team

completely so that it could run it according to its own wishes.

Theissen has been surprised by how much it takes to run a team rather than just an engine programme, but at least he has the continuity of technical director Willy Rampf and chief designer Seamus Mullarkey to take them into 2006, although future campaigns may have a very different technical line-up. One face that will be missing, though, is chief engineer Jacky Eeckelaert, who is being replaced from within by Mike Krack.

Nick Heidfeld has been recruited from Williams to lead the driving side, with Jacques Villeneuve staying for a second season to provide continuity.

FOR THE RECORD

Country of origin:	Switzerland
Team base:	Hinwil, Switzerland
Telephone:	(41) 1937 9000
Website:	www.sauber.ch
Active in Formula One:	From 1993
Grands Prix contested:	217
Wins:	0
Pole positions:	0
Fastest laps:	0

2005 DRIVERS & RESULTS

Driver	Nationality	Races	Wins	Pts	Pos
Felipe Massa	Brazilian	19	-	11	13th
Jacques Villeneuve	Canadian	19	-	9	14th

THE TEAM

Team principal:	Mario Theissen
Technical director:	Willy Rampf
Engine director:	tba
Chief designer:	Seamus Mullarkey
Chief engineer:	Mike Krack
Team manager:	Beat Zehnder
Third driver:	tba
Chassis:	tba
Engine:	BMW V8
Tyres:	Michelin

NICK HEIDFELD

Backed by BMW, Nick is back at his spiritual home - Sauber - but this time he is expected to deliver.

In theory, Nick Heidfeld is returning to Sauber. Yes, the team for which he will race is based at the same headquarters at Hinwil in Switzerland and many of the crew will be the same as when he raced for the team in 2003, but its takeover by BMW and the introduction of up to 100 extra staff will boost its form.

It might take time and the fruits of this new union will most likely be tasted in 2007, but it's a career break for the unflashy German, particularly as he has signed a three-year contract that ought to see him as a grand prix winner before it has run its course.

Certainly, 2005 was the year that rebuilt the reputation of this driver who pushed Juan Pablo Montoya all the way in Formula 3000 in 1998, with Williams' technical director Sam Michael raving with enthusiasm about his approach to driving. Second place at Monaco and pole position at the Nurburgring also helped his cause.

As it is, he's now a team leader in a team that's looking to go places, with BMW so keen to have him that they paid Williams to release him from his contract.

TRACK NOTES

Nationality:	GERMAN
Born:	10 MAY 1977, MOENCHENGLADBACH, GERMANY
Website:	WWW.NICK-HEIDFELD.DE
Teams:	PROST 2000, SAUBER 2001-03, JORDAN 2004, WILLIAMS 2005, BMW SAUBER 2006

CAREER RECORD

First Grand Prix:	1999 AUSTRALIAN GP
Grand Prix starts:	99
Grand Prix wins:	0
	best result: second, 2005 Monaco and European GPs
Poles:	1
Fastest laps:	0
Points:	56

JACQUES VILLENEUVE

Jacques was caught in a negative media frenzy last year, but he hung on in there and started to perform.

Few former world champions can have faced as many calls for them to stand down as Jacques did in 2005.

Jacques has never been one to care about the opinions of others, and he'd hoped that joining sleepy Sauber would let him concentrate on what he loves best - racing - rather than the PR-driven activities of other teams. After being shown the way home by team-mate Felipe Massa in the first three races and with Peter Sauber failing to guarantee he would race on beyond Imola, he'll have been delighted by his drive to fourth in the San Marino GP. This was sixth on the track, but he was promoted after the exclusion of both BARs.

This secured his place for the rest of 2005, and so Jacques stays on for 2006, although he can't feel safe, as BMW will want to introduce its own driver for 2007, perhaps leaving Jacques time to concentrate on a film being made about his late father, Gilles.

TRACK NOTES

Nationality:	CANADIAN
Born:	9 APRIL 1971, ST JEAN-SUR-RICHELIEU, CANADA
Website:	WWW.JACQUES.VILLENEUVE.COM
Teams:	WILLIAMS 1996-98, BAR 1999-2003; RENAULT 2004; SAUBER 2005; BMW SAUBER 2006

CAREER RECORD

First Grand Prix:	1996 AUSTRALIAN GP
Grand Prix starts:	155
Grand Prix wins:	11
	1996 European GP, British GP, Hungarian GP, Portuguese GP, 1997 Brazilian GP, Argentinian GP, Spanish GP, British GP, Hungarian GP, Austrian GP, Luxembourg GP

MF1 RACING

It's sink or swim for the team now known as MF1 Racing – formerly Jordan – for it haemorrhaged staff last year as the new owner made his mark. Now serious expenditure is required to turn it around again and avoid it just being a straggler.

The yellow of Jordan has been replaced by grey, red and white

It was a mess at Jordan in 2005, the final year before the team changed their name to MF1 Racing. The new ownership was in place, but little else was and the Silverstone HQ appeared to have a revolving door at its entrance as staff came and, more frequently, went.

Owner Alex Shnaider was scarcely seen in the paddock after his £16 million takeover. One problem was the fact that cars continued to be run in Jordan yellow and the team couldn't be rebranded until 2006.

Managing director Colin Kolles wasn't the most popular man in the paddock, which is one of the reasons sporting director Trevor Carlin quit, to be replaced by Adrian

Burgess. Matters improved when Johnny Herbert was introduced as sporting relations manager and this at least encouraged the press to drop by.

The busiest stream of traffic into the motorhome, though, was of prospective buyers, with former Jordan ace Eddie Irvine among their ranks. The team may well be sold, but Shnaider has just done some deals in the steel manufacturing world and may yet start investing in the team. Whether it's enough to make it competitive by 2008, as is his stated aim, remains to be seen, however. For now, the one saving grace is the Toyota V8 engine that the car will have in its tail.

FOR THE RECORD

Country of origin:	England
Team base:	Silverstone, England
Telephone:	(44) 01327 850800
Website:	www.midlandf1.com
Active in Formula One:	From 1991 (as Jordan until 2006)
Grands Prix contested:	250
Wins:	4
Pole positions:	2
Fastest laps:	2

2005 DRIVERS & RESULTS

Driver	Nationality	Races	Wins	Pts	Pos
Narain Karthikeyan	Indian	19	-	5	18th
Tiago Monteiro	Portuguese	19	-	7	16th

THE TEAM

Team principal:	Alex Shnaider
Managing director:	Colin Kolles
Technical director:	James Key
Sporting director:	Adrian Burgess
Sporting relations manager:	Johnny Herbert
Chief designer:	John McQuilliam
Chief engineer:	Gerry Hughes
Team manager:	Dominic Harlow
Third driver:	Andy Stevenson
Chassis:	Midland M16
Engine:	Toyota V8
Tyres:	Bridgestone

CHRISTIJAN ALBERS

Stranded when Minardi was sold, Christijan had to call on his sponsors again for a second crack at Formula One.

Unusually for a Dutchman, Christijan doesn't smile much, but any vestige of happiness was wiped away last autumn when the Minardi team for which he'd been racing was sold to Dietrich Mateschitz. At a stroke, his hopes for a second year in Formula One with the team were scuppered as the Austrian drinks magnate had drivers of his own to place there in its new life as Scuderia Toro Rosso.

So, Christijan, who peaked with a fifth place in the widely boycotted US Grand Prix but otherwise never finished higher than 11th, was back on the market. Thanks to his sponsors he landed a ride with the team that had been Jordan until it too was sold. It's now MF1 Racing.

Having chased the Jordans throughout 2005 in the battle not to finish last in the races, Christijan will now be driving for the team, albeit in their new grey, red and white livery. With Tiago Monteiro staying on as his team-mate, it'll be interesting to see what progress Christijan can make in his second season in single-seaters after a successful spell racing touring cars.

TRACK NOTES

Nationality:	DUTCH
Born:	APRIL 16, 1979, EINDHOVEN, HOLLAND
Website:	WWW.CHRISTIJAN-ALBERS.NL
Teams:	MINARDI 2005, MIDLAND 2006

CAREER RECORD

First Grand Prix:	2005 AUSTRALIAN GP
Grand Prix starts:	19
Grand Prix wins:	0
	best result: fifth, 2005 US GP
Poles:	0
Fastest laps:	0
Points:	4
Honours:	
2003 GERMAN TOURING CAR RUNNER-UP, 1999 GERMAN FORMULA THREE CHAMPION,	

TIAGO MONTEIRO

Picked as the top rookie last year, Tiago still had to call on sponsorship to ensure he stayed on board for 2006.

Tiago didn't arrive in Formula One in 2005 with glowing credentials. No-one expected miracles from anyone when the Jordan continued to drop off the pace as other teams developed their machinery. However, the very least expected of a driver is to demonstrate progress. Slower than his more-fancied team-mate Narain Karthikeyan to start with, this

intelligent driver showed that at least the team could rely upon him to be there at the end. Indeed, he seemed infallible as he racked up finish after finish. Better still, he had his day of days when he benefited after seven teams withdrew from the US GP to finish third at Indianapolis, attracting calls from Portugal's president and prime minister, both of which helped when it came to attracting sponsors for 2006. Better still, Tiago finished eighth on merit in the Belgian GP, a result that impressed the sport's insiders even more. Amazingly, it was only at the following race, the 17th of the 19 rounds that he failed to reach the finish.

TRACK NOTES

Nationality:	PORTUGUESE
Born:	24 JULY, OPORTO, PORTUGAL
Website:	WWW.TIAGORACING.COM
Teams:	JORDAN 2005, MIDLAND 2006

CAREER RECORD

First Grand Prix:	2005 AUSTRALIAN GP
Grand Prix starts:	19
Grand Prix wins:	0
	best result: third, 2005 US GP
Poles:	0
Fastest laps:	0
Points:	6
Honours:	
2004 FORMULA DALLARA NISSAN V6 RUNNER-UP,	

SCUDERIA TORO ROSSO

Minardi is no more, for now is the dawn of Scuderia Toro Rosso, with Red Bull funds set to take the underfinanced team forward as never before. This will be a season from which to build, with the monetary boost likely to show in 2007's car.

This will be a holding year for this renamed team

Everyone's favourite minnows, Minardi, are no more. Team principal Paul Stoddart and founder Giancarlo Minardi have gone, but many of the staff have stayed on. The biggest change, apart from Franz Tost moving across from BMW Motorsport to take the helm, is the arrival of money from Red Bull, something that will change the team's image forever.

Now known as Scuderia Toro Rosso (Team Red Bull in Italian), they will continue to operate from their Italian base for another two years, but may well be moved elsewhere after that. Of more immediate concern, after the takeover, was which chassis it would be allowed to use, either last year's Red Bull

RB1 or the Minardi PS05. There was also a debate about whether it would stick with plans to run a rev-capped Cosworth V10, as equivalency debates raged, or be forced to run a V8, with all of the costs of modifying either chassis to fit.

The driver line-up includes the driver with the fastest sounding name in Formula One: Scott Speed. His involvement will boost interest from American fans; something very much in line with Red Bull's promotional plans.

The change of ownership casued great consternation in Holland as both Christijan Albers and Robert Doornbos had seemed set to remain for 2006 and now found themselves without a ride.

FOR THE RECORD

Country of origin:	Italy
Team base:	Ledbury, England and Faenza, Italy
Telephone:	(39) 0546 696111
Website:	www.redbullracing.com
Active in Formula One:	From 1985 (as Minardi until 2006)
Grands Prix contested:	341
Wins:	0
Pole positions:	0
Fastest laps:	0

2005 DRIVERS & RESULTS

Driver	Nationality	Races	Wins	Pts	Pos
Christijan Albers	Dutch	19	-	4	19th
Robert Doornbos	Dutch	8	-	0	n/a
Patrick Friesacher	Austrian	11	-	3	21st

THE TEAM

Team principal:	Franz Tost
Managing director:	tba
Technical director:	Gabriele Tredozi
Chief designer:	tba
Chief engineer:	Andrew Tilley
Team manager:	Massimo Rivola
Third driver:	Neel Jani
Chassis:	tba
Engine:	Cosworth V8
Tyres:	Michelin

SCOTT SPEED

America is so vital to Formula One that having an American driver is a must. Here's one and he's quick.

Mario Andretti was a fabulous world champion. His son Michael was not. It was in 1993 that Michael headed back Stateside before the season was out and ever since Formula One fans from the US have lacked a driver to call their own.

Thanks to Red Bull, Scott is now ready to show whether he can impress on this most exacting stage, for not only did the energy drink giant finance his racing in Europe over the past two seasons, but it has also bought Minardi in order to have a second team into which to place its drivers.

Speed will have to treat this as a learning year as he steps up from GP2 and A1GP, and he'll have to keep reminding those who wonder why he's not winning, that he's effectively racing for perennial backmarkers Minardi, albeit with a new livery.

According to paddock whispers, Scott will also have to learn not to have towering rages when things don't work as he'd like them to. The speed is there, it's just a question of doing well enough to attract the attentions of a team higher up the order - even Red Bull Racing - for 2007.

TRACK NOTES

Nationality:	AMERICAN
Born:	24 JANUARY, 1983, MANTECA, USA
Website:	WWW.SCOTT SPEED.COM
Teams:	SCUDERIA TORO ROSSO 2006

CAREER RECORD

First Grand Prix:	2006 BAHRAIN GP
Grand Prix starts:	0
Grand Prix wins:	0
Poles:	0
Fastest laps:	0
Points:	56
Honours:	2004 EUROPEAN & GERMAN FORMULA RENAULT CHAMPION, 2001 US FORMULA RUSSELL CHAMPION

VITANTONIO LIUZZI

Frustration will have been Vitantonio's overriding feeling last year, but he should see plenty of action in 2006.

Toeing the party line isn't the easiest thing to do if you're frustrated, but Vitantonio put on a brave face at being kept on the sidelines most of last season. Indeed, contesting the fourth to seventh rounds, from Monaco where he scored first time out to the Nurburgring, was all he got. Thereafter, he waited for another chance: it never came.

It comes as little surprise then that he drove his heart out in a 1960s Plymouth Barracuda at the Goodwood Revival, winning a legion of new fans in a car that offered less than mechanical perfection. That's one of the great things about Tonio: he's upbeat and a joy to have around.

Looking to 2006, Red Bull's purchase of Minardi, now Scuderia Toro Rosso, at least offers him a chance to show his undoubted racing skills. It's an opportunity he will grab with both hands, even though the car will be less competitive than the one he drove briefly for Red Bull Racing last year.

TRACK NOTES

Nationality:	ITALIAN
Born:	6 AUGUST 1981, LOCOROTONDO, ITALY
Website:	WWW.LIUZZI.COM
Teams:	RED BULL 2005, SCUDERIA TORO ROSSO 2006

CAREER RECORD

First Grand Prix:	2005 SAN MARINO GP
Grand Prix starts:	4
Grand Prix wins:	0
	(best result: eighth, 2005 San Marino GP)
Poles:	0
Fastest laps:	0
Points:	1
Honours:	2004 FORMULA 3000 CHAMPION

SUPER AGURI RACING

New teams are rare in Formula One and this one boosts the number of outfits on the starting grid from ten to 11, a welcome move for the forthcoming season. Oddly enough, Super Aguri Racing is thought to have come into being simply to assuage Honda's guilt at dropping Takuma Sato from its works team for 2006.

Bizarre as this may seem, that was how rumours of the creation of a Honda B team surfaced just before autumn's Japanese GP. It was thought this would placate Japanese fans when it became clear that Rubens Barrichello and Jenson Button would be driving for Honda (formerly BAR) in 2006, with Sato left out in the cold.

But then everyone clammed up, and it took a while before further details emerged. When they did, in stuttering fashion, it became clear that the team would be under the aegis of former grand prix driver Aguri Suzuki and, therefore, would be known as Super Aguri Racing.

At the time, it seemed certain that Sato would be joined by long-time BAR test driver Anthony Davidson, a team-mate in British Formula Three in 2001. Since the team's announcement took so long to happen, though, Davidson played safe and signed up to remain where he was, as test driver for Honda Racing. As this book closed for press,

the second drive looked set to go to Sakon Yamamoto, the driver who shone as Jordan's third driver at the Japanese GP. Should the team become competitive, though, Davidson is likely to be drafted back into the second race seat. Japanese racing car manufacturer Dome – a marque long associated with Honda – were also inked in, albeit operating from the defunct Arrows team's HQ at Leafield in Oxfordshire.

Having been spotted in negotiation at the Chinese GP, former Ferrari team manager Daniele Audetto was the link in this. (He has also worked for Arrows.) Indeed, with time incredibly tight to sort out a chassis worthy of the name in time for the new season, it will be with Arrows' A23 chassis, from when the team folded in 2002, that Super Aguri will begin its campaign, with its own chassis coming on stream later in the season. At least the supply of competitive Honda V8s is guaranteed.

At time of going to press, Super Aguri Racing are considered likely competitors in 2006.

FOR THE RECORD

Country of origin:	Japan
Team base:	Leafield, England
Telephone:	tba
Website:	tba
Active in Formula One:	From 2006
Grands Prix contested:	0
Wins:	0
Pole positions:	0
Fastest Laps:	0

DRIVERS' 2005 STATISTICS

Driver	Nationality	Races	Wins	Pts	Pos
Takuma Sato (BAR)	Japanese	16	0	1	23
Sakon Yamamoto	Japanese	00	0	00	Pos

THE TEAM

Team principal	Aguri Suzuki
Technical director:	Mark Preston
Chief designer:	Paul Bowen
Chief engineer:	Jacky Eeckelaert
Team manager:	Kevin Lee
Third driver:	tba
Chassis:	tba
Engine:	Honda V8
Tyres:	Michelin

TAKUMA SATO

Takuma must rebuild his reputation this year. The trouble is he'll have to do it with an all-new team.

It was an *annus horriblis* for Takuma last year. He missed the Malaysian GP as he was unwell, was disqualified from fifth place at the San Marino GP on his return, then banned from the next two events for a technical irregularity with BAR's cars. On top of that, he failed to score until the 13th round at the Hungaroring, and then over-drove after that, winning few friends for clashing with other drivers, notably Michael Schumacher and Jarno Trulli.

In between these two crashes, he was also dropped from what has just become Honda Racing - formerly BAR - and what had seemed like a rosy future was looking far less like one. Aware of the backlash in Japan, rumours surfaced of a Honda Junior team that would run both him and Anthony Davidson, as Japanese fans took umbrage when he was replaced by Rubens Barrichello.

One thing for sure is that any new team like this will be a step back from the team that Japan's best-ever driver has left. What is also certain is that Takuma hasn't become a bad driver overnight. It's just that he seemed to lose focus in 2005 and tried too hard to land a top result.

TRACK NOTES

Nationality:	JAPANESE
Born:	28 JANUARY 1977, TOKYO, JAPAN
Website:	WWW.TAKUMASATO.COM
Teams:	JORDAN 2002, BAR 2003-05, SUPER AGURI RACING 2006

CAREER RECORD

First Grand Prix:	2002 AUSTRALIAN GP
Grand Prix starts:	54
Grand Prix wins:	0
	best result: third 2004 US GP
Poles:	0
Fastest laps:	0
Points:	40
Honours:	
	2001 BRITISH FORMULA THREE CHAMPION

SAKON YAMAMOTO

As announced beyond the 11th hour, Super Aguri Racing looked like snapping up Sakon to be its second driver.

With Super Aguri's involvement in doubt up to and even after the closing of the entry list for this year's World Championship, it was only with Christmas upon us that Sakon started being mentioned as the likely team-mate for Takuma Sato in this new team. Yamamoto was little known in Formula One. Indeed, had he not shone when he was the Jordan team's third driver

for last October's Japanese GP, he would not have featured on anyone's radar at all. That he outpaced regular Jordan drivers Tiago Monteiro and Narain Kathikeyan on his home track certainly raised a few eyebrows, and his timing in doing so was impeccable. It meant that the 23-year-old vaulted past many compatriots just as a new Japanese team was in the pipeline.

*At time of going to press, Yuji Ide (team-mate to champion Motoyama) and Kousuke Matssura who spent 2005 with Aguri Suzuki's Indycar team were also in the frame to be SAR's second driver.

TRACK NOTES

Nationality:	JAPANESE
Born:	9TH JULY 1982, TOYOHASHI CITY, JAPAN
Website:	WWW.SAKON - YAMAMOTO.COM
Teams:	SUPER AGURI RACING 2006

CAREER RECORD

First Grand Prix:	2006 Bahrain GP
Grand Prix Starts:	0
Grand Prix Wins:	0
Poles:	0
Fastest Laps:	0
Points:	0
Honours:	
	1999 FA CLASS JAPANESE KART CHAMPION,
	1997 FA2 CLASS LOCAL KART CHAMPION.

However well prepared a team might be, mechanics will always burn the midnight oil

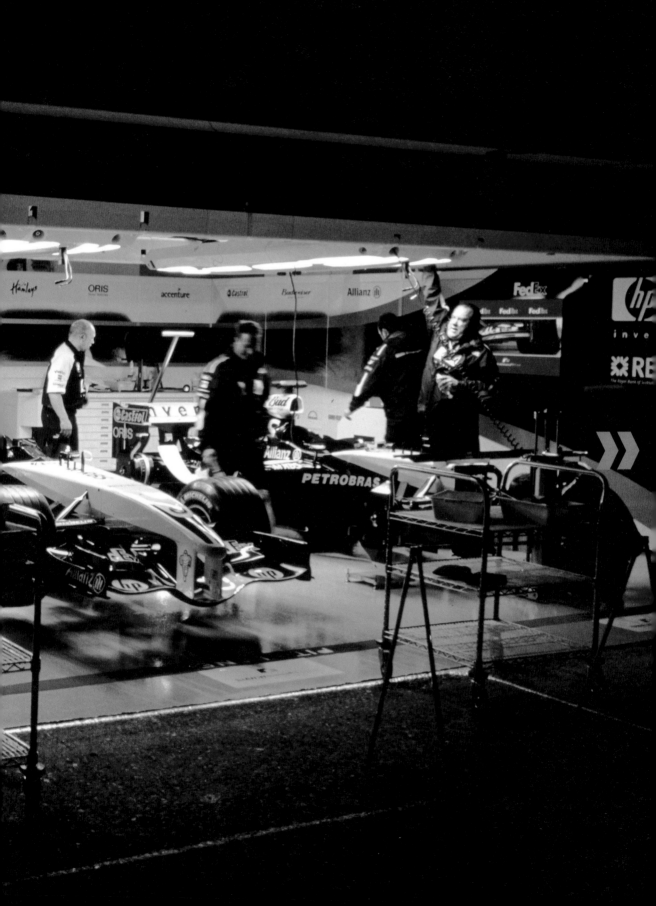

Turkish delight is no longer just a confection, but a circuit outside Istanbul as well...

HONDA'S LONG GESTATION

Over forty years after it first entered Formula One racing, Japanese car-maker Honda is to become sole owner of BAR Honda. They previously held a 45 per cent stake in the team and are now thought to be planning a second F1 team next season.

1964-1968: after joint Lotus and Brabham project collapses, Honda makes F1 debut at Nurburgring with state-of-the-art aluminium monocoque chassis and revolutionary load-bearing transverse-mounted engine. Honda withdraws from motor-racing after poor fifth season

RA271 claimed Honda's first win in Mexico, 1965

1983-1987: return to F1 with Spirit Honda followed by contract to supply Williams engines. FW10 claims first win in Dallas, 1984

Williams
McLaren

CONSTRUCTORS' CHAMPIONSHIPS
1986-1987
1988-1991

1988-1992: Honda joins McLaren, going on to win four further successive Constructors' Championships, but pulls out at end of 1992

MP4/4 driven by Alain Prost and Ayrton Senna won 15 out of 16 races in 1988 – the most successful car in F1 history

BAR Honda

2000-2006: agrees to supply British American Tobacco with engines for the new BAR team, extending deal in 2001 to chassis development. EU legislation banning tobacco advertising on F1 leads BAT to sell stake in BAR

2006 drivers Rubens Barrichello and Jenson Button

MAKING THE TYRES WORK

The single-race tyre rule was a defining factor in 2005's race strategies – it was clearly evident at Monaco when tyre wear left Renault struggling. With tyres expected to last over 50 per cent longer, choosing the right combination is crucial.

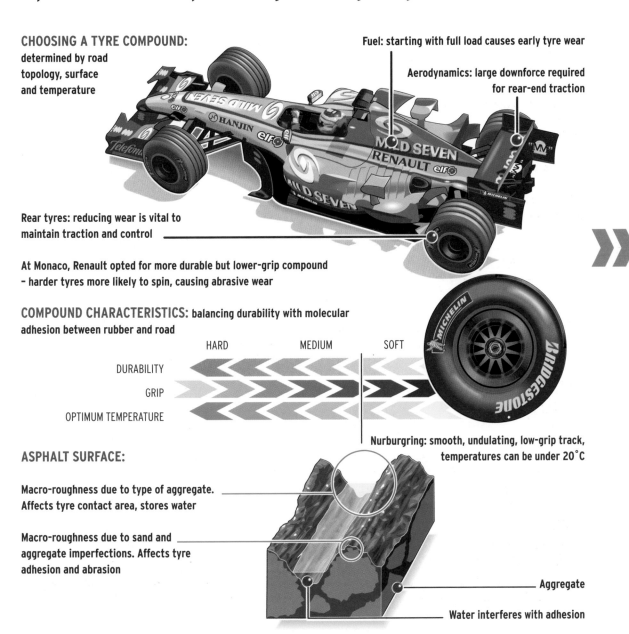

CHOOSING A TYRE COMPOUND: determined by road topology, surface and temperature

Fuel: starting with full load causes early tyre wear

Aerodynamics: large downforce required for rear-end traction

Rear tyres: reducing wear is vital to maintain traction and control

At Monaco, Renault opted for more durable but lower-grip compound – harder tyres more likely to spin, causing abrasive wear

COMPOUND CHARACTERISTICS: balancing durability with molecular adhesion between rubber and road

HARD — MEDIUM — SOFT

DURABILITY

GRIP

OPTIMUM TEMPERATURE

Nurburgring: smooth, undulating, low-grip track, temperatures can be under 20°C

ASPHALT SURFACE:

Macro-roughness due to type of aggregate. Affects tyre contact area, stores water

Macro-roughness due to sand and aggregate imperfections. Affects tyre adhesion and abrasion

Aggregate

Water interferes with adhesion

V8 ENGINES FOR 2006

Many technical changes seem draconian when they are announced, but, actually, they end up making little difference to the fan. Will the loss of 600cc and two cylinders for 2006 be one of those? Or will it belittle the category?

Every now and again – and nowadays more often than not – the Formula One rule book is given a shake-up. For 2006, it's not aerodynamic tweaking that will be making the diffence; it's what's happening in the engine bay. The V10 engines have been shown the door and the capacity of the engines that will replace them are to be cut by two cylinders and also reduced in cubic capacity, from 3000 to 2400cc.

Rest assured: although power output is expected to drop by as much as 200bhp, to 750 – the V8s will rev at up to and even over 20,000rpm – this year's cars will still be blindingly fast. The drivers will be able to recognize what the stopwatch will detect, but for race fans trackside the difference will be hard to identify. Some drivers called the V8s

"Mickey Mouse" in initial testing, but it will be the same for all of them.

One of the advantages of the V8s is that the constructors feel they will be reliable, something that's imperative with the two-race rule. Indeed, Mercedes' Norbert Haug was critical of this rule last year as he reckoned that it was detrimental to the racing as the penalty for any failure – a ten-place grid demotion – was draconian.

Another advantage might be the V8's fuel economy, with some reckoning that they may be able to run non-stop in grands prix due both to their economy and the fact their smaller size will allow for larger fuel tanks.

The change was instigated by the sport's governing body in the interests of reducing the speeds of the cars, to keep them in check

with the parameters of the circuits used and thus increase driver safety. Perhaps more pertinently, the change was made in the interests of cutting costs and thus keeping Formula One affordable to the teams and manufacturers in order to restore the number of cars in the World Championship from its 2005 level of ten teams (20 cars) to the 26 cars and more that used to be the norm.

Back in 1989 when, as it happens, the sport was dominated by cheap V8s, up to 39 cars were turning up for the right to fight to qualify. As many as 13 of those had to negotiate a first-four-past-the-post pre-qualifying session simply to reach the stage that all teams have been guaranteed of late entry to qualifying. Even then, four of the 30-car qualifying field would fail to make the cut.

If Toyota's new V8 engine is a strong one, then the German-based Japanese team could join the ranks of winners in 2006

Mercedes are hoping their new V8 engine will be good enough to keep the team challenging for race wins in 2006

Formula One has to work harder for its corn in the 21st century and Minardi – now Scuderia Toro Rosso – declared last year that it would have to stick with V10s. Since it didn't have a works engine deal, it couldn't afford to change its chassis to accommodate one of the new V8s. Heads were scratched and it was agreed that the Anglo-Italian team, which has existed on the breadline since it came into F1, would be allowed to stick with a V10, albeit with a rev limit to keep its power output on a level with that of the other nine teams who had swapped over to V8s. A suggested level of strangulation could be achieved through the fitting of a 77mm air restrictor and a rev limit of 16,700rpm. This is down as much as 300rpm on the free-revving screamers of the end of 2005 that led to Honda hitting the fabled 1000bhp mark in the season-closing races.

The majority of manufacturers were less than happy with the change to V8s, feeling that they would cost the teams more than the V10s, as the new engines would have to be built from scratch and couldn't simply be developments of the 2005 versions. BMW team principal Mario Theissen was one such protesting voice, with Honda and Mercedes joining BMW in threatening to take legal action against the FIA for its enforced change of the regulations. Among their charges is that the V10 engine rules had been set to remain in place under Formula One's binding contract, the Concorde Agreement, until the end of 2007. Theissen said that the cost argument didn't stack up, as BMW had effectively lost the development costs that had already gone into their 2006 V10. Indeed, there were many last summer who felt that the FIA's engine rule change was simply a product of the FIA's agenda to confront the manufacturers who were pushing it for a greater share of Formula One's television revenue.

Whatever, V8s are here and the engine builders will have spent the winter eking the most power possible out of them, ready for the first race of the season.

When Cosworth V8s were cheap, little teams like Onyx joined the ranks in 1989

The FIA Formula One World Championship has undergone a period of expansion and reorganisation. There was talk of extending it even further for 2006, to take in a new grand prix in Mexico. However, that race is now not going to happen and the championship calendar will remain at 19 grands prix. Still, this is a figure that ensures the teams, drivers, engineers and mechanics will have little chance of a rest between now and the end of the season.

Indeed, the trend in recent seasons, as the number of grands prix has risen from 16 to 19, has been for an increase in back-to-back races – those held on consecutive weekends – and a three-week gap in August, to allow the exhausted parties to rejoin their families for a holiday or simply to reacquaint themselves with that place called home.

The will-it-won't-it saga of Mexico's race is one that has been played out many times over the past decade or so, as ambitious countries or individuals have jockeyed to land the support for a grand prix. Russia, India, Indonesia, the Lebanon, Egypt, Cyprus, Romania and Libya are but a few of those who have tried to join the gang, while Mexico is on the list of those, including South Africa and Argentina, who have attempted to regain their place at motorsport's top table after having lacked the funds to continue in the past.

This time, Mexico's efforts weren't concentrated on restoring its circuit in Mexico City, but on bringing the race to a brand-new track in its tourist region near Cancun. However, in the end, the deal was never done.

Following on from the introduction of a wave of new circuits in Malaysia, Bahrain, China and Turkey – a circuit that became an instant classic on its debut such was the level of praise from teams

KNOW THE TRACKS

and drivers – in the past few seasons and the transformation of the circuit layouts of both Hockenheim and the Nurburging, some of the longstanding circuits now feel very traditional.

This is no bad thing, however, with the likes of Monza, Spa-Francorchamps, Monaco and Silverstone – all circuits that hosted rounds of the inaugural Formula One World Championship in 1950 – providing a link with the past that the likes of Sepang, Sakhir, Shanghai and Istanbul won't be able to do for years to come. Silverstone has plans to leap from the ranks of the old into those of the new with a £600 million modernisation plan.

The older circuits may lack the cutting-edge design of the newer ones, although this mainly relates to the circuit infrastructure and buildings, but they all have a discernible character, something that any Formula One fan is able to identify with the quickest of glances at a photograph. They have history on their side and instantly conjure up images of grands prix in the past when the best of the drivers produced epic races in their quest for glory. Nowhere is this more apparent than Monaco, the street circuit with its world-famous stretch along the waterfront past the yachts of the rich and famous.

Several circuits fall into the middle ground, somewhere between the old and the new. Imola is the pick of these due to the way that its blacktop twists and bucks around its parkland setting, while Suzuka stands out for its landmark Ferris wheel and corners such as its tricky uphill Esses. The Circuit de Catalunya, home of the Spanish Grand Prix, is technically excellent, but has yet to mark its place in history, something that can also be said of France's Formula One venue, Magny-Cours. Both are good places to go and watch racing, but attaining a soul isn't something that happens overnight. Standing at the very back of the queue for elevation to the rank of the loved, though, is the Hungaroring. This is a track that is never likely to win over many fans as its cramped, narrow layout requires drivers to perform superhuman acts to stop the race from becoming a procession.

Then there are the two North American circuits, tracks that could hardly be more different. The Montreal circuit snakes its way around a tiny island on the St Laurence River in complete contrast to the Indianapolis Motor Speedway, where massive grandstands dwarf the track at its feet. Head south of the equator to Brazil and the down-at-heel but charming Interlagos is, yet again, completely different from any other venue on the race calendar.

Sheer diversity is one of the best features of Formula One, but, wherever the circus goes, what binds it all together is the passion of the fans in the grandstands, the noise of the cars and the red-hot intensity of the racing.

BAHRAIN

Racing in Bahrain took Formula One to pastures new, taking it into a desert for the first time, to a land of sand, rock, palm trees and heavily watered grass verges.

Leading circuit architect, Hermann Tilke – yes, him again – was given a brief to build a circuit on a patch of rocky desert next to a camel farm. Better still, it was underwritten by a near open-ended cheque book. Money was simply not a problem, but excellence was demanded. This was certainly a blank canvas to work with and he decided to give it some character by splitting it into two notional sectors, the desert and the oasis, with the main grandstands, pit buildings and paddock in the oasis sector.

In addition to this split-personality of desert and oasis, Tilke gave the 14-turn layout some trademark touches, such as four straights leading into tight corners. Turn 1 is the first, with its quick feed into a tightish Turn 2, not dissimilar to that at Sepang.

After a short straight to tight Turn 4, the track hits one of its most exciting sectors, the downhill sweepers between Turn 5 and Turn 7, leading to the Turn 8 hairpin. The grandstand behind the paddock provides an excellent view of this and also of the back straight, which is entered by a tricky, off-camber left-hander, Turn 10.

From Turn 11, the circuit disappears into the far reaches of its desert section before coming back to the watered grass verges of the start-finish straight through slow Turn 14.

Wind blowing copious amounts of sand from the surrounding desert on to the track is, however, a perpetual problem.

INSIDE TRACK

BAHRAIN GRAND PRIX

Date:	**12 March**
Circuit length:	**3.366 miles/5.417km**
Number of laps:	**57**
Telephone:	**00 973 406222**
Website:	**www.bahraingp.com.bh**

PREVIOUS WINNERS

2004	**Michael Schumacher** FERRARI
2005	**Fernando Alonso** RENAULT

I have a dream: The Bahrain International Circuit at Sakhir was created after a massive push from Crown Prince Shaikh Salman bin Hamad Al Khalifa, an ardent motor-racing fan who was able to put the requisite pressure on the government to finance the scheme. Putting one over on its flashier neighbour Dubai was also seen as a good thing by the locals, as was all the tourism that the grand prix would generate.

Fast workers: The deal to hold a grand prix was signed in September 2002, yet the circuit was still ready in time for its debut, at the start of April 2004.

Island hopping: The main island of Bahrain, Bahrain Island, is home to the circuit, but there are 35 other islands, although many of them are tiny as the entire kingdom covers just 273 square miles.

I'm stuck on you: A special glue had to be applied to the sandy areas beyond the kerbs and rumble strips around the circuit for 2005, as errant drivers were bringing stones back onto the track that were large enough to puncture tyres.

Keeping your cool: This can be tricky unless you are in an air-conditioned VIP suite, as trackside temperatures can hit 50 degrees. Fortunately, humidity is low.

Watch your heads: A Gulf Air Boeing 747 did a low-level flypast to mark the opening of the circuit in 2004.

Circuit map

- **100** Gear/kph
- **100** Gear/mph
- **0** Timing sector
- Key Corners

Turn 4 — **2** 105 / 63
Turn 6 — **3** 200 / 125
Turn 5
Turn 10 — **2** 80 / 50
T 7 — **4** 215 / 135
Turn 9
Turn 13 — **3** 170 / 105
Turn 12
Turn 8 — **2** 90 / 56
Turn 3 — **3** 190 / 120
Turn 2 — **2** 120 / 75
Turn 1 — **1** 80 / 50
Turn 11 — **6** 300 / 186
6 320 / 200
6 320 / 200
START — **3**
Turn 14 — **2** 95 / 60

2005 POLE TIME: **Alonso (Renault)**, 3m01.902s*, 133.232mph/214.406kph

2005 FASTEST LAP: **De la Rosa, 1m31.447s, 132.392mph/213.054kph**

2005 WINNER'S AVERAGE SPEED: 128.681mph/207.082kph

LAP RECORD: **M Schumacher (Ferrari), 1m30.252s, 134.260mph/216.061kph, 2004**

*AGGREGATE OF TWO LAPS

SEPANG

Nobody likes the heat or the humidity very much, but the facilities are excellent and the Sepang circuit offers plenty of opportunities for overtaking.

If you want to give drivers the chance to overtake, offer them a long straight that is entered via a slow corner with another tight turn at the far end. Then make it wide and stand back to enjoy the fun. This is what ubiquitous circuit designer Hermann Tilke did when the Malaysians asked for a world-class racing facility.

Even from a standing start from halfway down the start-finish straight, there's distance aplenty for the field to slipstream and jostle for position into the first corner, Pangkor Laut. Actually, this tight right is a true hairpin, as it keeps on going past 180 degrees. And it's harder than most hairpins in terms of positioning too, as it feeds immediately into a tight

left, making a driver's line out of the first turn very important if he wants to try a move into Turn 2.

The circuit then opens out through a long right onto a straight before rising into the 90-degree right at Langkawi, with the apex on a crest. The flow picks up again through a left-right sequence, reaching the highest point at the 80-degree right at Klia on to another small straight. Doubling back at the Berjaya Tioman hairpin, a final twisting section of the circuit follows before drivers have to position themselves for a quick entry on to the back straight. This is so they can get a tow to the final corner, a left-hand hairpin, the approach to which provides them with their best chance of overtaking.

INSIDE TRACK

MALAYSIAN GRAND PRIX

Date:	**19 March**
Circuit length:	**3.444 miles/5.542km**
Number of laps:	**56**
Telephone:	**00 60 3 85262000**
Website:	**www.malaysiangp.com.my**

PREVIOUS WINNERS

1999	**Eddie Irvine** FERRARI
2000	**Michael Schumacher** FERRARI
2001	**Michael Schumacher** FERRARI
2002	**Ralf Schumacher** WILLIAMS
2003	**Kimi Raikkonen** McLAREN
2004	**Michael Schumacher** FERRARI
2005	**Fernando Alonso** RENAULT

Arrive by train: The circuit is linked by railway, both to the nearby international airport and to downtown Kuala Lumpur, which is 20 miles away.

This way and that: The two-sided grandstand along the start-finish straight is designed so that half of the circuit can be seen from either side.

Keeping in the shade: Shade is very important for spectators as temperatures can soar to 40 degrees and beyond. Giant fans attached to hoses are positioned along the shopping mall between the two sides of the main grandstand, spraying a welcome cooling breeze.

Action aplenty: David Coulthard proved in 1999 that Michael Schumacher could be passed, even in his pomp, catching the German unawares into Turn 2. Schumacher tried a similar move at the same point in 2003, but got it wrong and punted Jarno Trulli's Renault into a spin.

A head for heights: The Petronas Twin Towers in downtown Kuala Lumpur are the tallest skyscrapers in the world, at 1,483 feet, although the tips are often shrouded in smog at this incredibly humid time of year.

Circuit map

0 | **100** Gear/kph
100 Gear/mph

0 Timing sector

Key Corners

1 **78 / 49** Pangkor Laut chicane

Turn 2 **1** **78 / 49**

Turn 3 **5** **251 / 156**

6 **306 / 190**

2 **110 / 68** Langkawi

5 **245 / 152** Turn 5

Genting **4** **216 / 134**

2 **85 / 53**

Turn 7 **3** **180 / 112**

3 **179 / 111** Klia

START **3**

Sunway Lagoon **2** **107 / 67**

1 **76 / 47**

2 **193 / 120** Turn 10

2

Turn 12 **5** **247 / 154**

Turn 11 **2** **139 / 86**

2005 POLE TIME: **Alonso (Renault), 3m07.672s*, 132.128mph/212.630kph**
2005 FASTEST LAP: **Raikkonen (McLaren), 1m35.483s, 129.865mph/208.988kph**

*AGGREGATE OF TWO LAPS

2005 WINNER'S AVERAGE SPEED: **126.397mph/203.407kph**
LAP RECORD: **Montoya (Williams), 1m34.223s, 131.595mph/211.772kph, 2004**

MELBOURNE

Despite losing its pole position at the start of the grand prix calendar, Melbourne is still a big attraction with great weather and an enthusiastic set of fans.

Jetlag aside, the Australian GP is a popular one. This isn't because the circuit in Melbourne's Albert Park is a great one, because it isn't. It's because the city is one of the best to visit: the fans bubble with enthusiasm and the weather is good. Until this year, because it used to be the first race on the calendar, it was where the teams and drivers finally discovered whether it was going to be a good year or not for them.

All drivers who have raced here before, and even those who have only practised it on their home computers, are aware that the first corner is a sharpish right followed almost immediately by a left. In itself, this sequence is benign, but on the first lap of the race it's a good thing that there's

a large gravel trap to collect the fallen.

Turn 3 is reached via a straight bound by concrete walls, making it feel like a funnel as the cars burst out into the light at this tight right. After a left and a right, the drivers enter another tunnel through the trees. Then comes the back section on the park's golf course. Not only is this faster, but it is also more open, with a lake on the drivers' right. Broken up by the Clark Chicane and the esses at Turn 11, it comes to an end at the right-hander at Ascari. It then enters the trees again until just before Senna, a tricky left that's the last corner but one.

Overtaking is very tricky, but a good exit from the final corner gives drivers a chance into Turn 1.

INSIDE TRACK

AUSTRALIAN GRAND PRIX

Date:	**2 April**
Circuit length:	**3.295 miles/5.303km**
Number of laps:	**58**
Telephone:	**00 61 3 92587100**
Website:	**www.grandprix.com.au**

PREVIOUS WINNERS

1997	**David Coulthard** McLAREN
1998	**Mika Hakkinen** McLAREN
1999	**Eddie Irvine** FERRARI
2000	**Michael Schumacher** FERRARI
2001	**Michael Schumacher** FERRARI
2002	**Michael Schumacher** FERRARI
2003	**David Coulthard** McLAREN
2004	**Michael Schumacher** FERRARI
2005	**Giancarlo Fisichella** RENAULT

Been here before: The World Championship didn't arrive in Melbourne until 1997, but Albert Park had hosted the Australian GP before, in 1953 and again in 1956, with Stirling Moss winning the latter non-championship event.

Handy from the city: Albert Park is just a short tram ride from Melbourne's central business district and city centre. Better still, with trams arriving every few minutes along all four sides of the site, there's no need for spectators to get jammed in car parks for hours.

First, but not second: David Coulthard won the first World Championship round here in 1997 and was set to make it two in a row when Mika Hakkinen pitted from the lead in 1998. His McLaren team-mate misheard a call from the pitwall, however, and was waved straight through, with Coulthard moving over to honour a pre-race agreement that, whichever of them led into the first corner, would go on to win.

Up, up and away: Ralf Schumacher experienced one of the most dramatic moments in the circuit's history when his Williams got airborne over Rubens Barrichello's Ferrari at the start of the 2002 race.

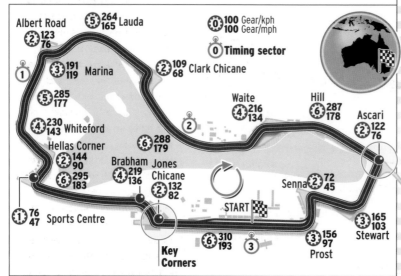

2005 POLE TIME: Fisichella (Renault), 3m01.460s*, 131.057mph/210.906kph
2005 FASTEST LAP: Alonso (Renault), 1m25.683s, 138.452mph/222.807kph
*AGGREGATE OF TWO LAPS

2005 WINNER'S AVERAGE SPEED: 133.705mph/215.167kph
LAP RECORD: M Schumacher (Ferrari), 1m24.125s, 141.016mph/226.933kph, 2004

IMOLA

The teams rejoice when they arrive at Imola, not because it's the world's best track, but because it's close to home after the season-opening fly-aways.

It has been years since people started saying that Imola was past it, a crumbling anachronism. The pitlane is narrow, the garages are below standard and the paddock behind them is cramped by the proximity of a river. There's still something magical about the place, however. This stems not only from the spring blossoms decorating this park-like setting, but also from the fact that many teams unveil their new cars after running interim chassis in the first few races.

Since the dreadful events of 1994 (see sidebar), chicanes have broken the flow of the track. The result of this is that the start of the opening lap, around Tamburello, is now more interesting, as the drivers use the kerbs in their attempts to gain a place.

Unfortunately, the track is a shadow of its former self thereafter.

The second chicane, at Villeneuve, prevents drivers from being able to make a move into the uphill, left-handed hairpin at Tosa, unless they have an appreciable speed advantage.

The climb up to the circuit's highest point, at Piratella, down through the Acque Minerali and up again to the chicane at Variante Alta is a classic strip of track, but sadly not one that offers much in the way of chances to pass. The double-apex downhill Rivazza does, but there's very little space and contact is frequent.

The end of the lap is simpler than of old, with just a simple chicane at Variante Bassa back on to the start-finish straight.

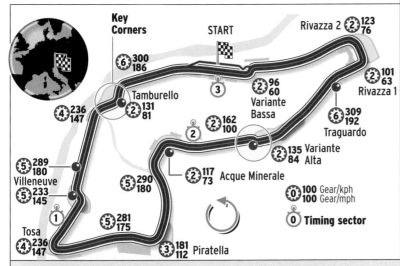

2005 POLE TIME: Raikkonen (McLaren),
2m42.880s*, 135.442mph/217.963kph
2005 FASTEST LAP: M Schumacher (Ferrari),
1m21.858s, 134.810mph/216.946kph

2005 WINNER'S AVERAGE SPEED:
129.925mph/209.084kph
LAP RECORD: M Schumacher (Ferrari),
1m20.411s, 137.230mph/220.840kph, 2004

*AGGREGATE OF TWO LAPS

NURBURGRING

Unloved when it was relaunched, the modern Nurburgring is starting to win over some fans, as it offers some easily achievable overtaking points.

Gone are the days when a grand prix at the Nurburgring meant a long, long lap twisting through the Eifel forest, with humps over which the cars would take off and the odd banked corner to keep the drivers on their toes. All that belongs to the dim and distant past. Its last grand prix was back in 1976, and the fans have long since settled for a goodish circuit next to the same forest.

Changes made by Hermann Tilke before the 2002 race have rendered the first corner unrecognisable. No longer is it a right-left esse with a huge gravel trap to catch errant cars. Now, a right-hand hairpin starts the Mercedes Arena complex, followed by a tightish left. Then there's gentle banking around to another left and finally a right on to the short straight that used to be the opening right-left. Action is guaranteed going into the new first turn, especially on the opening lap.

The track sweeps through a fast left into the Ford Kurve and then down to the Dunlop hairpin. From here, the track rises through a sweeper to the third-gear left at the top of the hill, the Michelin Kurve.

A good line through the following right, the Bit Kurve, can provide a driver with a tow down the hill and then up the other side into the NGK Chicane.

This is one of the key overtaking points. If a driver fails to get by at that point, there's always a chance to do so going into the final right-hander as long as the driver ahead slides wide on the exit of the chicane.

INSIDE TRACK

EUROPEAN GRAND PRIX

Date:	**7 May**
Circuit length:	**3.198 miles/5.148km**
Number of laps:	**60**
Telephone:	**00 49 2691 923060**
Website:	**www.nuerburgring.de**

PREVIOUS WINNERS

1995	**Michael Schumacher**	BENETTON
1996	**Jacques Villeneuve**	WILLIAMS
1998*	**Mika Hakkinen**	McLAREN
1999	**Jonny Herbert**	STEWART
2000	**Michael Schumacher**	FERRARI
2001	**Michael Schumacher**	FERRARI
2002	**Rubens Barrichello**	FERRARI
2003	**Ralf Schumacher**	WILLIAMS
2004	**Michael Schumacher**	FERRARI
2005	**Fernando Alonso**	RENAULT

*As the Luxemburg GP

Unfit for racing: In 1976, even before they had raced over the 14-mile, 174-turn Nurburgring Nordschleife, drivers said that the track was no longer safe enough to host a grand prix. When that race nearly claimed the life of Niki Lauda, its fate was settled, at least as far as Formula One was concerned, although it's still used by club racers today.

Go for a spin: If you turn up at the Nurburgring at any time besides grand prix week, you can pay a small fee and take your road car or motorbike around the Nordschleife.

Revisit the past: The circuit contains an excellent museum on its infield, filled with cars, bikes and photographs of the famous corners of the mighty Nordschleife.

New for old: Built over the start-finish straight and the surrounding area of the Nurburgring Nordschleife, the current circuit hosted a grand prix for the first time in 1984, when Alain Prost won the European GP there for McLaren. The new track hosted a German GP for the one and only time the following year.

Circuit Map

Hatzenbach Bogen (6) 289/180

(6) 310/193

NGK Chicane (2) 107/67

Bit Kurve (3) 161/100

(1) 89/55 — Mercedes Arena

(2) 128/80

(2) 113/70 — Coca-Cola Curve

Michelin (3) 148/92

START

(3)

(1) 75/46 — Castrol-S

Audi-S (5) 226/140

(5) 258/160

(1)

(4) 196/122

(2) 112/70 — Ford

Key Corners

(0) 100 Gear/kph / 100 Gear/mph

(0) Timing sector

(2) 94/58 — Dunlop Kehre

2005 POLE TIME: Heidfeld (Williams),
1m30.081s, 127.805mph/205.673kph
2005 FASTEST LAP: Alonso (Renault),
1m30.711s, 126.955mph/204.305kph

2005 WINNER'S AVERAGE SPEED:
123.392mph/198.571kph
LAP RECORD: M Schumacher (Ferrari),
1m29.468s, 128.719mph/207.144kph, 2004

BARCELONA

A track that is well known to drivers as a result of the endless testing that is done here, the Circuit de Catalunya offers a little bit of everything.

The first corner at the Circuit de Catalunya is always a place of much incident. Not only is it approached down one of the longest straights used in Formula One, but the drivers enter at speed through a fourth-gear final corner. This means that the cars are nudging 200mph as they drop down to the first corner, Elf, where they start to try and scrub off sufficient speed to negotiate the second-gear right-hander. In fact, it's effectively a right-left, with Turn 2 of Elf effectively being conjoined.

If all goes well on the approach to Elf, a slipstream both caught and used offers the best opportunity for drivers to overtake, either by diving down the inside or by braving it out around the outside, so that they are on the better line for the second part of the corner.

It's uphill from here, turning right through Renault and then twice right at Repsol. The track then starts to dip down through the tricky left at SEAT, which requires a clean exit to enable the driver to carry speed down to the following left-hander, before rising sharply to Campsa. After cresting the hill through this right-hander, there's a short straight down the hill to La Caixa, a corner that was reprofiled to less-than-unanimous praise for 2004. Banc Sabadell is a slow and climbing double right, before the cars accelerate hard downhill and slingshot through Europcar to try and hit the straight with as much speed as possible.

INSIDE TRACK

SPANISH GRAND PRIX

Date:	**14 May**
Circuit length:	**2.875 miles/4.627km**
Number of laps:	**66**
Telephone:	**00 34 93 5719771**
Website:	**www.circuitcat.com**

PREVIOUS WINNERS

1996	**Michael Schumacher** FERRARI
1997	**Jacques Villeneuve** WILLIAMS
1998	**Mika Hakkinen** McLAREN
1999	**Mika Hakkinen** McLAREN
2000	**Mika Hakkinen** McLAREN
2001	**Michael Schumacher** FERRARI
2002	**Michael Schumacher** FERRARI
2003	**Michael Schumacher** FERRARI
2004	**Michael Schumacher** FERRARI
2005	**Kimi Raikkonen** McLAREN

We've been here before: Located just to the north of Barcelona, the circuit is the third situated in and around the city, following on from Pedralbes which hosted the Spanish GP in 1951 and 1954 and from Montjuich Park that did so in 1969, 1971, 1973 and 1975, but never returned after an accident killed four spectators in the last of these races.

A lucky break?: The Circuit de Catalunya was given the Spanish GP in 1991 as Martin Donnelly was nearly killed in a huge accident at the Jerez circuit in Andalucia the year before.

Olympic winners: The city of Barcelona underwent intensive modernisation in time to host the Olympic Games in 1992, with the dock area turned into the fashionable Port Olimpic and the main stadium built in Montjuich Park.

Two wheels to four: Motorcycle racing has long been Spain's first love, but when Fernando Alonso started winning grands prix from 2003 onwards, the crowds flocked in. An extra 20,000 fans travelled from his home region of Asturias to watch him in 2004. No other Spanish driver had previously won a grand prix.

Circuit map

- **100** Gear/kph / **100** Gear/mph
- **0** Timing sector
- **Key Corners**
- Campsa **4** **221**/**137**
- Repsol **2** **131**/**81**
- **6** **286**/**178**
- **2** **97**/**60**
- **4** **229**/**142**
- Renault **3** **187**/**116**
- **2** **137**/**85** Elf
- **2** **145**/**90**
- **6** **316**/**196**
- Banc Sabadell **2** **118**/**73**
- **4** **237**/**147** Europcar
- **2** **114**/**71** La Caixa
- **4** **228**/**142** New Holland
- START

2005 POLE TIME: **Raikkonen (McLaren),**
2m31.421s*, 139.748mph/224.892kph
2005 FASTEST LAP: **Fisichella (Renault),**
1m15.641s, 136.840mph/220.212kph

*AGGREGATE OF TWO LAPS

2005 WINNER'S AVERAGE SPEED:
130.397mph/209.844kph
LAP RECORD: **See fastest lap**

MONACO

If you want different, Monaco is different. From its casino, yachts and beautiful people to its narrow, bumpy blacktop, there's nowhere quite like it.

The main thing people who watch their Formula One on television need to know about Monaco is that the circuit is far narrower and infinitely steeper than it appears on your screens at home. In addition, the crash barriers that line its length are never more than a few inches away from the racing line: their height and the buildings beyond them make the drivers feel as though they are in a tunnel long before they reach the one beneath the Grand Hotel (formerly Loews).

The start-finish straight bends to the right, making it hard for those at the back of the grid to see the starting lights. From here, it's a short blast to Ste Devote, with the barriers ready to claim any cars that bounce off each other.

Next, it's up, up, up before commitment is demanded by Massanet, the left-hander with a blind exit into Casino Square. As soon as the drivers drift through the following right-hander, the track's crown is noticeable on the drop to Mirabeau and on down to the hairpin in front of the Grand Hotel. There's precious little room as the track dips through two rights and plunges the drivers into the darkness of the tunnel.

Blinking in the daylight as they emerge, the drivers have to slow over a crest from 180mph to less than 35mph in order to take the harbour-front chicane. Then they accelerate again towards Tabac and the opened-out Piscine section, before completing the lap with the hairpin at La Rascasse and the bumpy, up-and-over right-hander, Antony Nogues, that spits the cars back past the pits.

INSIDE TRACK

MONACO GRAND PRIX

Date:	**28 May**
Circuit length:	**2.075 miles/3.339km**
Number of laps:	**78**
Telephone:	**00 377 93152600**
Website:	**www.acm.mc**

PREVIOUS WINNERS

1996	**Olivier Panis** LIGIER
1997	**Michael Schumacher** FERRARI
1998	**Mika Hakkinen** McLAREN
1999	**Michael Schumacher** FERRARI
2000	**David Coulthard** McLAREN
2001	**Michael Schumacher** FERRARI
2002	**David Coulthard** McLAREN
2003	**Juan Pablo Montoya** WILLIAMS
2004	**Jarno Trulli** RENAULT
2005	**Kimi Raikkonen** McLAREN

When is a straight not a straight?: At Monaco, where even the start-finish straight is nothing of the sort, arcing as it does to the right. This isn't surprising, however, as the circuit runs around a town that came into existence long before cars were invented and where nothing is straight. Only the section alongside the harbour can pertain to be a straight.

Join the high rollers: Partying in Monaco is not advised unless you have very deep pockets. Even the highly paid drivers gasp at the price of drinks in the top nightclubs, such as Jimmy'z. As for the casino, you'll need some notes of seriously high denominations to impress there.

The need for speed: Monaco has an incredibly high ratio of supercars on its roads, but with its strict speed limits there is hardly a metre of road on which many of them actually need to change out of first gear.

Changing of the guard: Having died just before last year's race, 2005 was the first time that a Monaco GP had not been presided over by Prince Rainier since the inaugural race was won by "Williams" in 1929.

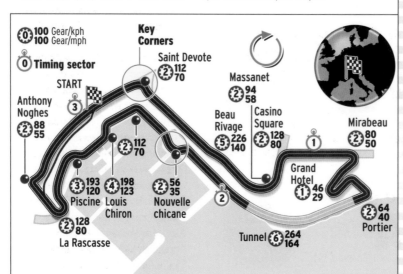

100 Gear/kph
100 Gear/mph

Timing sector

Key Corners

Saint Devote 112 70

Massanet 94 58

Beau Rivage 226 140

Casino Square 128 80

Mirabeau 80 50

START

Anthony Noghes 88 55

Grand Hotel 46 29

Piscine 193 120

Louis Chiron 198 123

Nouvelle chicane 56 35

Portier 64 40

La Rascasse 128 80

Tunnel 264 164

2005 POLE TIME: **Raikkonen (McLaren),**
2m30.323s*, 99.386mph/159.939kph
2005 FASTEST LAP: **M Schumacher (Ferrari),**
1m15.842s, 98.517mph/158.540kph
*AGGREGATE OF TWO LAPS

2005 WINNER'S AVERAGE SPEED:
92.279mph/148.502kph
LAP RECORD: **M Schumacher (Ferrari),**
1m14.439s, 100.373mph/161.527kph, 2004

SILVERSTONE

It's fast, it's open, it's awash with a sense of history and, not only that... it also provides the perfect setting for some of the best racing of the year.

Nips and tucks may have been applied over the years, but the essence of the circuit that hosted the first round of the inaugural Formula One World Championship back in 1950 remains to this day. A lap of Silverstone may not have the flat-out flow of old, but it remains one of Formula One's superior challenges.

First up is Copse, a right-hander that offers just enough space for drivers to have a go at passing. What follows at Maggotts is perhaps the biggest treat of all, as this left kink feeds into the Becketts esses. This is one of the toughest sections of track anywhere, as the g-forces throw the cars this way and that as they attempt to hold their ideal line through the sequence of bends and hit the Hangar Straight with as much speed as possible.

Passing is possible into Stowe, although the tighter exit into the dip at Vale introduced a few years back reduces the number of lines that drivers can take. Likewise, Club has lost its flow, but this slightly uphill, right-hander shows which cars have traction and which do not.

The Abbey chicane is tight, the dive under the bridge at Bridge scary, but passing is possible for the brave into Priory. Many, however, prefer instead to get close through the sequence of bends before Luffield in order to get a tow down the start-finish straight and line up a move into Copse.

INSIDE TRACK

BRITISH GRAND PRIX

Date:	**11 June**
Circuit length:	**3.194 miles/5.140km**
Number of laps:	**60**
Telephone:	**01327 857271**
Website:	**www.silverstone-circuit.co.uk**

PREVIOUS WINNERS	
1996	**Jacques Villeneuve** WILLIAMS
1997	**Jacques Villeneuve** WILLIAMS
1998	**Michael Schumacher** FERRARI
1999	**David Coulthard** McLAREN
2000	**David Coulthard** McLAREN
2001	**Mika Hakkinen** McLAREN
2002	**Michael Schumacher** FERRARI
2003	**Rubens Barrichello** FERRARI
2004	**Michael Schumacher** FERRARI
2005	**Juan Pablo Montoya** McLAREN

Busy overhead: The number of helicopters buzzing overhead could persuade a first-time race-goer that they had arrived in Vietnam in the 1960s. However, it's just VIP guests being dropped off, with the amount of traffic making it the busiest airstrip in Europe for the day.

Central location: For those not arriving by helicopter, Silverstone's location near the heart of England, 15 miles south-west of Northampton, makes it easy to reach. The circuit used to be famous for its traffic jams, but the opening of the A43 bypass has transformed ingress and egress.

Changes in store: Years of debate about the future of Silverstone are finally over, following the signing of a five-year extension for hosting a grand prix. This has led to money being released not only to revamp the pits and paddock but also to update its facilities. These include a new motorsport academy, an innovation centre and "incubator" business units, in a quest to turn it into the world's leading centre of motorsport excellence. The circuit is expected to maintain its current format.

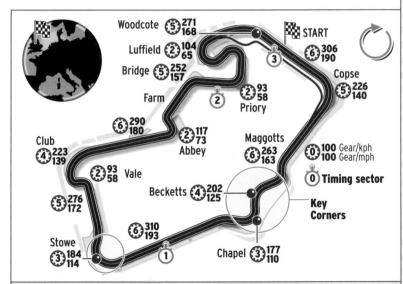

Woodcote (5) 271/168
Luffield (2) 104/65
Bridge (5) 252/157
Farm
Club (4) 223/139
(6) 290/180
(2) 93/58 Vale
(5) 276/172
(6) 310/193
Stowe (3) 184/114
(1)
Becketts (4) 202/125
Chapel (3) 177/110
Abbey (2) 117/73
Priory (2) 93/58
Maggotts (6) 263/163
(2)
START
(3)
(6) 306/190
Copse (5) 226/140
(0) 100/100 Gear/kph Gear/mph
(0) Timing sector
Key Corners

2005 POLE TIME: Alonso (Renault),
1m19.905s, 143.901mph/231.575kph
2005 FASTEST LAP: Raikkonen (McLaren),
1m20.502s, 142.834mph/229.858kph

2005 WINNER'S AVERAGE SPEED:
136.067mph/218.968kph
LAP RECORD: M Schumacher (Ferrari),
1m18.739s, 146.059mph/235.048kph, 2004

MONTREAL

It may look benign, but this circuit is a car breaker, with its combination of long straights and hairpins putting a strain on both the transmission and the brakes.

The Circuit Gilles Villeneuve is tailor-made for action on the opening lap, with the track kinking right after the start-finish line and then feeding left and immediately right into the double-apex, Coin Senna. There's never enough space for all of the drivers to get through unscathed.

For those that do, it's hard on the power as they go up through the gears to tackle a sequence of esses along the lakeside. The drivers are unable to find the time to look up and admire the cityscape views across the Saint Laurence River, especially as the track is lined with concrete walls situated behind the narrowest of grass verges.

With the flow interrupted by a second-gear left-right, it then opens out for the run down to the end furthest from the pits. This is the hairpin in front of a bank of temporary grandstands and it is also the place where drivers sometimes attempt an overtaking move.

Then it's hard on the power again as the cars go down the circuit's longest straight, with the former Olympic rowing lake to their left, all the way to the chicane that completes the lap. The wall on its exit has drawn in many of the sport's top drivers over the years.

Many try to make their move on the way in, but there really is very little room. Getting a clean exit from this chicane is vital too, as it enables you to carry speed down the start-finish straight for a possible passing manoeuvre into that first left-hander.

INSIDE TRACK

CANADIAN GRAND PRIX

Date:	**25 June**
Circuit length:	**2.710 miles/4.361km**
Number of laps:	**70**
Telephone:	**001 514 350 0000**
Website:	**www.grandprix.ca**

PREVIOUS WINNERS

1996	**Damon Hill**	WILLIAMS
1997	**Michael Schumacher**	FERRARI
1998	**Michael Schumacher**	FERRARI
1999	**Mika Hakkinen**	McLAREN
2000	**Michael Schumacher**	FERRARI
2001	**Ralf Schumacher**	WILLIAMS
2002	**Michael Schumacher**	FERRARI
2003	**Michael Schumacher**	FERRARI
2004	**Michael Schumacher**	FERRARI
2005	**Kimi Raikkonen**	McLAREN

Founding father: Gilles Villeneuve, the late father of Jacques, remains Canada's greatest racing hero. He provided the circuit with a home winner on its debut in 1978 and the circuit was duly named after him following his death in the Belgian GP at Zolder in 1982.

Don't wave now: In 1991, Nigel Mansell suffered the ignominy of waving to the crowds in the grandstands as he rounded the Casino hairpin for the final time in a clear lead, only to stall his Williams and drop back to finish second behind Nelson Piquet's Benetton.

Our furry friends: Look out for the marmots that burrow in the grass verges around the track and pop their heads up as cars flash by.

Row, row, row your boat: The rowing lake used in the 1976 Olympic Games is behind the paddock. It's the venue for an annual raft race between the Formula One teams.

Strange buildings: The island on which the circuit is built was the site of the Expo World Trade Fair in 1967 and some of the futuristic pavilions from that time still remain and can be spotted in the background.

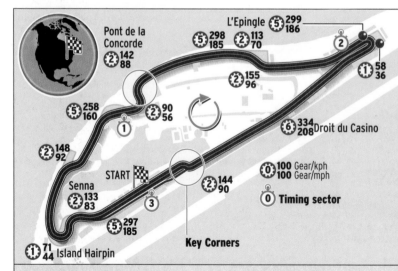

Pont de la Concorde · L'Epingle · Droit du Casino · Senna · Island Hairpin · START · Key Corners

| | Gear/kph |
| 0 | Gear/mph |

Timing sector

2005 POLE TIME: Button (BAR), 1m15.217s, 129.705mph/208.730kph

2005 FASTEST LAP: Raikkonen (McLaren), 1m14.384s, 131.157mph/211.067kph

2005 WINNER'S AVERAGE SPEED: 123.506mph/198.754kph

LAP RECORD: Barrichello (Ferrari), 1m13.622s, 132.511mph/213.246kph, 2004

INDIANAPOLIS

It will be with bated breath that the Formula One circus returns to the Indianapolis Motor Speedway after the tyre-related debacle of last year.

A simple difference between a Formula One car and an Indycar is that the latter is made to drive around banked ovals and the former around road circuits. At the Indianapolis Motor Speedway, Formula One is faced with a short stretch of banked corner, but this was enough to send Michelin into a spin last year as it had failed to assess the g-force loading correctly for either of the types of tyre that it brought to the event. The farce that culminated in 14 of the 20 cars failing to take the race start is chronicled in the report on pp94-5.

However, a lap of the circuit is predominantly on the level stuff to which the teams are more accustomed.

The start-finish straight is wide, with the pit lane some way back from the pit wall beyond a grass verge. To the drivers' left, the grandstands dwarf the cars. The track takes on more of a Formula One feel when it turns right and then left on to the infield.

After three rights, a double-apex left and another tight right, the track feeds onto its back straight. At the end of this, Turn 8 provides a possible passing point. The best chance a driver has of overtaking is to get a good exit from Turn 11 and then carry that speed up onto the banking at Turn 12 and through Turn 13 – the corner where Ralf Schumacher keeps hitting the wall – in order to be in the slipstream of the car ahead down the long drag to Turn 1.

INSIDE TRACK

UNITED STATES GRAND PRIX

Date:	2 July
Circuit length:	2.606 miles/4.195km
Number of laps:	73
Telephone:	001 317 481 8500
Website:	www.my.brickyard.com

PREVIOUS WINNERS

2000	**Michael Schumacher** FERRARI
2001	**Mika Hakkinen** McLAREN
2002	**Rubens Barrichello** FERRARI
2003	**Michael Schumacher** FERRARI
2004	**Michael Schumacher** FERRARI
2005	**Michael Schumacher** FERRARI

Two big ones: The circuit's main race remains the Indianapolis 500, a race run every year since 1911, with the NASCAR race, the Brickyard 400, a favourite since stock-car racing arrived here in 1994. Both races fill the circuit to its 350,000 capacity.

Racing in reverse: The main circuit at the Indianapolis Motor Speedway – the 2.5-mile oval – runs in the opposite, anti-clockwise direction for the Indy 500 and Brickyard 400.

Together, but not together: Indianapolis Motor Speedway played host to a round of the World Championship every year between 1950 and 1960, but this only occurred so that the Indy 500 could appear on the calendar, with not one regular F1 car or driver turning up to take part. Ironically, cross-pollination only started in the mid-1960s, when the F1 teams entered specially modified cars and started winning, bringing an end to the front-engined racers that previously prevailed.

A sporting kinda town: Indianapolis has long been the home of American motor racing, but the past decade saw a push to promote it as a general sporting haven, with major promotions to boost its basketball, baseball and ice hockey teams.

Gear/kph 100 / Gear/mph 100   **0 Timing sector**

Turn 12 (5) 275/171
Turn 11 (2) 134/83
Turn 9 (1) 59/37
2
Turn 5 (4) 243/151
Turn 7 (2) 115/72
(5) 300/186
Turn 4 (2) 130/81
(1) 72/45 Turn 10
(2) 111/69 Turn 11
Hulman Boulevard
Turn 2
Turn 6
Key Corners
(3) 194/121
Turn 3
START
Turn 13
Turn 1 (2) 123/76
(6) 343/213
(3)
(6) 316/196

2005 POLE TIME: Trulli (Toyota), 1m10.625s, 132.837mph/213.770kph

2005 FASTEST LAP: M Schumacher (Ferrari), 1m11.497s, 131.217mph/211.163kph

2005 WINNER'S AVERAGE SPEED: 123.480mph/198.713kph

LAP RECORD: Barrichello (Ferrari), 1m10.399s, 133.207mph/214.366kph, 2004

MAGNY-COURS

Said to possess the smoothest racing surface on the Formula One calendar, Magny-Cours is a great racing circuit, but it seems destined to remain unloved.

The reason that no one appears to like Magny-Cours is not due to the track itself, but to the fact that the circuit is miles from anywhere. Slap bang in the middle of France, it's an unavoidable fact that there are no cities of note nearby, no top hotels and little to do away from the circuit.

However, the track itself offers more than enough of a challenge to keep the drivers entertained.

It drops away from the start line down to the long, long Estoril corner, where a good line on exit is vital as it feeds on to the circuit's longest straight that climbs through a kink to the highest point, the Adelaide hairpin. If you want entertainment, this is where the majority of it happens, as it's great for drivers diving out of the tow of the car ahead and then trying to leave their braking as late as possible. Many have to use the kerbs and rumble-strips on the exit to complete their moves.

Then it's back down the hill through another kink to the wide hairpin and then all the way back up again to the top, with the compression at Imola making entry to Chateau d'Eau rather tricky.

This right, onto a downhill straight, is key for those looking to attempt a pass into the penultimate corner, Lycee, although a further chance is provided if a quick exit can be achieved through the chicane on to the start-finish straight.

INSIDE TRACK

FRENCH GRAND PRIX

Date:	**16 July**
Circuit length:	**2.741 miles/4.411km**
Number of laps:	**70**
Telephone:	**00 33 3 86218000**
Website:	**www.magny-cours.com**

PREVIOUS WINNERS

1996	**Damon Hill** WILLIAMS
1997	**Michael Schumacher** FERRARI
1998	**Michael Schumacher** FERRARI
1999	**Heinz-Harald Frentzen** JORDAN
2000	**David Coulthard** McLAREN
2001	**Michael Schumacher** FERRARI
2002	**Michael Schumacher** FERRARI
2003	**Ralf Schumacher** WILLIAMS
2004	**Michael Schumacher** FERRARI
2005	**Fernando Alonso** RENAULT

A golden history: No country has as much racing history as France, home to the first-ever car race in 1894 between Paris and Rouen and to the first grand prix, held in 1906 at Le Mans. It has moved its grand prix around, though, holding it at a staggering 15 circuits, including seven since the World Championship began in 1950. There's even talk of the race returning to a revamped Paul Ricard, a track that last held the race in 1990.

A window to the past: Not every circuit has a museum, but those that do are all well worth a visit, with Magny-Cours' revealing just what a jump the track made in the late 1980s when it was transformed with government assistance from a little-fancied club racing circuit into one of the most modern tracks in the world.

An international touch: To give the upgraded circuit a cosmopolitan feel following its transformation to international standard, many of the corners were named after other circuits, including Estoril, Adelaide, the Nurburgring and Imola.

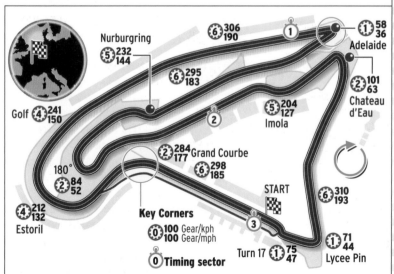

2005 POLE TIME: **Alonso (Renault)**, 1m14.412s, 132.608mph/213.401kph

2005 FASTEST LAP: **Raikkonen (McLaren)**, 1m16.423s, 129.118mph/207.786kph

2005 WINNER'S AVERAGE SPEED: 128.984mph/207.570kph

LAP RECORD: **M Schumacher (Ferrari)**, 1m15.377s, 130.910mph/210.669kph, 2004

HOCKENHEIM

No circuit offers a stadium section like Hockenheim: the noise and colour of the fans packed into the grandstands is one of the highlights of the year.

German fans demand action and there are few circuits on the F1 calendar that offer a first corner which provides as many incidents as Hockenheim. Year after year, drivers are caught out as they run out of space either into or out of this right-hander. And, year after year, the crowd bays its delight with klaxons blaring, especially if the fallen include any of Michael Schumacher's rivals. Although he kept out of trouble in 2005, Kimi Raikkonen is a regular visitor to the gravel trap and tyre wall here.

The unromantically named Einfahrt Parabolica offers a chance for overtaking on its approach, but its narrowing exit means a clear speed advantage is normally needed if an overtaking manoeuvre is to succeed. The best course of action is to get up close on the exit, so that a driver can then catch a tow along the left-arcing Hochgeschwindigkeits Kurve into the Spitzkehre hairpin.

The sequence of bends that follows is fiddly, but overtaking is still possible on arrival into the stadium section at the Mobil 1 Kurve. After this drivers tend to run in close formation through the twisty Sachs Kurve and on over a gentle brow through the Sudkurve – where Montoya fell off in qualifying last year – on to the start-finish straight to start all over again. As at many other circuits, exit speed from the final corner is crucial for those looking to mount a challenge along the start-finish straight into the first corner of the following lap.

INSIDE TRACK

GERMAN GRAND PRIX

Date:	30 July
Circuit length:	2.842 miles/4.574km
Number of laps:	67
Telephone:	00 49 6205 95005
Website:	www.hockenheimring.de

PREVIOUS WINNERS

1996	**Damon Hill**	WILLIAMS
1997	**Gerhard Berger**	BENETTON
1998	**Mika Hakkinen**	McLAREN
1999	**Eddie Irvine**	FERRARI
2000	**Rubens Barrichello**	FERRARI
2001	**Ralf Schumacher**	WILLIAMS
2002	**Michael Schumacher**	FERRARI
2003	**Juan Pablo Montoya**	WILLIAMS
2004	**Michael Schumacher**	FERRARI
2005	**Fernando Alonso**	RENAULT

It's a lottery: Few circuits have thrown up so many different winners over the past decade, with nine different drivers succeeding during that period. Michael Schumacher is the only driver to have won more than once – fittingly perhaps seeing it is his home grand prix.

Avoid the village people: Hockenheim is in the middle of the countryside and local villages offer few places to stay or eat. Head instead for the medieval city of Heidelberg or to the town of Schwetzingen.

Going green: The "country" loop of the circuit that was used until 2001 is fast disappearing, as trees are planted along its length. The ultimate intention is to blend this section of the high-speed track in with the forests that surround it.

All change: To understand the history of the circuit, there is an excellent museum behind the Nordkurve grandstand, with photographs, cars and bikes dating right back to the circuit's inception in 1929 when the track had a near five-mile lap, part of which ran much closer to the town centre. It was used in its early days as a test circuit by Mercedes.

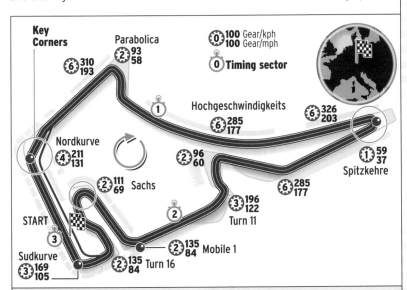

Key Corners

Parabolica (2) 93 / 58

(6) 310 / 193

(0) 100 Gear/kph / 100 Gear/mph

(0) **Timing sector**

Hochgeschwindigkeits (6) 285 / 177

(6) 326 / 203

Nordkurve (4) 211 / 131

(2) 96 / 60

(1) 59 / 37 Spitzkehre

(2) 111 / 69 Sachs

(3) 196 / 122 Turn 11

START

(3)

(2) Mobile 1 (2) 135 / 84

Sudkurve (3) 169 / 105

(2) 135 / 84 Turn 16

2005 POLE TIME: Raikkonen (McLaren), 1m14.320s, 137.664mph/221.539kph

2005 FASTEST LAP: Raikkonen (McLaren), 1m14.873s, 136.660mph/219.923kph

2005 WINNER'S AVERAGE SPEED: 132.128mph/212.630kph

LAP RECORD: Raikkonen (McLaren) 1m13.780s

HUNGARORING

It's always hot and often humid. The track is tight and twisty, making overtaking difficult, so it comes as little surprise that many a move here ends up with a collision.

The passing of time can surprise. How is it that 20 years have passed since Formula One ventured behind the Iron Curtain? In fact, younger Formula One fans may only have heard of the Iron Curtain in history lessons. The calendar doesn't lie, however, and the Hungaroring is no longer thought of as one of the new circuits, a mantle since assumed by the likes of Sepang, Sakhir, Shanghai and Istanbul.

The track is always well worth a visit, since the views offered to spectators are excellent as the circuit flows between two sides of a valley. The drivers, by contrast, have little time for the place, as it offers few challenging corners and overtaking is very tricky; all of which makes being stuck behind a slower car a time-consuming nightmare.

The main straight dips on the approach to Turn 1, a double-apex corner that catches out many on the opening lap. Those that keep out of trouble there often find themselves caught out at Turn 2, as the track drops away through the kink at Turn 3.

Rising up the far side of the valley, Turn 4 offers the sternest challenge. Once the drivers double back through Turn 5, they are on the level through a series of twists until they reach Turn 11, where they dive down again before rising for the recently reprofiled final sequence of corners. A good exit is essential to ensure that they get a run into Turn 1, which is literally the only chance for overtaking.

INSIDE TRACK

HUNGARIAN GRAND PRIX

Date:	**6 August**
Circuit length:	**2.722 miles/4.381km**
Number of laps:	**70**
Telephone:	**00 36 2 844 1861**
Website:	**www.hungaroring.hu**

PREVIOUS WINNERS

1996	**Jacques Villeneuve** WILLIAMS
1997	**Jacques Villeneuve** WILLIAMS
1998	**Michael Schumacher** FERRARI
1999	**Mika Hakkinen** McLAREN
2000	**Mika Hakkinen** McLAREN
2001	**Michael Schumacher** FERRARI
2002	**Rubens Barrichello** FERRARI
2003	**Fernando Alonso** RENAULT
2004	**Michael Schumacher** FERRARI
2005	**Kimi Raikkonen** McLAREN

A tale of two cities: Due to the circuit's restrictive format limiting overtaking, the Hungarian GP is one of the few where a visit to the closest city can be as exciting as the race itself. Or in the case of Budapest, that should read two cities, as they face each other across the River Danube, with Buda on one side and Pest on the other.

Raiding parties: You'll see hordes of fans bearing the blue and white Finnish flag. Mika Hakkinen used to do well here and Kimi Raikkonen won last year. These fans have another reason to visit the grand prix closest to their homeland: Hungary's Magyar language is the only one in Europe, other than theirs, that stems from the arrival of Attila the Hun and his Mongol hordes in 445.

A limited blood line: Hungarian driver Ferenc Szisz won the first-ever grand prix in France in 1906, but the cupboard has been all but bare for Hungarian drivers since then, with just Zsolt Baumgartner, who dabbled with Jordan and Minardi in 2003 and 2004, reaching the Formula One stage.

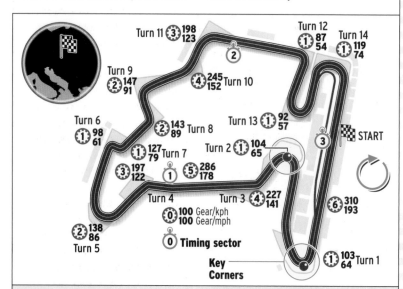

2005 POLE TIME: M Schumacher (Ferrari), 1m19.882s, 122.671mph/197.411kph
2005 FASTEST LAP: Raikkonen (McLaren), 1m21.219s, 120.667mph/194.186kph

2005 WINNER'S AVERAGE SPEED: 117.357mph/188.859kph
LAP RECORD: M Schumacher (Ferrari), 1m19.071s, 123.828mph/199.461kph, 2004

ISTANBUL

New for 2005, Turkey's only international standard racing circuit was an instant hit with drivers and fans alike, some of its corners proving real tests.

Turkey made many countries that were Formula One wannabes jealous when it vaulted to the head of the queue and landed a race deal for 2005. Then came the serious matter of building a new circuit from scratch. As is now the case the world over, favoured circuit architect Hermann Tilke was brought in to craft a racing facility of which the country could be proud.

There were certainly problems along the way, with construction budgets running over and the threat of political unrest stemming from problems with the Kurdish population in the east of the country, but the Istanbul Park circuit arrived not only on time but proved a real test for, as well as a substantial hit with, the drivers.

The lap starts with a short sprint to the dipping first corner. Unusually, this is a left-hander as, even more unusually, the circuit runs in an anti-clockwise direction.

After a long arc to the right, the sequence of corners from Turn 3 to Turn 6 is predominantly twisting in nature before the first straight of note which also twists back on itself. Out of Turn 9, however, the track opens out on to a long straight that runs through a kink, Turn 11, before reaching the best overtaking point of the lap, the braking zone for the tight left at Turn 12.

With the corner onto the start-finish straight also a slow one, drivers will look to hitch a tow down the straight for another possible passing move into Turn 1.

INSIDE TRACK

TURKISH GRAND PRIX

Date:	**27 August**
Circuit length:	**3.318 miles/5.340km**
Number of laps:	**58**
Telephone:	**(90) 216 418 5222**
Website:	**www.formula1-istanbul.com**

PREVIOUS WINNERS

2005	**Kimi Raikkonen** McLAREN

Going green: The first race against the clock was to complete the circuit in time for its inaugural race at the end of last August. However, development is due to continue for years to come, with circuit chief Mumtaz Tahincioglu reckoning that it will take until the third year for the circuit to look at its best, by which point the grass should have grown on the banks and hillsides around the track and the trees matured.

Security threat: The Kurdish separatist movement gave cause for concern before the first Turkish Grand Prix last year when they carried out a series of small bomb blasts near the circuit and several fatal ones further afield aimed at affecting the country's burgeoning tourist industry. The teams declared that it would be "business as usual", as had been the case when Bahrain hosted its opening grand prix in 2004 at a time of much political unrest in the Middle East. To ensure the safety of all present, the circuit employed 1,000 security guards.

Two-pronged campaign: Turkey's arrival on the world motorsport stage has been a sudden one: it hosted a round of the FIA World Rally Championship for the first time in 2003 before hosting its inaugural grand prix last year. No Turkish driver has yet made an impact at the highest level of the sport, although Can Artam stepped up from Formula One's feeder formula GP2 last year to be the third driver for Jordan at the Turkish Grand Prix.

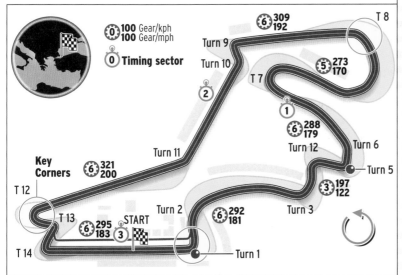

2005 POLE TIME: Raikkonen (McLaren), 1m26.797s, 136.581mph/219.795kph
2005 FASTEST LAP: Montoya (McLaren), 1m24.770s, 138.096mph/222.167kph

2005 WINNER'S AVERAGE SPEED: 133.673mph/215.116kph
LAP RECORD: **See fastest lap (left)**

MONZA

This is the daddy of all Formula One circuits, a fast-flowing track that has been in use since 1922. It's a true favourite and not just for Ferrari fans.

Walk through the park at Monza, squint at the track and you could be forgiven for thinking that only the peripherals have changed. Sure, the banking has long since been abandoned, but the level sections have altered in remarkably few ways over its 84-year history. The main change is the insertion of three chicanes, added in 1972 simply to keep the cars' speeds in check. Other than that, the trees that surround much of the track have grown taller and some of the buildings are shabbier, but the circuit is all but the same.

The lap starts with the run to the first chicane, a right-left opening on to the run through the once-mighty Curva Grande. This chicane is good for overtaking, not only on the first lap when the field is bunched, but on any lap, as drivers can use a tow down the start-finish straight. The sight of a car getting it wrong over the kerbs in an attempt to pass can happen at any stage of the race.

The same is true of the second chicane, a left-right sequence. The Lesmos that follow have been less daunting since the trees on the outside were chopped down. The test now is to carry as much speed as possible on to the run down to the third chicane at Variante Ascari, where exit speed is vital as it feeds onto the back straight.

The final corner of the lap is the Parabolica, out of which drivers pray that they'll achieve slingshot speed on to the long and wide main straight.

INSIDE TRACK

ITALIAN GRAND PRIX

Date:	10 September
Circuit length:	3.600 miles/5.793km
Number of laps:	53
Telephone:	00 39 39 24821
Website:	www.monzanet.it

PREVIOUS WINNERS

1996	**Michael Schumacher** FERRARI
1997	**David Coulthard** McLAREN
1998	**Michael Schumacher** FERRARI
1999	**Heinz-Harald Frentzen** JORDAN
2000	**Michael Schumacher** FERRARI
2001	**Juan Pablo Montoya** WILLIAMS
2002	**Rubens Barrichello** FERRARI
2003	**Michael Schumacher** FERRARI
2004	**Rubens Barrichello** FERRARI
2005	**Juan Pablo Montoya** McLAREN

The Red Sea: The fanatical Ferrari fans, known as the *tifosi*, can make Monza an intimidating place for drivers of other teams, as Mika Hakkinen discovered when he spun off at the first chicane in 1999 while leading and was jeered as he cried in frustration. It was even worse for another McLaren driver in 1976, when Ferrari hero Niki Lauda's title rival James Hunt was spat at as he walked back to the pits after retiring from the race.

A fatal start: One of Monza's darkest days came in 1978 when a mass shunt off the startline led to Ronnie Peterson being hospitalised with leg injuries. The Lotus driver died later that night.

You can bank on it: The remaining section of the famous banking is still on the inside of the circuit just before the first chicane, arcing incredibly steeply round to the right to where it used to cross over the current circuit as it heads back from the second Lesmo towards Variante Ascari. The matching banking at the far end, beyond Parabolica, has long since been demolished.

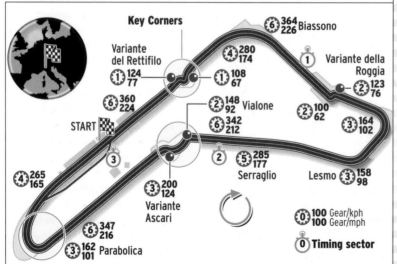

Key Corners

⑥ 364 / 226 Biassono
④ 280 / 174
① Variante della Roggia
Variante del Rettifilo
① 124 / 77
① 108 / 67
② 123 / 76
⑥ 360 / 224
② 148 / 92 Vialone
② 100 / 62
③ 164 / 102
START
⑥ 342 / 212
③
②
⑤ 285 / 177 Serraglio
Lesmo ③ 158 / 98
④ 265 / 165
③ 200 / 124
Variante Ascari
⓪ 100 / 100 Gear/kph / Gear/mph
⑥ 347 / 216
⓪ **Timing sector**
③ 162 / 101 Parabolica

2005 POLE TIME: **Raikkonen (McLaren),** 1m20.878s, 160.241mph/257.871kph
2005 FASTEST LAP: **Raikkonen (McLaren),** 1m21.504s, 159.000mph/255.874kph

2005 WINNER'S AVERAGE SPEED: **153.545mph/247.095kph**
LAP RECORD: **Barrichello (Ferrari),** 1m21.046s, 159.899mph/257.321kph, 2004

SPA-FRANCORCHAMPS

Wherever they race, Formula One cars excite people but they are in their pomp at Spa-Francorchamps, a track considered by many to be the world's greatest.

Like Monaco, Spa-Francorchamps is even more hilly in real life than it appears on television. Even the parts that look flat are on an incline. This, combined with its setting in the Ardennes forests, makes it all the more magical, especially as some of the corners really test the drivers.

The blast from the grid to the first corner, the La Source hairpin, is a short one and, as contact is frequent here, it's very easy for drivers to have a wing knocked out of shape or a diffuser split. The track is wide enough for all sorts of exit lines, but drivers have to get back on to the racing line as they dive down the hill past the old pits to Eau Rouge. This legendary corner is a left flick and then hard right as the hill rises abruptly, with another flick to the left at the crest.

A long climb up to Les Combes follows, with the braking zone for this chicane offering a popular point for overtaking. From Malmedy, the track dips again, through the Rivage hairpin and down to the tricky, off-camber, double-apex left at Pouhon. The slope eases off through the Fagnes twisters.

After the track's lowest point, Stavelot, it's hard on the power on the homeward leg, with Blanchimont a frightening corner at 185mph. The Bus Stop section has been simplified into a single, rather than a double, chicane before the cars reach the short start-finish straight.

INSIDE TRACK

BELGIAN GRAND PRIX

Date:	17 September
Circuit length:	4.333 miles/6.973km
Number of laps:	44
Telephone:	00 32 8727 5138
Website:	www.spa-francorchamps.be

PREVIOUS WINNERS

1995	**Michael Schumacher** BENETTON
1996	**Michael Schumacher** FERRARI
1997	**Michael Schumacher** FERRARI
1998	**Damon Hill** JORDAN
1999	**David Coulthard** McLAREN
2000	**Mika Hakkinen** McLAREN
2001	**Michael Schumacher** FERRARI
2002	**Michael Schumacher** FERRARI
2004	**Kimi Raikkonen** McLAREN
2005	**Kimi Raikkonen** McLAREN

Wet and dry: No circuit has weather as changeable as Spa-Francorchamps. One minute it can be bright sunshine, the next minute, torrential rain. Fog has also been known to hang between the trees and prevent morning track sessions. To make matters more complicated, it was not infrequent for the original 9.236-mile circuit to be soaking in the section near the pits, yet bone dry on its far section in the next valley, forcing drivers to be on maximum alert at all times.

Old and new: Visitors to Spa-Francorchamps should take time to trace the route of its original grand prix circuit. Instead of turning right at Les Combes, it carries on down public roads and arcs left over the crest of the hill before eventually spearing into the forest then rejoining today's circuit at the current Stavelot corner.

History on display: The magnificence and danger of the original circuit is captured in an excellent museum in the town of Stavelot, including photographs showing the track in all its former savage glory.

Key Corners

Raidillion (6) 297 185

(6) 330 205

(3) 177 110

(1)

(3) 140 87

Les Combes

(6) 290 180 Pouhon

(3) 177 110 Rivage

(5) 265 165

(6) 290 180 Eau Rouge

(6) 297 185

(3) 140 87

Fagnes

(3) 170 106

(3)

(2) 90 56 Bus Stop

(6) 305 190 Blanchimont

START

(2) 64 40 La Source

(0) 100 Gear/kph
100 Gear/mph

(2)

(0) Timing sector

Stavelot (5) 245 100

2005 POLE TIME: Montoya (McLaren), 1m46.391s, 146.618mph/235.947kph

2005 FASTEST LAP: R Schumacher (Toyota), 1m51.453s, 140.019mph/225.328kph

2005 WINNER'S AVERAGE SPEED: 127.119mph/204.569kph

LAP RECORD: Raikkonen (McLaren), 1m45.108s, 148.407mph/238.827kph, 2004

SHANGHAI

Formula One regulars were blown away by the Shanghai International Circuit on their first visit in 2004, as its excellent facilities set new standards for all to emulate.

The standard of finish on this circuit and its sheer architectural ambition are astonishing. They are a massive testament to the aspirations of China – and to Shanghai in particular – to present an image of excellence to the world.

Look beyond the massive and outlandish pit buildings and grandstands – as well as the twin wing-shaped edifices above the start-finish straight – and the black strip below is equally worthy of praise.

It's classic Hermann Tilke, with a tight first corner pouring straight into the 180-degree Turn 2, a bend that is gently banked to hold the cars in place followed by a hairpin at Turn 3.

If this sequence slows the cars to a near standstill, they are then able to unwind like a coil and fire themselves up to 180mph on the approach to another hairpin at Turn 6.

After a series of sweepers and a pair of tightish left-handers, there is a short straight up to a trio of bends that mimic Turns 1 to 3 in taking the drivers on a 270-degree twister on to the back straight. This is one of the longest straights in use in Formula One and it offers a fabulous chance to overtake on the entry to the hairpin at its conclusion.

There's more in store too, as drivers ought to be able to line up the car ahead out of the last corner and have a go at overtaking on the blast past the pits.

INSIDE TRACK

CHINESE GRAND PRIX

Date:	**1 October**
Circuit length:	**3.390 miles/5.450km**
Number of laps:	**56**
Telephone:	**00 86 2162520000**
Website:	**www.f1china.com.cn**

PREVIOUS WINNERS

2004	**Rubens Barrichello** FERRARI
2005	**Fernando Alonso** RENAULT

Pile drivers: The circuit is built on top of marshy ground. This would have defeated many, but the prize-winning construction project got around this by sinking 40,000 concrete piles, some as deep as 80 metres.

Symbolic gesture: The circuit echoes the shape of the Shang symbol, meaning "above" and is, of course, part of the name of the nearby city.

Colour-coded: Many of the circuit buildings are painted, or at least accented, in red and gold, traditional Chinese colours that symbolize success and wealth.

Drivers beware: Foreigners are not allowed to drive in China, which is just as well as the roads are extremely dangerous with the local drivers described as having all the aggression of Italian drivers, but without any of the skills.

Formula One seat-time: The race to be the first Chinese driver to compete in Formula One continues, with Dutch-born Ho-Pin Tung leading the way. He raced in Formula Three last year, featuring strongly in the German series, which puts him ahead of A1 GP racer Tengyi Jiang and McLaren-backed "Franky" Cheng Confu, currently in Formula Three.

A false start: China's first attempt to land a grand prix came to nothing when the Zhuhai circuit in the south of the country failed to step up from being a reserve race for the 1998 World Championship. It has yet to be completed to an acceptable standard.

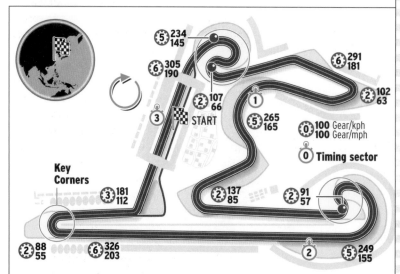

Key Corners

Timing sector

Gear/kph
Gear/mph

2005 POLE TIME: Alonso (Renault), 1m34.080s, 129.600mph/208.569kph
2005 FASTEST LAP: Raikonnen (McLaren), 1m33.242s, 130.770mph/210.443kph

2005 WINNER'S AVERAGE SPEED: 113.862mph/183.235kph
LAP RECORD: M Schumacher (Ferrari), 1m32.238s, 132.202mph/212.749kph, 2004

SUZUKA

Some drivers rank Spa-Francorchamps as their favourite circuit, but others prefer Suzuka. Either way, this is a place where the drivers have to work hard for their living.

Any driver who tells you that Suzuka is an easy circuit has either never been there or is not telling the truth. Its S Curves - Spoon Curve and, in particular, its 130R - deserve considerable respect.

On a clear day you can see the sea in the distance, but the drivers don't have time for that as they head down the hill to the First Curve. This is narrow on entry and only opens out on exit as the track turns uphill after its second apex.

The slope steepens as it reaches the S Curves and a mistake into any part will be magnified by the wrong line into the next. Out of this, the drivers are faced with Dunlop Curve at the crest of the hill, before the track slopes down through Degner

to Crossover, a corner that is unique in Formula One since it feeds the track under a bridge that carries the latter section of the lap.

Climbing into the Hairpin, the track continues to rise all the way through a long right arc that tightens at the end before the entry of Spoon Curve, another corner that appears to go on forever before spitting the cars onto the blast back towards the pits, down to Crossover.

Having crossed back over the bridge, 130R comes and goes in a flash at 170mph. Then it's hard on the anchors for Casio Triangle, a tricky chicane that drops away from entry to exit before feeding onto the start-finish straight.

INSIDE TRACK

JAPANESE GRAND PRIX

Date:	8 October
Circuit length:	3.608 miles/5.806km
Number of laps:	53
Telephone:	00 81 593 783620
Website:	www.suzukacircuit.co.jp

PREVIOUS WINNERS

1996	**Damon Hill** WILLIAMS
1997	**Michael Schumacher** FERRARI
1998	**Mika Hakkinen** McLAREN
1999	**Mika Hakkinen** McLAREN
2000	**Michael Schumacher** FERRARI
2001	**Michael Schumacher** FERRARI
2002	**Michael Schumacher** FERRARI
2003	**Rubens Barrichello** FERRARI
2004	**Michael Schumacher** FERRARI
2005	**Kimi Raikkonen** McLAREN

Staying power: Japanese fans stay longer after the race than anywhere except Silverstone - where there's an after-race concert - as the traffic is so bad that many people elect to sit in the grandstands opposite the pits and watch the crews pack their gear...

Is there a new rival?: Fuji Speedway, the circuit on the slopes of Mount Fuji that hosted the inaugural Japanese Grand Prix in 1976 has been revamped by Toyota and is now vying with Suzuka to claim the race again, perhaps with the losing party ending up hosting a race called the Pacific Grand Prix, as the Tanaka International circuit did in 1994 and 1995.

Tempestuous weather: The arrival of Typhoon 22 threatened the Japanese Grand Prix in 2004, but it swerved away at the last moment, allowing the race to go ahead.

Unusual partners: Japan is full of curious juxtapositions, but one of the weirdest is the fact that the Suzuka circuit is part of an amusement park, with its twisting blacktop sited next to rides in which children are carried aloft inside giant insects.

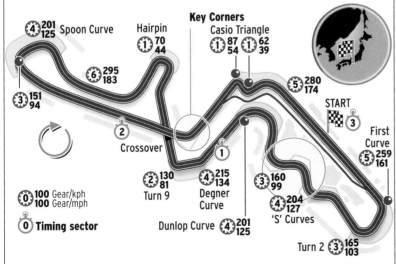

Key Corners

Spoon Curve — (4) 201 / 125
Hairpin — (1) 70 / 44
Casio Triangle — (1) 87 / 54 — (1) 62 / 39
(6) 295 / 183
(5) 280 / 174
(3) 151 / 94
START (3)
First Curve — (5) 259 / 161
Crossover — (2)
(1)
(2) 130 / 81 — Turn 9
Degner Curve — (4) 215 / 134
(3) 160 / 99
(4) 204 / 127 — 'S' Curves
Dunlop Curve — (4) 201 / 125
Turn 2 — (3) 165 / 103

(0) 100 Gear/kph / 100 Gear/mph
(0) **Timing sector**

2005 POLE TIME: **R Schumacher (Toyota),** 1m46.106s, 122.410mph/196.996kph
2005 FASTEST LAP: **Raikkonen (McLaren),** 1m31.080, 141.890mph/228.342kph

2005 WINNER'S AVERAGE SPEED: **128.796mph/207.267kph**
LAP RECORD: **See fastest lap (left)**

INTERLAGOS

The facilities may be a little frayed around the edges, but this remains one of the great tracks visited by Formula One, with an atmosphere as outstanding as the layout.

Like the Nurburgring, Interlagos is a circuit that is a shadow of its former self, with its lengthy original layout still visible in the background. However, in contrast to the Nurburgring, the shortened version used today is still one of Formula One's great tracks.

From the moment the drivers accelerate up the start-finish straight – one that is recessed into a trench between the pitwall and the grandstand, which rises sheer from the concrete wall that lines its right-hand side – they know that a challenge lies ahead.

Especially as they can see the entry to the first corner, but no more. It plunges left over a crest and then turns immediately right into the Senna S. No sooner have the drivers turned through this than they have

to turn left through Curva do Sol on to the downhill straight to Descida do Lago, a corner where overtaking is a definite possibility, much to the delight of the enthusiastic fans in the grandstands which overlook it.

From here, it's uphill to the tricky, double-apex Ferradura, out of which the circuit flows to Laranja, then drops to Pinheirinho, before rising again to Contovelo and plunging to Mergulho. From the following corner, Junção, the drivers are then hard on the power all the way until just before they reach Curva 1 again, accelerating through the Arquibandas corner and on up to 190mph along this arcing straight in front of the massed grandstands, with every possibility of catching a tow to help with a move into the first corner.

INSIDE TRACK

BRAZILIAN GRAND PRIX

Date:	**22 October**
Circuit length:	**2.667 miles/4.292 km**
Number of laps:	**71**
Telephone:	**0055 11 813 3775**
Website:	**www.interlagos.com**

PREVIOUS WINNERS

1996	**Damon Hill** WILLIAMS
1997	**Jacques Villeneuve** WILLIAMS
1998	**Mika Hakkinen** McLAREN
1999	**Mika Hakkinen** McLAREN
2000	**Michael Schumacher** FERRARI
2001	**David Coulthard** McLAREN
2002	**Michael Schumacher** FERRARI
2003	**Giancarlo Fisichella** JORDAN
2004	**Juan Pablo Montoya** WILLIAMS
2005	**Juan Pablo Montoya** McLAREN

The most passionate fans: There's no place like Interlagos for a carnival atmosphere. Fans at Monza may have the most Ferrari flags, fans in Britain may have the most knowledge and fans in Germany may have the loudest airhorns, but fans in Brazil have the most passion, with some queuing overnight for admission.

A family affair: The Fittipaldis are still the only Brazilian family to have three of its family members race in Formula One, with Emerson and Wilson – who raced in the 1970s – followed by Wilson's son Christian in the 1990s.

A family outlook: BAR driver Rubens Barrichello will have to wait a while yet to see if his son makes it to Formula One, but Interlagos is in the family blood, as the family home looks out over the circuit.

Banking on the past: Monza wasn't the only circuit to lose a banked section of its layout when it was modernised, as the first corner at Interlagos was also banked, this time to the left. It can still be seen, lying abandoned in front of the grandstands between the Curva do Sol and the Descida do Sol.

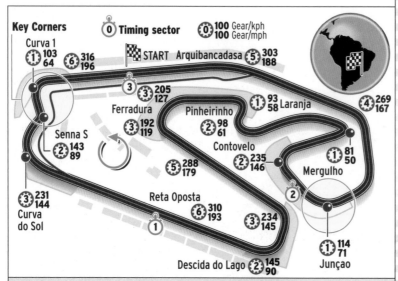

2005 POLE TIME: Alonso (Renault), 1m11.988s, 133.372mph/214.632kph
2005 FASTEST LAP: Raikkonen (McLaren), 1m12.268s, 132.855mph/213.800kph

2005 WINNER'S AVERAGE SPEED: 127.660mph/205.235kph
LAP RECORD: Montoya (Williams), 1m11.473s, 134.867mph/217.038kph, 2004

The twists and turns of Interlagos really make drivers work for their corn

REVIEW OF THE 2005 SEASON

This was the year in which Michael Schumacher's domination came to an end. With Ferrari and Bridgestone out of sorts, the path was clear for Renault and McLaren to hit the front, with Fernando Alonso coming out on top for Renault. He also became the youngest-ever world champion at the age of just 24.

There were many occasions between Michael Schumacher's first world title for Ferrari in 2000 – his third in all – and the end of 2004 when Formula One fans must have wondered if anyone else would ever be champion. Well, rule changes in 2005 dictated that there would be no tyre changes during pitstops. The trouble was, Ferrari were the only top team on Bridgestones and the lack of comparative testing hampered the Japanese engineers in their quest to maximize the performance of their tyres for this new format. On top of this, there was a further rule stating that engines must last for two grands prix.

Michael still weaved his magic to rank third overall, but the year was all about Fernando Alonso for Renault and Kimi Raikkonen for McLaren.

Renault were on the pace from the outset, with a change of weather helping Alonso's team-mate, Giancarlo Fisichella, to benefit from a new qualifying system to claim pole in Australia. He duly won, but Alonso's charge from the back to third was ominous.

Alonso won the next three races but, by the fourth round, McLaren resolved their problem of getting heat into their cars' tyres. Indeed, Raikkonen was pulling away in the San Marino GP when his engine failed. This was to be the first of many failures for the Mercedes V10 and these wore away at the Finn as he lost potential pole positions or wins. A last-lap blow-out at the Nurburgring provided some variety.

That said, Alonso drove beautifully to leave Fisichella in his shadow. What made things worse was that, if Renault had a mechanical failure, it invariably tended to afflict the Italian. Likewise, Montoya lost out at McLaren, first by missing two races after injuring a shoulder and then through accidents when he had regained his form.

Yet McLaren's strengths led to them taking the points lead with two races to go when Montoya led home a one-two in Brazil, a race in which third place was enough for Alonso to become world champion. In so doing, he beat Emerson Fittipaldi's record, set in 1972, by becoming the youngest-ever champion, at 24 years and 58 days.

The stage was set for the Japanese GP and McLaren suffered a blow when Jacques Villeneuve clashed with Montoya. Even victory for Raikkonen couldn't prevent Renault from taking the points lead and they capitalized on this in China, even before a raised drain cover triggered an end to Montoya's race. You could say that reliability won over speed, but Renault's speed by the end of the 2005 campaign was every bit as good as McLaren's.

Ferrari ended up third overall, but their form was patchy and it was only their one-two at the farce that was the US GP – a race boycotted by all seven teams using Michelins because of concerns over tyre safety – that kept them clear of the most improved team of the year: Toyota.

Jarno Trulli shone for the Japanese team, with second places in both rounds two and three. Seldom as quick in qualifying, Ralf Schumacher came on strong following the late-season introduction of the TF105B, qualifying on pole in Japan and finishing third in China.

Williams had an up-and-down season, but largely trailed away in the second half of the year after Nick Heidfeld and Mark Webber had both finished on the podium at Monaco. The team's partnership with BMW soured and it was known that they would be parting company for 2006, with BMW's thoughts turning to their buy-out of Sauber.

Most disappointing of all was BAR, who were runners-up to Ferrari in 2004. Disqualified after finishing third and fifth at Imola, BAR missed the next two races, claimed pole in Canada through Jenson Button, yet still didn't score a point until the tenth round. Their form improved thereafter, as shown by Button's third places in Germany and Belgium. By contrast, Takuma Sato appeared to panic at his tally of one point and kept crashing into rivals.

Sauber mainly scored points in races where others hit trouble, such as when Villeneuve took fourth at Imola once the BARs had been thrown out, with Felipe Massa matching that result in Canada.

Jordan and Minardi were treated to a one-off points haul in the US GP, with Jordan's Tiago Monteiro claiming a once-in-a-lifetime trip to the podium. Jordan was a troubled outfit, though, with finances too tight to progress. By contrast, Minardi made strides with their first new chassis for years. Then, at the end of the final race, they both effectively ceased to exist as Jordan will be known as Midland and Minardi as Scuderia Toro Rosso.

AUSTRALIAN GP

Giancarlo Fisichella drew first blood on his maiden outing for Renault after making the most of changing conditions to qualify on pole, but the team's real star was Fernando Alonso, who tigered his way through the field from 13th on the grid to finish third.

Happy, happier, exhausted: Barrichello, Fisichella and Alonso share the year's first podium

A tweaking of the rule book in 2005 introduced a two-part qualifying format in which the grid positions were decided on aggregate. The thinking behind this slightly confusing procedure was to spread interest in qualifying from Saturday afternoon to Sunday morning and to provide the fans with a reason to switch on their televisions on race morning, so that they could see who had made gains and who had tripped up.

The trouble was that the rain eased off midway through the Saturday afternoon session and one driver made the most of being presented with a gap in the weather to set provisional pole. This was Fisichella, on his first outing since rejoining many of his former Benetton mechanics and engineers at Renault. With more rain arriving almost as soon as he had completed his sole flying lap, no one was able to match his time; in fact, nobody even came close. As a result, the Italian took an advantage of nearly 2.1s into the Sunday session.

Making the most of his advantage, the team fuelled his car heavy for the second session so that he could start the race with an advantageous long opening stint. With others gambling along similar lines, only Williams' new signing, Mark Webber, went faster, albeit only by 0.01s. That left Fisichella on pole by close on 3s from Jarno Trulli's Toyota.

Demonstrating how the rain had shuffled the predicted order, Jacques Villeneuve started in fourth place on the grid for Sauber and David Coulthard fifth for Red Bull Racing (formerly Jaguar), one place ahead of team-mate Christian Klien. BAR's Jenson Button was only eighth, just ahead of McLaren's Juan Pablo Montoya and Kimi Raikkonen, with Ferrari's Rubens Barrichello 11th and reigning world champion Michael Schumacher in 18th out of 20, after he elected to change an engine and take the ten-place grid demotion this entailed.

The race was Fisichella's from start to finish, as he was headed only by cars out of sequence following each of his two pit stops. He did all that was needed and his win was an extremely popular one, since his is a talent that has received relatively meagre returns over the years.

Trulli gave Toyota plenty to cheer about in the first part of the race, but he was one of several drivers to suffer from degrading tyres: this was the first grand prix for years in which tyres were only allowed to be changed as a result of a puncture. Such was the drop-off in grip that the Italian slid down the order thereafter, missing out by one position on the single point that he would have gained by being in eighth place at race's end.

The biggest surprise of all in the early laps was Coulthard running third, after passing Webber into the first corner. He wasn't embarrassed by this elevated position and was able to resist Webber's fightback. After his first stop, the Scot ran second until he came in for his final pit stop, but he was ultimately unable to give his new team boss Christian Horner a podium result as Barrichello raced strongly through the order, chased by Alonso and this duo emerged from the final stops ahead of him.

Setting the race's fastest lap as he went, Alonso closed and closed on the Ferrari driver, but couldn't quite find a way by. Coulthard's fourth-place finish was bolstered by Klien's seventh.

So, first blood to Renault then, with a first- and a third-place finish, but what made their success all the sweeter was that Michael Schumacher failed to score a point. The reigning world champion collided with countryman Nick Heidfeld, whose Williams he squeezed off the track when he tried a passing manoeuvre into Turn 3. Perhaps Michael wasn't used to being overtaken.

Most disappointing of all, however, was Villeneuve. Despite starting fourth on the grid, the 1997 world champion produced a lacklustre performance, dropping to ninth on the first lap and continued his fall down the field to finish in a lapped 13th position. By contrast, his team-mate, Felipe Massa, went the other way, using a one-stop strategy to climb from 18th to tenth.

MELBOURNE ROUND 01

Date: 6 March 2005 Laps: **57** Distance: **191.117 miles/307.574km**
Weather: **Overcast and warm**

RACE RESULT

Position	Driver	Team	Result	Stops	Qualifying Time	Grid
1	**Giancarlo Fisichella**	Renault	1h24m17.336s	2	3m01.460s	1
2	**Rubens Barrichello**	Ferrari	1h24m22.889s	2	3m16.822s	11
3	**Fernando Alonso**	Renault	1h24m24.048s	2	3m17.466s	13
4	**David Coulthard**	Red Bull	1h24m33.467s	2	3m07.212s	5
5	**Mark Webber**	Williams	1h24m34.244s	2	3m04.996s	3
6	**Juan Pablo Montoya**	McLaren	1h24m52.369s	2	3m14.645s	9
7	**Christian Klien**	Red Bull	1h24m56.333s	2	3m07.477s	6
8	**Kimi Raikkonen**	McLaren	1h24m56.969s	2	3m15.558s	10
9	**Jarno Trulli**	Toyota	1h25m20.444s	2	3m04.429s	2
10	**Felipe Massa**	Sauber	1h25m31.729s	1	no time	18
11	**Jenson Button**	BAR	56 laps/engine	2	3m12.128s	8
12	**Ralf Schumacher**	Toyota	56 laps	3	3m22.717s	15
13	**Jacques Villeneuve**	Sauber	56 laps	2	3m06.846s	4
14	**Takuma Sato**	BAR	55 laps/engine	2	no time	20
15	**Narain Karthikeyan**	Jordan	55 laps	2	3m17.092s	12
16	**Tiago Monteiro**	Jordan	55 laps	2	3m20.329s	14
17	**Patrick Friesacher**	Minardi	53 laps	2	3m28.363s	16
R	**Michael Schumacher**	Ferrari	42 laps/accident damage	2	1m57.931s	19
R	**Nick Heidfeld**	Williams	42 laps/accident	2	3m09.130s	7
R	**Christijan Albers**	Minardi	16 laps/gearbox	0	1m49.230s	17

TALKING POINT: WHEN IS A RETIREMENT GENUINE?

A strange sight to F1 occurred during the penultimate lap of the race: two healthy cars withdrew to the pits and parked up. Both were BARs and the team did so out of choice. It didn't cost them any points, as Jenson Button had been running in 11th and Takuma Sato in 13th, but the reason for this bizarre action was that the team wanted to be able to change engines for the following race without incurring a ten-place grid demotion, something that it wouldn't otherwise be able to do following the introduction of the rule that an engine must last for two meetings.

Cunningly bending the rules to their advantage, Takuma Sato and Jenson Button of BAR

MALAYSIAN GP

Two races and two wins was Renault's perfect tally following the race in Kuala Lumpur, but this time it was Fernando Alonso who took the spoils, controlling proceedings from start to finish to leap to the head of the points table.

Starting a trend: Alonso leads the way from Trulli and Fisichella, kicking off a three-race winning streak that set him on the way to his title

This was no mere race win for Fernando Alonso – it was domination the like of which is seldom seen in Formula One. Certainly, Michael Schumacher in his pomp had produced a few runaway wins, but this was winning more in the style of Jim Clark in the 1960s or Jackie Stewart in the early 1970s. It was a cakewalk.

The Spaniard placed his Renault in pole position, by a quarter of a second over Jarno Trulli's much-improved Toyota. Perhaps making the point that he, rather than Giancarlo Fisichella, would have won the opening round at Melbourne had he not started back in 13th, he outqualified his Italian team-mate by 0.776s. These margins sound huge, but don't forget that these were the aggregate times of both a qualifying session on Saturday afternoon and another on Sunday morning, something

that wouldn't change for another five races. Even so, the front three were well clear of the rest, with Mark Webber going well for Williams and qualifying fourth overall, almost half a second further in arrears.

Any thoughts that Trulli might be able to take Toyota to new heights were dashed when he failed to get the jump on Alonso at the start. However, few ever get the better of Renault's renowned excellence off the line. Indeed, Trulli was careful to keep Fisichella behind him on the sprint to the first corner. Trulli then tried his best to stay in touch with Alonso, but the blue-and-yellow Renault eased clear and was never troubled again.

Trulli drove beautifully to give Toyota its first podium finish, but Fisichella wasn't as fortunate behind him, going out of the race after a clash with Webber over fourth

place after half-distance. Having damaged his front wing on a kerb, Fisichella slowed and Webber was joined by Toyota's Ralf Schumacher and his own team-mate Nick Heidfeld in a tight bunch that produced some great cut-and-thrust racing. Webber attacked Fisichella into the corner leading on to the back straight, but Fisichella got crossed up and needed room; room that he wasn't given, with the end result being that he bounced over the nose of the Australian's car, taking both out. Each blamed the other, but the driver left smiling was Heidfeld who, as a result, assumed third place.

Ralf Schumacher then lost a wing endplate and dropped away, leaving the road clear for Juan Pablo Montoya to claim fourth for McLaren, thus saving the day for the team after Kimi Raikkonen's earlier disappointment. The Finn stayed out longer than Fisichella and Webber before his first pit stop and rattled off a series of blinding laps, only to have his right rear tyre suffer a valve failure as he rejoined the race in third place. It cost him considerable time as he limped back to the pits.

If his high-profile showing in the Australian opener owed something to the fortune of qualifying well in a weather-affected lottery, David Coulthard showed that it wasn't all down to luck, as he kept out of trouble – save for a quick spin – to finish sixth, keeping many more-fancied runners, including Michael Schumacher, in his wake.

The reigning world champion was only able to finish seventh and, indeed, he was fortunate even to do that, as he was pressed in the closing laps by Coulthard's fast-improving team-mate, Christian Klien, in the second Red Bull Racing entry.

With Ferrari so used to winning, it was even more bewildering for Rubens Barrichello who thought that, because his car's handling was so bad, he must have had a puncture. It turned out that a piece of rubber foam had caught on the rear wing and this was cooking his rear tyres to such an extent that the Brazilian could hardly hold the car in a straight line. He eventually retired.

SEPANG ROUND 02

Date: **20 March 2005** Laps: **56** Distance: **192.878 miles/310.408km**
Weather: **Hot and humid**

RACE RESULT

Position	Driver	Team	Result	Stops	Qualifying Time	Grid
1	**Fernando Alonso**	Renault	1h31m33.073s	2	3m07.672s	1
2	**Jarno Trulli**	Toyota	1h31m58.063s	2	3m07.925s	2
3	**Nick Heidfeld**	Williams	1h32m05.924s	2	3m09.917s	10
4	**Juan Pablo Montoya**	McLaren	1h32m15.367s	2	3m10.090s	11
5	**Ralf Schumacher**	Toyota	1h32m25.590s	2	3m09.007s	5
6	**David Coulthard**	Red Bull	1h32m46.279s	2	3m09.700s	8
7	**Michael Schumacher**	Ferrari	1h32m53.724s	2	3m11.663s	13
8	**Christian Klien**	Red Bull	1h32m54.571s	2	3m09.589s	7
9	**Kimi Raikkonen**	McLaren	1h32m55.316s	2	3m09.483s	6
10	**Felipe Massa**	Sauber	55 laps	2	3m11.884s	14
11	**Narain Karthikeyan**	Jordan	54 laps	2	3m17.656s	17
12	**Tiago Monteiro**	Jordan	53 laps	2	3m17.962s	18
13	**Christijan Albers**	Minardi	52 laps	2	3m23.001s	20
R	**Rubens Barrichello**	Ferrari	49 laps/handling	2	3m11.502s	12
R	**Giancarlo Fisichella**	Renault	36 laps/accident	1	3m08.448s	3
R	**Mark Webber**	Williams	36 laps/accident	1	3m08.904s	4
R	**Jacques Villeneuve**	Sauber	26 laps/accident	1	3m12.995s	16
R	**Jenson Button**	BAR	2 laps/engine	0	3m09.832s	9
R	**Anthony Davidson**	BAR	2 laps/engine	0	3m11.890s	15
R	**Patrick Friesacher**	Minardi	2 laps/accident	0	3m21.186s	19

TALKING POINT: FERRARI WORRIED AT LACK OF PACE

Think Michael Schumacher and Ferrari and you conjure up images of smiling faces and winner's trophies. It seemed this would last for ever, but nothing does and there was concern for Ferrari at Sepang when Michael failed to qualify in the top 10 for the second race in succession. His showing in the Australian opener had been put down to changing weather conditions, but this time it was for real; his lap was only good enough for 13th place on the grid, 1.5s off pole. Fingers were pointed at Bridgestone tyres, but Ferrari couldn't be sure that things would improve when it upgraded from its F2004M to the F2005 for round three.

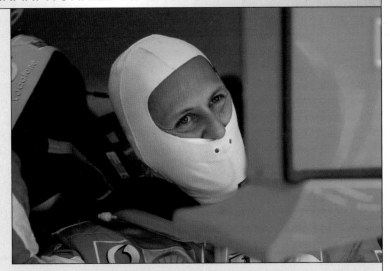

What a difference a year makes: Michael Schumacher with no reason to smile

BAHRAIN GP

Reigning world champion Michael Schumacher bounced back in Bahrain,
but the German genius could do nothing about Fernando Alonso, while a rare
Ferrari mechanical failure left Jarno Trulli to finish as the best of the rest.

Come and get me: Fernando Alonso was again the class of the field for Renault, who were beginning to open out a championship lead

With Fernando Alonso's early season form marking him out as the driver most likely to be crowned world champion at the season's end, it was fitting that the driver whom he seemed likely to topple, Michael Schumacher, should hit some improved form in the first outing for the new Ferrari F2005. And the seven-time world champion gave the Spaniard a stern test. That Alonso weathered it with hardly a ruffled hair is credit to the Renault driver. That the Ferrari should break in its pursuit, however, showed the extent to which the car was pushed: it was the first time for years that a Ferrari had broken down simply trying to live with the pace. Even better news for the Spaniard came after the race, when news emerged that he had not even used his Renault engine's full power (see sidebar).

So, advantage Renault, and most definitely advantage Alonso, as he left Sakhir with a ten-point championship lead.

Pole position was his for the second race in a row, this time by 0.455s from Schumacher, with Jarno Trulli again showing well to qualify not far behind for Toyota. Nick Heidfeld just edged out team-mate Mark Webber and Toyota's Ralf Schumacher to be fourth for Williams. McLaren continued to struggle over a single qualifying lap, as they failed to get the most from their tyres and Kimi Raikkonen lined up only ninth, two places behind the team's test driver, Pedro de la Rosa, a stand-in for Juan Pablo Montoya who had injured a shoulder playing tennis.

Alonso was pressed hard by Schumacher's Ferrari in the opening laps, but the Spaniard always seemed to have something in hand. Onlookers were never allowed to see exactly how much extra power he had in reserve, however, as the Ferrari ran off the track after a hydraulic failure and Schumacher was forced to coast back to the pits to retire.

Trulli took over in second place but never threatened Alonso. Indeed, the only driver making marked progress was Raikkonen, as he scythed his way past Ralf Schumacher and Heidfeld by running a longer first stint. It explained why he'd been off the pace in qualifying – he'd been running with a heavier fuel load. He then put pressure on Webber, whose car's rear-end grip was clearly lacking, and the Australian obliged by spinning, with Ralf Schumacher also nipping by before the the Williams driver rejoined the race.

De la Rosa was another driver on the move, but his lack of race time in recent seasons showed as he tried time and again to pass those ahead of him. It was entertaining, however, and he even set the race's fastest lap; his reward came when he demoted Webber for fifth place with just three laps to go.

Felipe Massa claimed seventh place, a lap down on Alonso. It looked as though he'd be followed home by his Sauber team-mate, Jacques Villeneuve, but a clash with David Coulthard took the Canadian out with two laps to go. The Scot then passed a gripless Rubens Barrichello on the final lap to claim the final point for Red Bull Racing. It was his third points score in a row.

BAR's season continued to go from bad to worse. After the embarrassment in Malaysia of seeing Jenson Button and Anthony Davidson (standing in for Takuma Sato who had a fever) both retire with engine failures after two laps, Button and Sato qualified only 11th and 13th respectively and both succumbed to transmission failure. This left the team down with Jordan and Minardi on zero points. Considering the disparity in budgets, especially now that Honda has a larger share in BAR, it was a disaster.

Honda's high-flying 2004 season, which propelled the team to second place overall, now seemed like a figment of the imagination.

BAHRAIN ROUND 03
Date: **3 April 2005** Laps: **57** Distance: **191.716 miles/308.523km**
Weather: **Very hot and bright**

RACE RESULT

Position	Driver	Team	Result	Stops	Qualifying Time	Grid
1	**Fernando Alonso**	Renault	1h29m18.531s	2	3m01.902s	1
2	**Jarno Trulli**	Toyota	1h29m31.940s	2	3m02.660s	3
3	**Kimi Raikkonen**	McLaren	1h29m50.594s	2	3m03.524s	9
4	**Ralf Schumacher**	Toyota	1h30m11.803s	2	3m03.271s	6
5	**Pedro de la Rosa**	McLaren	1h30m23.519s	2	3m03.373s	8
6	**Mark Webber**	Williams	1h30m33.232s	2	3m03.262s	5
7	**Felipe Massa**	Sauber	56 laps	2	3m05.302s	12
8	**David Coulthard**	Red Bull	56 laps	2	3m05.844s	14
9	**Rubens Barrichello**	Ferrari	56 laps	2	3m07.693s	20
10	**Tiago Monteiro**	Jordan	55 laps	2	3m09.428s	16
11	**Jacques Villeneuve**	Sauber	54 laps/suspension	2	3m07.983s	15
12	**Patrick Friesacher**	Minardi	54 laps	2	3m11.261s	19
13	**Christijan Albers**	Minardi	53 laps	3	3m10.422s	18
R	**Jenson Button**	BAR	48 laps/transmission	2	3m04.348s	11
R	**Takuma Sato**	BAR	27 laps/transmission	1	3m05.563s	13
R	**Nick Heidfeld**	Williams	25 laps/engine	1	3m03.217s	4
R	**Michael Schumacher**	Ferrari	12 laps/hydraulics	0	3m02.357s	2
R	**Giancarlo Fisichella**	Renault	4 laps/engine	1	3m03.765s	10
R	**Narain Karthikeyan**	Jordan	2 laps/electrics	0	3m10.143s	17
R	**Christian Klien**	Red Bull	0 laps/electrics	0	3m03.369s	7

TALKING POINT: NOT TAKING IT TO THE MAX

A revelation by Renault cast its rivals into depression: they may have won the first three grands prix, but the team had yet to turn its engines up to full power. The French manufacturer took a conservative approach to the first three races, all flyaways, in order to be sure its engines would last two races as required by the rulebook. Fernando Alonso and Giancarlo Fiischella were running with their revs restricted, though Alonso used a few more in the opening laps here to keep Michael Schumacher at bay. This race showed Renault was right to be cautious, as Fisichella was forced to retire early when a piston failed.

Renault appeared to be packing enough of a punch, but revealed there was more in store

SAN MARINO GP

Renault was made to fight at Imola, but Fernando Alonso weathered a fierce attack from Michael Schumacher to make it four wins out of four for Renault. However, when the race began, it seemed to be heading Kimi Raikkonen's way.

Pupil beats teacher: Fernando Alonso held off a reinvigorated Michael Schumacher to emphasise his ability to beat the seven-time champion

McLaren's failure to get sufficient heat into its Michelin tyres, to qualify the car in line with the abilities of the team, was rectified for Imola, thanks to bringing the MP4-20's weight distribution forward. It worked and Kimi Raikkonen claimed the team's first pole position of the year.

Better was to follow, as the Finn simply powered clear in the race, taking a 2s advantage on the opening lap, leaving Fernando Alonso's Renault in its wake. Indeed after eight laps, the McLaren driver was 3.5s in front, controlling the race as he pleased from Alonso, Jenson Button's BAR and Jarno Trulli's Toyota. But then a cv joint broke... and that was that. The race suddenly had a new leader and it could almost be said that the status quo had been re-established, with Renault at the front again, just as the team had been for all but a few laps that year.

Alonso had the upper hand on Button, but a driver who had started from 13th on the grid and who had advanced at this stage only to 11th was on the move.

His name was Schumacher and his Ferrari was handling just how he liked it to handle. Better still, he had started with more fuel on board than his rivals and would therefore be able to make the first of his two stops later than they did.

Indeed, he waited until lap 27 of 62, by which time he had climbed to third place as his rivals pitted. Furthermore, he was able to rejoin the race in the same position after a series of fast laps. Being the final driver in for the second round of pit stops even allowed Schumacher to entertain the *tifosi* by running in the lead for a couple of laps. On returning to the track with 11 laps to go, he'd outrun Button and was now up into

second place, with only Alonso to overhaul for a famous, fighting win, one that would have been far more exciting than his win-from-the-front victories of 2004.

The gap between the German and his heir apparent was just a few car lengths, but the seven-time world champion was anxious to take his first win of the campaign, particularly in front of this Ferrari-mad crowd. The trouble was, the Renault had superior traction out of the slow corners and Alonso was able to parry every thrust. So this is how they finished, the teacher trailing the pupil, who had not fluffed a single one of his lines.

Having dropped away in the heat of the battle, Button was third, 10s behind, but easily clear of, the second McLaren, driven this time by long-time test driver Alexander Wurz. He, too, had seconds to spare over

Takuma Sato in the second BAR. Sadly, however, BAR's first points of the year were not to stand (see sidebar).

This elevated Jacques Villeneuve to fourth place, offering the 1997 world champion some welcome cheer in a season of little fortune for Sauber, although he did cross the finish line some half a minute behind Sato.

The final points went to Jarno Trulli, who was elevated from seventh to fifth for Toyota following the exclusion of the BAR duo, Nick Heidfeld who shadowed him across the line, and Mark Webber in the second Williams. Webber just edged out Vitantonio Liuzzi, who enjoyed a strong run on his first outing for Red Bull Racing as part of his unusual mix-and-match swapping season with Christian Klien as the team assessed which of the junior drivers was the better bet.

Raikkonen wasn't the only frontrunner to fall, with Renault's opening-round victor Giancarlo Fisichella the first to retire, on lap 6, when he spun off at Tamburello while pressuring Heidfeld's Williams. Rubens Barrichello also dropped out when electrical gremlins struck after the first of his two planned pit stops. David Coulthard had hoped for better, but his Red Bull handled poorly after it was assaulted by Felipe Massa's Sauber at the start.

IMOLA ROUND 04

Date: **24 April 2005** Laps: **62** Distance: **189.897 miles/305.595km**
Weather: **Warm and dry but overcast**

RACE RESULT

Position	Driver	Team	Result	Stops	Qualifying Time	Grid
1	**Fernando Alonso**	Renault	1h27m41.921s	2	2m43.441s	2
2	**Michael Schumacher**	Ferrari	1h27m42.136s	2	2m47.244s	13
D	**Jenson Button**	BAR	1h27m52.402s	2	2m44.105s	3
3	**Alexander Wurz**	McLaren	1h28m09.475s	2	2m44.689s	7
D	**Takuma Sato**	BAR	1h28m16.704s	2	2m44.658s	6
4	**Jacques Villeneuve**	Sauber	1h28m46.363s	2	2m46.259s	11
5	**Jarno Trulli**	Toyota	1h28m52.179s	2	2m44.518s	5
6	**Nick Heidfeld**	Williams	1h28m53.203s	2	2m54.196s	8
7	**Mark Webber**	Williams	1h29m05.218s	2	2m44.511s	4
8	**Vitantonio Liuzzi**	Red Bull	1h29m05.685s	2	2m48.155s	15
9	**Ralf Schumacher**	Toyota	1h29m17.762s	2	2m45.416s	10
10	**Felipe Massa**	Sauber	61 laps	2	2m44.930s	18*
11	**David Coulthard**	Red Bull	61 laps	2	2m48.070s	14
12	**Narain Karthikeyan**	Jordan	61 laps	2	2m52.099s	15
13	**Tiago Monteiro**	Jordan	60 laps	4	2m54.252s	17
R	**Christijan Albers**	Minardi	20 laps/fluid leak	0	no time	20
R	**Rubens Barrichello**	Ferrari	18 laps/electrics	1	2m45.243s	9
R	**Kimi Raikkonen**	McLaren	9 laps/driveshaft	0	2m42.880s	1
R	**Patrick Friesacher**	Minardi	8 laps/clutch shaft	0	2m57.048s	19
R	**Giancarlo Fisichella**	Renault	5 laps/accident	0	2m46.710s	12

* RELEGATED TEN PLACES ON GRID FOR ENGINE CHANGE

TALKING POINT: BARS THROWN OUT

Post-race scrutineering threw up a shock: the BARs were excluded, scrapping hard-earned third- and fifth-place finishes for Jenson Button and Takuma Sato. The 007s were over the minimum weight limit, until they were emptied of fuel and discovered to be underweight. A secondary fuel tank – a 10–12 litre tank within the tank – was found that the team claimed was within the rules. However, the FIA said that there was a possibility it might be filled only at the final pit stop, concluding the team could have run the first part of the race underweight. BAR's penalty was not only disqualification from this race, but also a two-race ban.

Quick, slow, slow: third place became nothing for BAR, followed by a two-race ban

SPANISH GP

Robbed of victory at Imola, Kimi Raikkonen decided to make amends in Spain and, in so doing, left Fernando Alonso's home fans in no doubt whatsoever that their hero was going to have a massive fight on his hands for championship honours.

Kimi Raikkonen must have wondered where his season was heading after the first three grands prix. Fourth time out, at Imola, he was the class act and, despite the fact that mechanical failure curtailed his runaway victory, it came as a massive relief to him that he not only qualified on pole at the Circuit de Catlunya but that he also led every lap of the race for his first win since the 2004 Belgian Grand Prix. So great was his dominance, he wasn't even knocked off the top of the lap chart, even when he came in for either of his two pit stops. Indeed, Raikkonen was able to back off after his first stop and still finish close on half a minute clear of Alonso's previously dominant Renault. Small wonder then that he was seen to break from his taciturn norm for a smile or two afterwards.

Mark Webber had qualified his Williams second, but the Australian was unable to produce a drive that would have made both the team and engine partner BMW happy at a time when a split between the two parties was becoming ever more likely. At the start, the Australian was immediately demoted by both Alonso and Ralf Schumacher's Toyota, emphasising just how poor the Williams-BMW is off the line.

The order then had to settle down behind him, with Jarno Trulli fifth and Giancarlo Fisichella sixth, as the safety car was deployed – both Minardis had failed to start and were stationary on the track.

Once the safety car had withdrawn, Raikkonen simply streaked into an ever-extending lead, sometimes escaping by as much as 1s per lap, with Alonso unable to do anything about his pace.

One of the reasons that Alonso wasn't able to respond to the Finn was that his tyres were blistering and he had to ease off, meaning that Ralf Schumacher became a threat. After the first round of stops, though, Trulli had moved ahead of his team-mate, but a late first stop from Fisichella elevated him to second, benefiting from Alonso being stuck behind Raikkonen's refuelled, and thus heavier, car in the final two laps before his pit stop. It wasn't to be the Italian's race, though: his handling went so awry that he pitted for a new nose and he was only able to finish fifth after passing Webber in the closing laps.

Michael Schumacher was so late in for his first stop – not until just before half distance and seven laps later than Raikkonen – that he caused his rivals to think that he was attempting a one-stop strategy. They were wrong, but Michael's race was spoiled by not one, but two, tyre deflations. The first,

A double blow: one puncture may count as bad luck, but Michael Schumacher succeeded in picking up two

to his left rear, occurred just after he had inherited third place following Fisichella's unplanned stop. Incredibly, he was back in again two laps later with the front left flat.

Juan Pablo Montoya was back from his two-race recuperation and showed that the fire still burned as he made the most of his Michelins' ability to come up to temperature at a restart. He got the jump on Schumacher's Bridgestone-shod Ferrari when the safety car withdrew, righting a wrong from lap 1 when the German had usurped him after he had been pushed wide by Trulli.

However, the Colombian's injured shoulder was still not 100 per cent and he struggled, spinning once, although his refuelling rig failed to help his cause, malfunctioning and necessitating an extra stop, which left him to finish a lapped seventh.

Having been jumped at the start, Webber realised early on as he failed to re-pass Ralf Schumacher and Alonso that he wouldn't be able to keep to his pre-race plan of making three stops. Instead, he accepted that he would have to take on more fuel at each stop, coming in just twice. This, combined with vibrations caused by worn tyres, meant that he had fallen to sixth by the end of the race and was clearly deflated by the turn of events.

CATALUNYA ROUND 05
Date: **8 May 2005** Laps: **66** Distance: **189.677 miles/305.256km**
Weather: **Hot and bright**

RACE RESULT

Position	Driver	Team	Result	Stops	Qualifying Time	Grid
1	**Kimi Raikkonen**	McLaren	1h27m16.830s	2	2m31.421s	1
2	**Fernando Alonso**	Renault	1h27m44.482s	2	2m31.962s	3
3	**Jarno Trulli**	Toyota	1h28m02.777s	2	2m31.995s	5
4	**Ralf Schumacher**	Toyota	1h28m03.549s	2	2m31.917s	4
5	**Giancarlo Fisichella**	Renault	1h28m14.766s	2	2m32.830s	6
6	**Mark Webber**	Williams	1h28m25.372s	2	2m31.668s	2
7	**Juan Pablo Montoya**	McLaren	1h27m17.051s	3	2m33.472s	7
8	**David Coulthard**	Red Bull	65 laps	2	2m34.168s	9
9	**Rubens Barrichello**	Ferrari	65 laps	1	no time	16
10	**Nick Heidfeld**	Williams	65 laps	2	no time	17
11	**Felipe Massa**	Sauber	63 laps/wheel	2	2m34.224s	10
12	**Tiago Monteiro**	Jordan	63 laps	2	2h39.943s	18
13	**Narain Karthikeyan**	Jordan	63 laps	2	2m39.968s	13
R	**Jacques Villeneuve**	Sauber	51 laps/water leak	1	2m36.480s	12
R	**Michael Schumacher**	Ferrari	46 laps/puncture	2	2m33.551s	8
R	**Christijan Albers**	Minardi	19 laps/gearbox	0	2m41.141s	14
R	**Patrick Friesacher**	Minardi	11 laps/spun off	0	2m42.759s	15
R	**Vitantonio Liuzzi**	Red Bull	9 laps/spun off	0	2m35.302s	11

TALKING POINT: DRIVERS DEMAND SAFETY WHEN TESTING

As one of the four directors of the Grand Prix Drivers' Association, David Coulthard called upon the sport's governing body, the FIA, to improve safety standards at test sessions. The drivers were concerned that the medical facilities at many of the tests were far short of those enjoyed at grands prix, as was the number of marshals. With test runs longer than ever before – as teams performed more race-distance runs so that they could simulate the longer distances that their one-race tyres and two-race engines required – parts were becoming more stressed and there had been several large accidents.

Five-star rescue required: Michael Schumacher looks on as his Ferrari is collected

MONACO GP

The McLaren roadshow was really on a roll by the time it left Monaco. Kimi Raikkonen scored a second straight win to move into second place behind Renault's Fernando Alonso in the title chase, with all still to play for.

Monaco magic: Kimi Raikkonen gave Renault cause for concern as he dominated for McLaren

For the third race in succession, Kimi Raikkonen lined up in pole position. The margin over Fernando Alonso may have been small, but all the Finn had to do at this narrowest of circuits was to ensure he kept his McLaren ahead of the Spaniard's Renault at the start. Then, just as had been the case in Spain, Raikkonen simply motored clear, helped in no small part by the fact that Alonso's Renault struggled for grip from his hard-compound Michelins.

Also as had been the case in Spain, Mark Webber found his Williams embarrassed for acceleration at the start and dropped back from third to fifth as Giancarlo Fisichella used his Renault's excellent get-up-and-go to move ahead before the first corner, Ste Devote, followed by Jarno Trulli's Toyota.

The order then remained static until Trulli leapt from fourth to second on lap 25, although he did so only because Alonso and Webber pitted. The Italian driver was to hold

on to that position for a further 14 laps, as he was on a one-stop strategy. He wasn't the last to pit, however, as the McLarens came in several laps later. Raikkonen pitted and resumed without even ceding the lead to the best of the two-stoppers.

Raikkonen's team-mate, Juan Pablo Montoya, was having a far less serene meeting, though, having to fight his way forward after being made to line up 16th of the 18 cars after his time in the first qualifying session was declared void when he was adjudged to have brake-tested Ralf Schumacher in the fourth practice session. This caused an accident that also took out David Coulthard and Jacques Villeneuve. However, he behaved impeccably during the race and used his one-stop strategy to good effect to climb to an eventual fifth place – right on Alonso's tail – helped on his ascent by Trulli's coming together with Fisichella. This happened during lap 64 at the Grand Hotel Hairpin, and dropped the Renault driver from fifth to tenth since he had to wait before being able to rejoin the race as Montoya, Ralf Schumacher and both Ferrari drivers nipped past. Trulli didn't benefit from his lunge down the inside, though, as he had to pit for his car to be checked and would climb only as high as tenth by the end of the race.

More embarrassing than this melee, though, was the fate that befell Sauber's racers the lap before, when Villeneuve attempted to pass Felipe Massa into Ste Devote for eighth place. It was never on and he caused Peter Sauber apoplexy as they clashed. Both were able to continue the race, but all hope of points was lost.

With Raikkonen steaming along in the

lead, under no pressure from behind in the final third of the race, Alonso was having a harder time in second as his car lost grip when its tyres went off. The Williams drivers lined him up and first Nick Heidfeld – who had moved past Webber at their second pit stop – and then Webber got past, with Heidfeld benefiting when Alonso's attention wandered as he came up to lap the delayed Trulli at the chicane on lap 71. Webber then pressed hard and passed the Spaniard in the same place that his team-mate had overtaken him three laps earlier.

But it was what happened in the closing laps that really made the crowds scream with delight, as Alonso gave his all in trying to keep a train of cars behind him. The procession behind the Spaniard was led by Montoya, with Ralf Schumacher then Rubens Barrichello and Michael Schumacher almost in his shadows. Barrichello found no intra-team love on the final lap as Michael forced his way by at the chicane, showing as much aggression in his move into seventh as many might in attempting to take the lead. He was then so anxious to make it into sixth that brother Ralf was convinced he would take both of them off. Somehow, though, they managed not to clash as their wheels interlocked and they flashed across the finish line, with the Toyota still just ahead.

MONACO ROUND 06

Date: **22 May 2005** Laps: **78** Distance: **161.880 miles/260.520km**
Weather: **Warm and bright**

RACE RESULT

Position	Driver	Team	Result	Stops	Qualifying Time	Grid
1	**Kimi Raikkonen**	McLaren	1h45m15.556s	1	2m30.323s	1
2	**Nick Heidfeld**	Williams	1h45m29.433s	2	2m32.883s	6
3	**Mark Webber**	Williams	1h45m34.040s	2	2m31.656s	3
4	**Fernando Alonso**	Renault	1h45m52.043s	1	2m30.406s	2
5	**Juan Pablo Montoya**	McLaren	1h45m52.203s	1	no time	16
6	**Ralf Schumacher**	Toyota	1h45m52.733s	1	no time	17
7	**Michael Schumacher**	Ferrari	1h45m52.779s	2	2m34.736s	8
8	**Rubens Barrichello**	Ferrari	1h45m53.126s	2	2m34.983s	10
9	**Felipe Massa**	Sauber	1h46m03.563s	2	2m35.120s	11
10	**Jarno Trulli**	Toyota	77 laps	2	2m32.590s	5
11	**Jacques Villeneuve**	Sauber	77 laps	2	2m34.936s	9
12	**Giancarlo Fisichella**	Renault	77 laps	1	2m32.100s	4
13	**Tiago Monteiro**	Jordan	75 laps	1	2m43.078s	15
14	**Christijan Albers**	Minardi	73 laps	1	2m42.206s	14
R	**Vitantonio Liuzzi**	Red Bull	59 laps/accident damage	1	2m37.152s	12
R	**Patrick Friesacher**	Minardi	29 laps/accident	1	2m40.810s	13
R	**David Coulthard**	Red Bull	23 laps/accident damage	1	2m33.867s	7
R	**Narain Karthikeyan**	Jordan	18 laps/accident damage	3	2m43.442s	18

TALKING POINT: IRVINE LINES UP TAKEOVER OF JORDAN

The grand prix scene often resembles something of a soap opera, and never has this been so strongly the case as in Monaco. The big story here in 2005 was that former Jordan driver, Eddie Irvine, was being linked with a takeover of his old team. Irvine was in town as a frontman for a Russian syndicate, led by Routsam Tariko, that was looking to take the team off Alex Shnaider, the Canadian-domiciled Russian who had bought it from Eddie Jordan at the end of 2004, but who had seemingly lost interest. Whether this bid came to anything or not, it was typical of the stories that have become such a feature of this money-go-round.

Talking money: Eddie Irvine (right) was seen in the company of Jordan money man Ian Phillips

EUROPEAN GP

This race nearly produced a third win in a row for Kimi Raikkonen, but a late-race vibration – caused by a flat-spotted tyre – led to suspension failure on the final lap and the fast-closing Fernando Alonso blasted by to record his fourth win of the season.

Kimi Raikkonen's McLaren missed out on pole position for the first time since the third round but, once the race was under way, there was never any doubt that he was the man in control.

He blasted past Nick Heidfeld's pole-sitting Williams and, just as had been the case at Imola, Barcelona and Monaco, started to edge clear. All was not clear behind him, though, with contact aplenty at the first corner.

Mark Webber had started third, but his BMW engine's pick-up was as weak as ever and he ended up behind Jarno Trulli and Juan Pablo Montoya as they reached the Mercedes Arena. At that point, the Australian left his braking too late and hit Montoya, spearing himself into retirement. Montoya dropped down the order, the Ferrari drivers were also delayed and Ralf Schumacher had to pit for a new nose.

David Coulthard used all his experience to keep to the inside of the mayhem, promoting himself from 12th to fourth. He then led for Red Bull on lap 19 – the lap before his first stop – as Heidfeld pitted very early from second as he was running a three-stop strategy, something that proved that he had run with a light fuel load in qualifying.

Then his 2004 team-mate Raikkonen brought his McLaren in on lap 18. Coulthard's attempts to get out of the pits quickly were ruined when he was clocked at 1mph over the pitlane limit. The Scot was called in for a drive-through penalty, which dropped him a position.

Trulli had also been ahead of Coulthard in the early laps, but also incurred a drive-through penalty after his mechanics stayed on the grid within the final 15s before the start of the parade lap. This dropped the Toyota driver to ninth and, coupled with

Alonso's increase in speed, meant that the Renault driver was effectively Raikkonen's chief pursuer. Sure, Heidfeld was still second, but he still had two more stops to make and would thus fall away.

Raikkonen's romp to another victory was spoiled in three ways. First, when he had made the first of his two pitstops on lap 18 and it became clear that Alonso was running a longer first stint: he stayed out for an extra five laps, running light.

Then, on lap 30, Raikkonen had an off at Ford Kurve, damaging one of his bargeboards. Four laps later, while trying to lap Jacques Villeneuve into the Dunlop hairpin, he locked up and flat-spotted his right front tyre. It was this last problem that led to his demise.

When both he and Alonso had made their second and final pitstops, the Finn held a lead of 12s, but he was increasingly troubled

Push and you shall be rewarded: Fernando Alonso's pressure finally paid off and he took the lead on the very last lap

by vibrations caused by his flat-spotted tyre. He was able to keep up his lap times to start with, but the vibrations steadily worsened and Raikkonen also found that it was starting to blur his vision. Not surprisingly, his lap times dropped accordingly and Alonso started to close in, believing that he might be able to catch the Finn before the end of the race.

Logic dictated that McLaren might call Raikkonen in to change the tyre, but there was concern that the race stewards might not agree that the tyre was in a dangerous condition (see sidebar).

This, coupled with the fact that he wanted to act like the red-blood racer that he undoubtedly is, meant he raced on, eschewing any such safety-first tactics. On to the final lap he went, still 1.5s ahead of the fast-closing Alonso.

It looked as though he would hang on, but then his suspension collapsed as he approached the first corner. The car was pitched into the gravel trap, narrowly missing Jenson Button's BAR. So, the gamble had failed and Alonso darted past for a present that meant that his points' lead would be 32 rather than 20. Heidfeld was also elevated, to second place, with the three-stopping Barrichello not far behind and Coulthard finishing in a deserved fourth.

NURBURGRING ROUND 07

Date: 29 May 2005 Laps: 59 Distance: 191.914 miles/308.863km
Weather: **Warm but overcast**

RACE RESULT

Position	Driver	Team	Result	Stops	Qualifying Time	Grid
1	**Fernando Alonso**	Renault	1h31m46.648s	2	1m31.056s	6
2	**Nick Heidfeld**	Williams	1h32m03.215s	3	1m30.081s	1
3	**Rubens Barrichello**	Ferrari	1h32m05.197s	3	1m31.249s	7
4	**David Coulthard**	Red Bull	1h32m18.236s	3	1m32.553s	12
5	**Michael Schumacher**	Ferrari	1h32m37.093s	2	1m31.585s	10
6	**Giancarlo Fisichella**	Renault	1h32m38.580s	2	1m31.566s	9
7	**Juan Pablo Montoya**	McLaren	1h32m44.821s	2	1m30.890s	5
8	**Jarno Trulli**	Toyota	1h32m 57.739s	3	1m30.700s	4
9	**Vitantonio Liuzzi**	Red Bull	1h32m58.177s	2	1m32.642s	14
10	**Jenson Button**	BAR	1h33m22.434s	2	1m32.594s	13
11	**Kimi Raikkonen**	McLaren	58 laps/accident	2	1m30.197s	2
12	**Takuma Sato**	BAR	58 laps	3	1m32.926s	16
13	**Jacques Villeneuve**	Sauber	58 laps	2	1m32.891	15
14	**Felipe Massa**	Sauber	58 laps	3	1m32.205s	11
15	**Tiago Monteiro**	Jordan	58 laps	3	1m35.047s	17
16	**Narain Karthikeyan**	Jordan	58 laps	2	1m36.192s	19
17	**Christijan Albers**	Minardi	57 laps	3	1m36.239s	20
18	**Patrick Friesacher**	Minardi	56 laps	2	1m35.394s	18
R	**Ralf Schumacher**	Toyota	33 laps/accident	2	1m31.392s	8
R	**Mark Webber**	Williams	0 laps/accident	0		

TALKING POINT: TAKING A GAMBLE ON TYRES

Anyone witnessing the final laps of the European GP will have been given first-hand insight into the 2005 regulations which decreed that drivers were only allowed to use one set of tyres per race. For had Raikkonen elected to forfeit a possible win for a fresh set of tyres and certain points, his team couldn't have been sure they'd be allowed to make the change. The reason for this confusion is that the FIA stewards have to deem a tyre's condition dangerous for it to be changed and McLaren couldn't be certain that his flat-spotted tyre would count as a puncture and thus merit a change without penalty.

All in a spin: Raikkonen just misses Button as his suspension fails on the final lap

CANADIAN GP

To keep everyone guessing about the outcome of the championship, Kimi Raikkonen's mid-season charge continued in Montreal and his victory was all the sweeter as Fernando Alonso slammed his Renault into the wall while leading.

The walls bite: Jenson Button followed Alonso's lead in hitting one of the ever-present walls

Up front, Alonso was frustrated as he was capable of running faster than Fisichella, but his team-mate didn't allow him to get by, confident that his own pace was just right for preserving his tyres.

Delayed by Christian Klien's Red Bull before his first pitstop and subsequently by a faulty fuel hose during it, Alonso remained in second place, but the Spaniard took over the lead on lap 32, after Fisichella's gearbox hydraulics suddenly developed a mind of their own.

Montoya began to reduce Alonso's lead, dropping Raikkonen as the Finn's steering went awry. Then, on lap 39, Alonso made a rare slip and smote the wall at Turn 4 with his right rear wheel, leaving him to limp back to the pits to retire.

The McLarens were now running in first and second place, with Button third, Michael Schumacher fourth and Jarno Trulli fifth, but Button crashed out of the race when he clipped the kerb at the final chicane on lap 47 - just before the planned second round of pitstops - and was tipped into the unyielding wall.

Proving that this wasn't BAR's day, Sato had already earned the unfortunate accolade of having made the race's longest pitstop: he remained in the pits for fully 32 minutes as his crew changed the gearbox. This would never previously have been worth the effort, but with the finishing order now dictating the starting order for the next race's qualifying session, the team deemed it worthwhile. However, even this didn't work as well as had been hoped, since the Japanese driver spun out after his car's rear-end seized.

Just to show that they hadn't been idling during their two-race ban, BAR arrived at the Circuit Gilles Villeneuve with aero tweaks on their cars that clearly yielded dividends, as Jenson Button claimed pole with team-mate Takuma Sato sixth. However, once the race had started, it showed that the Englishman had achieved his lap time with the help of running with a light fuel load, as had Michael Schumacher, whose Ferrari lined up beside him.

As it happens, neither was to benefit from their front-row positions, as the Renaults on the second row powered past them at the start. Giancarlo Fisichella took the lead ahead of Fernando Alonso, with Button slotting into third and Juan Pablo Montoya diving past Schumacher at Turn 2 to be fourth. Worse still for Ferrari, Schumacher was forced wide as the Colombian came past and, in a flash, he dropped to sixth as Kimi Raikkonen also dived by.

The Renaults soon opened up a lead, helped by Button holding up the McLarens. With precious few places to overtake, the McLarens remained bottled up until lap 15, when Button pitted, and then started to haul in the Renaults.

There was an immediate outcome to Button's retirement: Montoya lost the lead and was disqualified from the race after illegally trying to rejoin it. This came about as the safety car was brought out while the wrecked BAR was cleared and pit crews along the pitwall had to decide whether their drivers would benefit from bringing their planned second pitstops forward by a lap or two (see sidebar).

With Montoya disqualified – many people said that the severity of his penalty was the result of his action, some time before, when he got into trouble for brake-testing his rivals in Monaco – Raikkonen was now in front, but Michael Schumacher had made up more than half a minute when the field sat behind the safety car and was right on his tail. There was nothing that the German could do in the final laps, though, and Raikkonen claimed his third win of the campaign.

With eight laps to go, Trulli was robbed of third place when a brake disc broke, promoting Barrichello to the final podium position, a result that owed everything to the fact that he had pitted a lap before the safety car had come out. Its timing led to him vaulting from eighth to fourth behind Trulli. Felipe Massa kept his Sauber ahead of Mark Webber's Williams for fourth place.

MONTREAL ROUND 08

Date: **12 June 2005** Laps: **70** Distance: **189.686 miles/305.270km**
Weather: **Warm and bright**

RACE RESULT

Position	Driver	Team	Result	Stops	Qualifying Time	Grid
1	**Kimi Raikkonen**	McLaren	1h32m09.290s	2	1m15.923s	7
2	**Michael Schumacher**	Ferrari	1h32m10.427s	3	1m15.475s	2
3	**Rubens Barrichello**	Ferrari	1h32m49.773s	2	no time	20
4	**Felipe Massa**	Sauber	1h33m04.429s	3	1m16.661s	11
5	**Mark Webber**	Williams	1h33m05.069s	2	1m17.749s	14
6	**Ralf Schumacher**	Toyota	69 laps	2	1m16.362s	10
7	**David Coulthard**	Red Bull	69 laps	2	1m16.890s	12
8	**Christian Klien**	Red Bull	69 laps	2	1m18.249s	16
9	**Jacques Villeneuve**	Sauber	69 laps	3	1m16.116s	8
10	**Tiago Monteiro**	Jordan	67 laps	3	1m19.034s	18
11	**Christijan Albers**	Minardi	67 laps	3	1m18.214s	15
R	**Jarno Trulli**	Toyota	62 laps/brakes	2	1m16.201s	9
D	**Juan Pablo Montoya**	McLaren	52 laps/passed red light	2	1m15.669s	5
R	**Jenson Button**	BAR	46 laps/accident	2	1m15.217s	1
R	**Nick Heidfeld**	Williams	43 laps/engine	1	1m17.081s	13
R	**Takuma Sato**	BAR	40 laps/brakes	2	1m15.729s	6
R	**Patrick Friesacher**	Minardi	39 laps/hydraulics	2	1m19.574s	19
R	**Fernando Alonso**	Renault	38 laps/accident	1	1m15.561s	3
R	**Giancarlo Fisichella**	Renault	32 laps/hydraulics	1	1m15.577s	4
R	**Narain Karthikeyan**	Jordan	24 laps/accident	1	1m18.664s	17

TALKING POINT: A LATE CALL COSTS MONTOYA

Juan Pablo Montoya's hopes of kick-starting a season that had failed to produce a podium position came to nothing when he was disqualified from the Canadian GP. His crime was to leave the pitlane when a red light was showing at the exit, but the damage had already been done: the lead that he had taken when the Renaults retired had been scuppered a lap earlier after his pit crew failed to call him in for a stop when the safety car was deployed – McLaren realised Montoya needed to come in just after he had passed the pit entry – enabling Raikkonen to make his stop and move into the lead.

Over and out: Montoya comes in to park up after being disqualified from the race

UNITED STATES GP

Pig-headedness is not an attractive trait at the best of times, but almost every single party involved in the United States Grand Prix displayed such behaviour. The outcome was that seven of the teams retired to the pitlane after the parade lap.

At least someone was happy: Tiago Monteiro celebrates his unexpected podium visit for Jordan

If you're going to make a fool of yourself, don't do it in front of the crowd that is deemed to be the most important to your welfare and, above all, don't stick two fingers up at those who pay the bills.

We will only know this year whether this action of insulting fans in the country where the customer is king has killed off F1 in its most lucrative market.

Yet, this is precisely what F1 did, with the parties involved playing hardball with each other with such machismo that no solution was found to a purported safety problem and the race was turned into a farce with just six cars: that's to say two

Ferraris enjoying a rare visit to the front of the field, plus what one pressroom wag described as "four cars making a noise" – perennial backmarkers Jordan and Minardi.

The root of the team's arguments was that cars running on Michelin tyres had had a series of accidents in practice, with Ralf Schumacher putting his Toyota into the wall on the Turn 13 banking at precisely the point where he had injured his back in the 2004 race.

His team's third driver, Ricardo Zonta, had already gone off after tyre failure at Turn 5. To make matters worse, McLaren and then Red Bull also reported concerns over their rear tyre wear.

After analysing their tyres through Friday night, Michelin admitted it could not guarantee the safety of either of the compounds it had brought to Indianapolis.

More inspection followed on Saturday and, on race morning, Michelin confirmed that its tyres were unsafe for racing and suggested that the seven teams using its rubber – BAR, Renault, Williams, McLaren, Sauber, Red Bull Racing and Toyota – ought to run no more than ten laps on a set.

With an hour to go until the race, circuit owner Tony George and F1 boss Bernie Ecclestone pushed for a chicane to be inserted at Turn 13 to ensure the Michelin teams would race, but Ferrari wouldn't agree to this and, despite the Michelin teams offering to forgo any points scored, the FIA rejected it.

With half an hour to go, it seemed as though an agreement had been reached when all 20 cars lined up on the grid, with Jarno Trulli on pole position ahead of Kimi Raikkonen, Jenson Button and Giancarlo Fisichella, as they all set off on the parade lap.

But the crowd was shocked to the core when all 14 Michelin runners peeled off into the pitlane, leaving Michael Schumacher on what had been the inside of the third row now sitting on what had become pole, with Rubens Barrichello behind him and then Tiago Monteiro's Jordan the next up, with five empty rows between them.

The engine notes, normally the dominant sound, could hardly be made out over the boos from the grandstands and many of the crowd opted to get up and leave in protest at the way that they were being duped.

If there was anything to be thankful for, it was that the Ferraris actually had quite a decent dice, with Barrichello tailing his team-mate, but finding himself in front when Michael Schumacher emerged from his first pitstop in second place a lap after the Brazilian had made his.

The honours were exchanged at the second time of asking, with Schumacher taking a lead that he wasn't going to lose, reaching the finish 1.5s ahead of his Brazilian team-mate. Monteiro could hardly contain himself after the race. He had been lapped, in his Jordan but there was nothing unusual in that, save for the fact that he had been lapped just the once.

What was almost freakishly divorced from the norm was that he was invited to visit the podium for finishing third, becoming the first Portuguese driver ever to do so. His Jordan team-mate, Narain Karthikeyan, the first Indian to drive in the Formula One World Championship, took until the tenth lap to move past Minardi's Christijan Albers for fourth place and remained there to the finish.

Fortunately, both Albers and Patrick Friesacher avoided mechanical failure, so that at least the few who stayed to watch the entire race still had six cars circulating at the finish.

INDIANAPOLIS ROUND 09
Date: **19 June 2005** Laps: **73** Distance: **190.150 miles/306.016km**
Weather: **Warm but overcast**

RACE RESULT

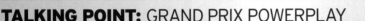

Position	Driver	Team	Result	Stops	Qualifying Time	Grid
1	**Michael Schumacher**	Ferrari	1h29m43.181s	2	1m11.369s	5
2	**Rubens Barrichello**	Ferrari	1h29m44.703s	2	1m11.431s	7
3	**Tiago Monteiro**	Jordan	72 laps	2	1m13.462s	17
4	**Narain Karthikeyan**	Jordan	72 laps	2	1m13.776s	19
5	**Christijan Albers**	Minardi	71 laps	3	1m13.632s	18
6	**Patrick Friesacher**	Minardi	71 laps	2	1m14.494s	20
R	**Jarno Trulli**	Toyota	0 laps/withdrew*	0	1m10.625s	1
R	**Kimi Raikkonen**	McLaren	0 laps/withdrew*	0	1m10.694s	2
R	**Jenson Button**	BAR	0 laps/withdrew*	0	1m11.277s	3
R	**Giancarlo Fisichella**	Renault	0 laps/withdrew*	0	1m11.290s	4
R	**Fernando Alonso**	Renault	0 laps/withdrew*	0	1m11.380s	6
R	**Takuma Sato**	BAR	0 laps/withdrew*	0	1m11.497s	8
R	**Mark Webber**	Williams	0 laps/withdrew*	0	1m11.527s	9
R	**Felipe Massa**	Sauber	0 laps/withdrew*	0	1m11.555s	10
R	**Juan Pablo Montoya**	McLaren	0 laps/withdrew*	0	1m11.681s	11
R	**Jacques Villeneuve**	Sauber	0 laps/withdrew*	0	1m11.691s	12
R	**Ricardo Zonta**	Toyota	0 laps/withdrew*	0	1m11.754s	13
R	**Christian Klien**	Red Bull	0 laps/withdrew*	0	1m12.132s	14
R	**Nick Heidfeld**	Williams	0 laps/withdrew*	0	1m12.430s	15
R	**David Coulthard**	Red Bull	0 laps/withdrew*	0	1m12.682s	16

* ALL MICHELIN-SHOD TEAMS WITHDREW ON TYRE-RELATED SAFETY GROUNDS

TALKING POINT: GRAND PRIX POWERPLAY

It is safe to say that nothing is ever quite as it seems in the grand prix world. Indeed, many felt that the argument that scuppered the United States GP had little to do with tyre safety, but more to do with the ongoing battle between the majority of the teams and the sport's governing body over the future of F1. With all of the top teams aligned to the proposed Grand Prix World Championship breakaway series scheduled for 2008 among those running on Michelins, this supposition certainly held water, as did FIA president Max Mosley's lack of desire to help them find a solution.

Not going to play: the Michelin runners peel off after the parade lap, to park up for the day

FRENCH GP

After Formula One's abject public humiliation at Indianapolis, it was absolutely essential that the sport bounced back in some style in France. And it did, especially in the case of Fernando Alonso who led the race from start to finish.

Renault, Renault, Renault: the home crowd show their true colours as they cheer Fernando Alonso on to an outstanding victory

After the hullaballoo at Indianapolis, lovers of Formula One craved a good, straightforward race with no politics. While there were certainly rumblings in the paddock (see sidebar), the drivers delivered on the track, albeit with one of them reducing all of his rivals to the role of also-rans.

That driver was championship leader Fernando Alonso and he delighted the home crowd by qualifying on pole position for Renault and then leading every lap to record his fifth win of the season. Good as this figure looks after ten rounds, it masked the fact that McLaren's Kimi Raikkonen had been the man to beat in each grand prix since the fourth of the season, save for Indianapolis, when all of the Michelin-shod runners had retired to the pits after the parade lap.

This time around, the Finn was unable to offer the sort of challenge he would have liked, and merited, as his Mercedes engine failed in practice on Friday and he was duly demoted ten places on the grid after a new one had been fitted. It meant he had to try to advance from 13th, just as Alonso had had to do in Australia. In fact, Raikkonen went one place better than the Spaniard had managed Down Under, working his way right through to second place by flagfall, meaning that he had lost just two points to his title rival, who did all he needed to win and no more. Mind you, that was still good enough to leave the other 18 drivers in the shade. It also meant that Renault's first win at home in France since Alain Prost did the honours in 1983 was in safe hands.

Jarno Trulli was unable to challenge Alonso from second place on the grid, despite producing a good effort in the early stages when he kept Michael Schumacher's Ferrari behind him, as the tyre deterioration suffered by his Toyota grew ever worse, leaving it short of rear-end grip.

Schumacher might have hoped he would then lay claim to the second step on the podium, but that discounted the pace of the McLarens. Starting back in eighth and 13th, both had little choice but to run a two-stop strategy rather than to come in three times like their rivals. This meant they would spend much of the race running with a heavier load of fuel than the frontrunning cars – thus increasing their lap times. However, it was thought that this was the only way they would be able to gain track position. It worked too, with Montoya climbing to second before his first pit stop and then Raikkonen emerging in that place when he made his first stop three laps later. It wasn't to be Montoya's day, though, as a pipe in his car's hydraulics failed, leaving him with a faltering gearbox.

If Montoya had reason to be glum then so did Nick Heidfeld, who pitted six times in his Williams because he felt its left rear corner was behaving strangely. It turned out to be a differential problem, but this wasn't detected until after the race, by which time he had fallen to 14th place. Team-mate Mark Webber was also in the wars: one of his hips was being cooked so much by a hot point in the cockpit that it necessitated cold water being poured into his cockpit at pit stops.

With Montoya out, Schumacher was able to finish third, 10s behind Raikkonen, but as the only other driver on the lead lap. Giancarlo Fisichella had risen to fourth in the second Renault, but had lost time with a fuel-rig glitch in his first pit stop, then had a floor stay break and finally stalled at his last pit stop, dropping him to sixth behind Jenson Button and Trulli. Amazingly, considering that BAR ranked second only to Ferrari in 2004, these were the team's first points of the 2005 campaign.

MAGNY-COURS ROUND 10

Date: **3 July 2005** Laps: **70** Distance: **191.746 miles/308.586km**
Weather: **Hot and bright**

RACE RESULT

Position	Driver	Team	Result	Stops	Qualifying Time	Grid
1	**Fernando Alonso**	Renault	1h31m22.233s	3	1m14.412s	1
2	**Kimi Raikkonen**	McLaren	1h31m34.038s	2	1m114.559s	13
3	**Michael Schumacher**	Ferrari	1h32m44.147s	3	1m14.572s	3
4	**Jenson Button**	BAR	69 laps	2	1m15.051s	7
5	**Jarno Trulli**	Toyota	69 laps	2	1m14.521s	2
6	**Giancarlo Fisichella**	Renault	69 laps	3	1m14.887s	6
7	**Ralf Schumacher**	Toyota	69 laps	2	1m15.771s	10
8	**Jacques Villeneuve**	Sauber	69 laps	2	1m15.699s	5
9	**Rubens Barrichello**	Ferrari	69 laps	3	1m14.832s	6
10	**David Coulthard**	Red Bull	69 laps	3	1m16.434s	15
11	**Takuma Sato**	BAR	69 laps	3	1m14.655s	4
12	**Mark Webber**	Williams	68 laps	3	1m15.885s	12
13	**Tiago Monteiro**	Jordan	67 laps	3	1m18.047s	19
14	**Nick Heidfeld**	Williams	66 laps	6	1m16.207s	14
15	**Narain Karthikeyan**	Jordan	66 laps	3	1m17.857s	17
R	**Juan Pablo Montoya**	McLaren	46 laps/hydraulics	1	1m15.406s	8
R	**Christijan Albers**	Minardi	37 laps/puncture	2	1m18.335s	20
R	**Patrick Friesacher**	Minardi	33 laps/puncture	2	1m17.960s	18
R	**Felipe Massa**	Sauber	30 laps/hydraulics	3	1m15.566s	9
R	**Christian Klien**	Red Bull	1 lap/fuel pressure	0	1m16.547s	16

TALKING POINT: TEAMS WANT MAX MOSLEY OUT

Having been told that they would be punished for their role in the debacle that was the United States GP – when the field was reduced to six cars – the majority of team owners wanted the man who runs the sport, Max Mosley, to stand down. As many as seven out of the ten teams proposed to select a candidate to stand against him in the FIA presidential elections in October 2005. The teams behind this move were most likely BAR, McLaren, Minardi, Renault, Sauber, Toyota and Williams – all of the teams that support a manufacturers' breakaway championship for 2008 after the end of the Concorde Agreement that binds them until 2007.

The focus of attention: Max Mosley under scrutiny as he talks to Ferrari's Jean Todt

BRITISH GP

Renault versus McLaren had been the pattern of the season and the British Grand Prix was no different from any of the other rounds. This time, though, it was Alonso against Montoya, not Raikkonen. And Montoya took the chequered flag.

The full Monty: Juan Pablo Montoya leads Alonso and Raikkonen as he heads for his first grand prix win for McLaren

The two championship contenders, Fernando Alonso and Kimi Raikkonen, were true to their positions in the title race after qualifying in first and second. However, Raikkonen's guns had already been spiked: he suffered engine failure in practice for the second race in succession and, with it, the consequent ten-place grid demotion. He blamed poor engine preparation and was left with a mountain to climb. All he could do was pray that his McLaren team-mate Montoya would prevent Alonso from taking the maximum haul of ten points.

This is precisely what the Colombian managed to do by finishing almost 3s ahead of the Spaniard, not only retricting him to an eight-point haul, but also putting his own season back on track after a shaky start. He made his move right from the off, powering past Jenson Button on the run to Copse. He kept the hammer down as Alonso hugged the inside line and attacked into Maggotts. He was level rather than in front, so bravery was required, as well as sense from both him and Alonso as they ran side by side into the Becketts complex, before the Colombian edged ahead. Once in front, Montoya was topped only during the pit stop sequences and regained the lead when Alonso made his second stop late in the race.

Shortly before Alonso's final stop, there had been activity in the Renault pit as Giancarlo Fisichella was called in from third place on lap 46 for his final stop. The Italian had been called in from Alonso's tail after working his way forward from sixth on the grid and had been hoping to stop on lap 50 as he reckoned that he would emerge ahead of Alonso and, possibly, Montoya, to take the lead. For whatever reason, the most likely being to ensure that Alonso scored as many points as possible, Fisichella was called into the pits ahead of schedule.

With team orders banned, this is all a team can do to manipulate proceedings; anything too obvious on the track, such as one driver slowing to let a higher-ranked team-mate come through, would lead to punishment. But it mattered little in the end as his engine stalled in the pit stop and this dropped him to fourth place.

Past him into third came Raikkonen, who set the race's fastest lap on the final lap, showing Montoya that he could have won had he not been forced to start back in 12th.

For the second race in a row, Button came away with points. Having started second, though, he might have expected more than the four that he picked up for finishing fifth, but he lost a place at each of his two pit stops, firstly to Fisichella and then to Raikkonen on his second visit.

Just to show how far off the pace they had fallen, Ferrari had to make do with sixth and seventh for Michael Schumacher and Rubens Barrichello. This backed up team boss Jean Todt's comments that the team had "gone backwards in 2005". A shortage of grip was the main problem.

At least the Ferraris finished ahead of the Toyotas, which were eighth and ninth, with Trulli falling from fifth on the grid to miss out on a point, with the Japanese cars again struggling for grip as the race advanced. In fact they weren't that fast at the outset, as any of the drivers in the queue that formed behind Trulli would attest. Indeed, this was why Raikkonen lost so much time getting to the frontrunners – he had been forced to bide his time behind Trulli and Michael Schumacher – and could only get by after they had been called in for their first pit stops while he ran a longer first stint.

The Toyota drivers had more reason to smile than Williams's, though (see sidebar), as Mark Webber and Nick Heidfeld trailed in lapped, in 11th and 12th, to emphasize the team's decline.

SILVERSTONE ROUND 11
Date: **10 July 2005** Laps: **60** Distance: **191.603 miles/308.355km**
Weather: **Warm and bright**

RACE RESULT

Position	Driver	Team	Result	Stops	Qualifying Time	Grid
1	**Juan Pablo Montoya**	McLaren	1h24m29.588s	2	1m20.382s	3
2	**Fernando Alonso**	Renault	1h24m32.327s	2	1m19.905s	1
3	**Kimi Raikkonen**	McLaren	1h24m44.024s	2	1m19.932s	12
4	**Giancarlo Fisichella**	Renault	1h24m47.502s	2	1m21.010s	6
5	**Jenson Button**	BAR	1h25m09.852s	2	1m20.207s	2
6	**Michael Schumacher**	Ferrari	1h25m44.910s	2	1m21.275s	9
7	**Rubens Barrichello**	Ferrari	1h25m46.155s	3	1m20.906s	5
8	**Ralf Schumacher**	Toyota	1h25m48.800s	2	1m21.191s	8
9	**Jarno Trulli**	Toyota	1h25m50.439s	2	1m20.459s	4
10	**Felipe Massa**	Sauber	59 laps	2	1m22.495s	16
11	**Mark Webber**	Williams	59 laps	2	1m21.997s	11
12	**Nick Heidfeld**	Williams	59 laps	2	1m22.117s	14
13	**David Coulthard**	Red Bull	59 laps	2	1m22.108s	13
14	**Jacques Villeneuve**	Sauber	59 laps	2	1m21.352s	10
15	**Christian Klien**	Red Bull	59 laps	2	1m22.207s	15
16	**Takuma Sato**	BAR	58 laps	1	1m21.114s	7
17	**Tiago Monteiro**	Jordan	58 laps	2	no time	20
18	**Christijan Albers**	Minardi	57 laps	2	1m24.576s	18
19	**Patrick Friesacher**	Minardi	56 laps	2	1m25.566s	19
R	**Narain Karthikeyan**	Jordan	10 laps/electrics	0	1m23.583s	17

TALKING POINT: WILLIAMS STILL IN THE DARK AERODYNAMICALLY

In 2004, Williams took a brave direction with its "walrus-nosed" FW26 but had to ditch it when it didn't work. This time around, they were also left scratching their heads when the FW27 proved not to be the class of the field. Even with a revised aero package – including new sidepod chimneys and winglets – introduced at the French GP, matters failed to improve (either there or at Silverstone), forcing the team's technical chiefs to press on. Paddock insiders reckoned that engine supplier BMW was forcing the team to run its V10s at such limited revs in Friday practice to preserve engine life that it was costing them vital chassis set-up time.

Aerodynamic evolution: Williams was trying everything to develop the FW27

GERMAN GP

Failure is infuriating, but all the more so when the race is there for the taking, as Kimi Raikkonen found, not for the first time, when his McLaren failed him once more and victory was handed on a plate to his arch-rival, Fernando Alonso.

Kimi who? Montoya, Alonso and Button celebrate furiously on the Hockenheim podium

This should have been Kimi Raikkonen's race, pure and simple. He qualified his McLaren on pole position and led with ease from Fernando Alonso's Renault through to the first round of pit stops.

He came in for the first of his two planned stops three laps after the Spaniard and still emerged in the lead. And there he stayed until lap 35 of the scheduled 67 when, sitting on a lead of 11s, his steering went heavy, the throttle stopped responding

and the MP4-20 simply coasted to a halt, its hydraulic pressure gone, its race run: a tuppeny-threepenny bleed nipple on the gearbox that had not been tightened properly was to blame.

To make matters all the more galling, he was the only one of the 20 starters not circulating at the finish, meaning that he would also suffer from being the first out to qualify at the following grand prix in Hungary.

Worse still, this left Alonso to collect all ten points, to boost his points' lead to 36. Raikkonen's team-mate, Juan Pablo Montoya, gave his all in coming home second, but his charge had been made all but futile by giving just that little bit more than his all into the final corner of his qualifying lap, flinging the car off the circuit and clouting the tyre barrier.

This meant that he had to start from the back row, making his drive through to second all the more meritorious. However, had he started from the second or third row the result of this race could have been very different.

In order to make his way through the field, McLaren sent Montoya out with a heavy fuel load and he made the first of his two pit stops shortly after his rivals, elevating him from eighth before they started pitting to fifth afterwards.

This ascent was helped no end by a stunning opening lap that saw him climb from 19th to 11th. Raikkonen's retirement made this fourth, then he moved past front-row starter Jenson Button and Michael Schumacher's Ferrari into second place just before his final pit stop. He then emerged in that position and held it to the finish, albeit crossing the line more than 20s behind Alonso.

Having finally resumed his scoring ways at the French GP, Button was in the points for the third race in a row, taking his first podium of 2005 by finishing third just a couple of seconds behind Montoya.

At one point in the closing stages, it looked as though that place might go to Michael Schumacher, but the Ferrari driver was struggling with an increasing lack of grip and he fell to fourth after his second and final pit stop. He then lost one more place to Giancarlo Fisichella's Renault into the hairpin, with just two laps left to run. Had the race lasted a lap longer, he would probably have dropped a further place, as brother Ralf was holding a watching brief in his Toyota.

However, Ralf's record of going for the kill against his older brother remains rather patchy, so perhaps Michael would have held on after all.

Meanwhile, Scotsman David Coulthard collected his seventh set of points for 2005, which was no poor tally for a team that was expected to operate at a lower level entirely. He finished a fraction of a second behind Ralf, having been demoted by him at the last round of pit stops.

Felipe Massa took the final point, for eighth, after advancing from 13th as several more fancied runners struggled, including Rubens Barrichello (who chose too hard a tyre), Jarno Trulli (who suffered a puncture and then a drive-through penalty), Mark Webber (who was hit by Takuma Sato on the opening lap and lost 11 laps while repairs were made) and Nick Heidfeld (whose handling deteriorated after running fifth until his first pit stop).

HOCKENHEIM ROUND 12

Date: **24 July 2005** Laps: **67** Distance: **190.424 miles/306.458km**
Weather: **Warm, dry and overcast**

RACE RESULT

Position	Driver	Team	Result	Stops	Qualifying Time	Grid
1	**Fernando Alonso**	Renault	1h26m28.599s	2	1m14.904s	3
2	**Juan Pablo Montoya**	McLaren	1h26m51.168s	2	no time	19
3	**Jenson Button**	BAR	1h26m53.021s	2	1m14.759s	2
4	**Giancarlo Fisichella**	Renault	1h27m19.186s	2	1m14.927s	4
5	**Michael Schumacher**	Ferrari	1h27m20.289s	2	1m15.006s	5
6	**Ralf Schumacher**	Toyota	1h27m20.841s	2	1m15.689s	12
7	**David Coulthard**	Red Bull	1h27m21.299s	2	1m15.679s	11
8	**Felipe Massa**	Sauber	1h27m25.169s	2	1m16.009s	13
9	**Christian Klien**	Red Bull	1h27m38.417s	2	1m15.635s	10
10	**Rubens Barrichello**	Ferrari	66 laps	3	1m16.230s	15
11	**Nick Heidfeld**	Williams	66 laps	2	1m15.403s	7
12	**Takuma Sato**	BAR	66 laps	3	1m15.501s	8
13	**Christijan Albers**	Minardi	65 laps	2	1m17.519s	16
14	**Jarno Trulli**	Toyota	64 laps/pneumatics	6	1m15.532s	9
15	**Jacques Villeneuve**	Sauber	64 laps	2	1m16.012s	14
16	**Narain Karthikeyan**	Jordan	64 laps	5	no time	20
17	**Tiago Monteiro**	Jordan	64 laps	4	1m18.599s	18
18	**Robert Doornbos**	Minardi	63 laps	4	1m18.313s	17
NC	**Mark Webber**	Williams	55 laps	3	1m15.070s	6
R	**Kimi Raikkonen**	McLaren	35 laps/hydraulics	1	1m14.320s	1

TALKING POINT: RAIKKONEN FURIOUS AT MECHANICAL FAILURES

By this stage of the championship, Kimi Raikkonen ought to have been hot on Fernando Alonso's heels in the title race, but yet another mechanical failure, again while leading, left him 36 points adrift as he stormed away from Hockenheim. He was so angry that he didn't even speak to the press. Following on from consecutive engine failures that had cost him ten grid positions at each of the previous two races, his love for all things McLaren and Mercedes was wearing thin. Team boss Ron Dennis admitted to "running the cars on the edge" in their quest for speed, but this failure wasn't down to that.

Why the long face? Kimi Raikkonen listens to explanations as to why his car let him down again

HUNGARIAN GP

Fernando Alonso had little luck this time out. However, when push came to shove, McLaren were left disappointed for the second race in succession as they lost a potential one-two finish, but at least this time one of their drivers came out on top.

That driver was Kimi Raikkonen and the Finn's triumph became all the more important when Fernando Alonso could only finish a lapped 11th and his failure to score a point meant that the gap between them was reduced by ten points to 26.

In contrast to his successes earlier in the season, Raikkonen's win was anything but simple, however. Check the results and you will see that he had a finishing margin of close on 36s over the next driver home, Michael Schumacher, but such were the flashes of form that went unfulfilled that Schumacher might have been able to win, his own team-mate Juan Pablo Montoya probably should have won, while Alonso's day was spoiled as early as the first corner on lap 1 when he damaged his car's nose, only to lose it completely shortly afterwards.

In short, a great deal was happening around the tight twists and turns of the Hungaroring. As ever, it was hot and humid, but that appeared to suit Bridgestone and Ferrari as Michael Schumacher used their softer-compound tyres to record a simply blinding qualifying lap. He took pole by 0.9s, an enormous margin, especially around a track as short as this, with a lap time of 1m20s. He'd opted to run with a light fuel load as he pitted ahead of many rivals, but this was a tactic that had worked for him before at this circuit where overtaking is so hard.

Raikkonen qualified only fourth, behind Montoya and Toyota's Jarno Trulli, but he was up to second by the first corner as Montoya pushed Trulli wide and he simply dived down the inside. Trulli's woes didn't end there, as he was hit up the rear by

Rubens Barrichello's Ferrari, while his own team-mate, Ralf Schumacher, took evasive action and left no space at all for Alonso. The Spaniard got onto the grass on the inside in his attempt to avoid contact, but his car's nose took a hit all the same.

Most spectacular of all at this first corner, though, was Christian Klien, as the Austrian's Red Bull RB1 was flipped into an aerial roll by Jacques Villeneuve's Sauber. Fortunately, it landed on its wheels, but its race was run.

Red Bull Racing's bad luck doubled before the lap was out as Alonso's damaged nose detached and flew off in front of the pack. With little time to see it as Takuma Sato and Mark Webber jinked around it, and no time to avoid it, David Coulthard hit it head on and he too crashed out of the race as it

Mind the gap: Kimi Raikkonen takes the chequered flag to reduce the margin of Alonso's lead and haul him back into his sights once more

wrecked his front suspension and tipped him into the barriers.

If you thought that this was incident aplenty, Montoya had already suffered more than his share of surprises, having damaged his McLaren's bargeboards in a freak incident on the grid when he hit one of BAR's generators. Frantic repairs followed and all seemed well as he ran strongly on a two-stop strategy, leading twice in the process, but a driveshaft failed when he was in front before his second scheduled stop and this may well have been a result of this unusual impact.

Either way, it made Raikkonen's life easier, as he was now in front and able to make his third and final pit stop without losing the lead to win unchallenged. Michael Schumacher would have pushed harder had he not been demoted by the Finn at the time of their second stops, but the German then chose to back off and make sure of second place.

There were two Schumachers on the podium for the first time since the 2004 Japanese GP, with Ralf right on Michael's tail but unable to pass, just as had been the case at Hockenheim. Trulli endured dreadful handling after that first corner shunt, but still finished fourth, with BAR collecting points through Jenson Button in fifth and Sato in eighth for his first point of the season.

HUNGARORING ROUND 13

Date: **31 July 2005** Laps: **70** Distance: **190.552 miles/306.663km**
Weather: **Very hot, dry and sunny**

RACE RESULT

Position	Driver	Team	Result	Stops	Qualifying Time	Grid
1	**Kimi Raikkonen**	McLaren	1h37m25.552s	3	1m20.891s	4
2	**Michael Schumacher**	Ferrari	1h38m01.133s	3	1m19.882	1
3	**Ralf Schumacher**	Toyota	1h38m01.681s	3	1m20.964s	5
4	**Jarno Trulli**	Toyota	1h38m19.773s	3	1m20.839s	3
5	**Jenson Button**	BAR	1h38m24.384s	2	1m21.302s	8
6	**Nick Heidfeld**	Williams	1h38m33.927s	2	1m22.086s	12
7	**Mark Webber**	Williams	69 laps	2	1m23.495s	16
8	**Takuma Sato**	BAR	69 laps	2	1m21.787s	10
9	**Giancarlo Fisichella**	Renault	69 laps	3	1m21.333s	9
10	**Rubens Barrichello**	Ferrari	69 laps	3	1m21.158s	7
11	**Fernando Alonso**	Renault	69 laps	3	1m21.141s	6
12	**Narain Karthikeyan**	Jordan	67 laps	2	1m25.057s	18
13	**Tiago Monteiro**	Jordan	66 laps	4	no time	20
14	**Felipe Massa**	Sauber	63 laps	2	1m22.565s	14
R	**Christijan Albers**	Minardi	59 laps/hydraulics	4	1m24.443s	17
R	**Jacques Villeneuve**	Sauber	56 laps/fire damage	2	1m22.866s	15
R	**Juan Pablo Montoya**	McLaren	41 laps/driveshaft	1	1m20.779s	2
R	**Robert Doornbos**	Minardi	26 laps/hydraulics	1	1m25.484s	19
R	**David Coulthard**	Red Bull	0 laps/accident	0	1m22.279s	13
R	**Christian Klien**	Red Bull	0 laps/accident	0	1m21.937s	11

TALKING POINT: BUTTON WANTS TO RENEGE ON WILLIAMS DEAL

A year on from saying "no comment" on seemingly any number of occasions at the Hungaroring when asked whether he was going to leave BAR for Williams, Jenson Button started saying the same thing all over again. This time it was in response to questions about why he had done an about-face and decided to try and back out of a deal to go to Williams for 2006. Put simply, he thought there was a better chance of success with Honda-backed BAR in 2006 and beyond.
This made a mockery of the contract he had signed with Willams and did very little for either his or the sport's image.

Facing the music: BAR's Nick Fry and Gil de Ferran flank Button as he is grilled by the press

TURKISH GP

Kimi Raikkonen made good his championship challenge with a second straight win, but it was the stunning new circuit that impressed the most. Fernando Alonso was well beaten, but salvaged second place on the penultimate lap when Montoya's McLaren ran wide.

Raikkonen first, Alonso second was the story of the Turkish GP at the all-new Istanbul Park circuit. It was good news for the Finn, but even better news for the Spaniard, since it meant that Raikkonen had only clawed back two points from his points lead, leaving Alonso 24 points ahead with five grands prix to run. In other words, he was still on course for his first world title and it left Raikkonen praying he could keep on winning and that the Renault driver would have to retire from a race or two.

Until two laps before the finish, however, it looked as though Alonso would have to settle for third, with Juan Pablo Montoya trailing Raikkonen home for what would have been McLaren's first one-two finish since the Austrian GP in 2000. However, as the Colombian lapped Tiago Monteiro for the third time, he pulled across sharply in front of the Jordan driver, braked early – as one of his tyres was flat-spotted – and left the Portuguese driver with nowhere to go but into the back of him. Both spun and time was lost, but Montoya was able to rejoin the race still in second place, albeit with Alonso now hard on his heels. Defending for all he was worth, Montoya then ran wide at Turn 8 on the penultimate lap.

Alonso was through into second place in a flash as the Colombian toured the acres of tarmac run-off and rejoined the circuit. Montoya blamed a broken diffuser from the Monteiro shunt for his error, but doubt was later cast on the extent of the damage.

So, despite qualifying on pole and driving beautifully to lead every lap of the race, Raikkonen scarcely dented Alonso's advantage and left Turkey chastened by the fact that, for all his strong form, mechanical failures earlier in the season might well have blown his title hopes.

Jenson Button ought to have been a feature at Istanbul, but he started back in 13th place on the grid after having run wide when on potential pole pace in qualifying. He scythed through the field, passing both Red Bulls and both gripless Ferraris to reach third place by the first of his two pit stops. The English driver levelled out in sixth, then passed Toyota's Jarno Trulli at the second round of pit stops to finish an eventual fifth. But it could, and perhaps should, have been higher.

Raikkonen was in a class of his own in Turkey's first-ever grand prix and was never headed as he raced from pole position to the chequered flag

The place ahead of him, fourth, was claimed by Giancarlo Fisichella in the second Renault. He'd got the jump on Raikkonen at the start and led around the first lap, but was usurped before he reached the start-finish straight again and had no answer to Raikkonen's escape. He was also passed by team-mate Alonso on lap 2, either unable to live with his pace or perhaps conveniently letting him through so that the Spaniard could go for maximum points for his title challenge. Either way, a fuel-rig problem ruined Fisichella's day at his first stop, leaving him adrift of the frontrunners, but clear of those behind.

Compared to the Williams drivers, Fisichella had it lucky, for they were troubled by right rear tyres that would suddenly deflate. Eventually, it led to the team withdrawing them from the fray, but not before Mark Webber had had a coming-together with Michael Schumacher that spun the German and removed his front wing. Webber was furious with the seven-time world champion for moving across him, even though the Australian was a lap down and clearly faster. Schumacher also failed to finish.

Sixth place went to Trulli, easily clear of the pair of Red Bulls, with David Coulthard finishing ahead of Christian Klien to bring welcome points for the team.

ISTANBUL PARK ROUND 14

Date: **21 August 2005** Laps: **58** Distance: **192.388 miles/309.603km**
Weather: **Hot, dry and sunny**

RACE RESULT

Position	Driver	Team	Result	Stops	Qualifying Time	Grid
1	**Kimi Raikkonen**	McLaren	1h24m34.454s	2	1m26.797s	1
2	**Fernando Alonso**	Renault	1h24m53.063s	2	1m27.050s	3
3	**Juan Pablo Montoya**	McLaren	1h24m54.089s	2	1m27.352s	4
4	**Giancarlo Fisichella**	Renault	1h25m12.427s	2	1m27.039s	2
5	**Jenson Button**	BAR	1h25m13.758s	2	1m30.063s	13
6	**Jarno Trulli**	Toyota	1h25m29.874s	2	1m27.501s	5
7	**David Coulthard**	Red Bull	1h25m43.750s	2	1m29.764s	12
8	**Christian Klien**	Red Bull	1h25m46.076s	2	1m28.963s	10
9	**Takuma Sato**	BAR	1h26m24.441s	1	no time*	20
10	**Rubens Barrichello**	Ferrari	57 laps	2	1m29.369s	11
11	**Jacques Villeneuve**	Sauber	57 laps	2	no time	17
12	**Ralf Schumacher**	Toyota	57 laps	2	1m28.594s	9
13	**Robert Doornbos**	Minardi	55 laps	2	no time	17
14	**Narain Karthikeyan**	Jordan	55 laps	3	no time	18
15	**Tiago Monteiro**	Jordan	55 laps	3	1m30.710s	14
R	**Christijan Albers**	Minardi	48 laps/withdrew	4	1m32.186s	15
R	**Michael Schumacher**	Ferrari	32 laps/crash damage	3	no time	19
R	**Nick Heidfeld**	Williams	29 laps/tyres	2	1m27.929s	6
R	**Felipe Massa**	Sauber	28 laps/engine	1	1m28.419s	8
R	**Mark Webber**	Williams	20 laps/tyres	2	1m27.944s	7

* SATO'S TIME (1M30.175S) DISALLOWED FOR IMPEDING WEBBER'S FLYING LAP

TALKING POINT: CIRCUIT PROVES A MASSIVE HIT

Everyone who attended the inaugural Turkish GP was wowed by the circuit. They had all seen Hermann Tilke-designed tracks before, but this was different. It had a change of gradient for starters, which made entry to some corners blind, plus a corner with four apexes. In short, it made the drivers work. Formula 1 ringmaster Bernie Ecclestone described it as Spa-like – and compliments come no higher than that. Rubens Barrichello said: "The first corner is the sort of place where you feel you are always telling yourself you can brake later and later, so it's quite interesting."

Hermann Tilke has come up with a track which makes the drivers work

ITALIAN GP

Juan Pablo Montoya's tyre wear was worrying and it had already tripped up team-mate Kimi Raikkonen after a remarkable charge up the order, but the Colombian held his nerve to win at Monza, with title aspirant Fernando Alonso close behind.

Montoya leads the pack through the chicane on the opening lap, with Alonso, Button, Trulli, Satto, Schumacher and Barrichello tucked in behind

In years to come, Kimi Raikkonen may wake up in a cold sweat, nightmarishly re-living the engine failures that scuppered his 2005 title hopes again and again. Nowhere was this more unfortunate than at Monza, where he suffered his third engine failure in practice. He had been right on the pace in each of the practice sessions and was primed to scorch off to the victory he required to keep his title fight with Renault's Fernando Alonso going to the final - or even penultimate - round. That he scorched to the fastest time in qualifying counted for little, as the engine change meant that he would have to start in 11th once his ten-place grid penalty had been applied. What was remarkable, though, was that the Finn's McLaren had achieved this pole time in a car that was carrying more fuel than any other. Indeed, this was his main

hope for making up places as those ahead of him called in for their first pit stop.

The plan worked well, as team-mate Juan Pablo Montoya led away from the front of the grid and importantly kept Raikkonen's arch-rival Alonso out of the top spot. Slow initial progress, as the Finn laboured with the extra weight of his fuel load, was followed by a remarkable ascent to second before he called in for his pit stop on lap 25. Resuming in fifth and setting a startling pace, he looked sure to haul in the leaders. Unbeknown to them, he was fuelled to the end of the race and on course for victory. However, three laps later, Raikkonen was in the pits again, this time to replace a flat tyre. When he rejoined he was back in 12th, one place lower than his starting position. Thus Raikkonen set about mounting another charge, but this was spoiled by

a spin that allowed Jarno Trulli to re-pass him. Chastened, Raikkonen regained the place to finish an eventual fourth, 5s behind Giancarlo Fisichella's Renault.

Fortunately for Raikkonen, Montoya controlled the race and prevented Alonso from winning, but the result meant that the Finn lost another three points to the Spaniard and was now 27 points behind with just four races to run.

As is almost inevitable at Monza, the first chicane was the scene for a collision on the opening lap. This time it was David Coulthard who was in the wars, as the Scot had to stop more suddenly than the pursuing Mark Webber expected after Fisichella did the same in front of him. The Red Bull driver had to pit for a replacement nose, as did Webber, but Coulthard was also afflicted thereafter by dreadful handling and only after the race did he discover that his bargeboard had been knocked out of true.

Williams' other driver for the day was not Nick Heidfeld but Antonio Pizzonia. The German was forced to stand down, as he was still suffering from the effects of an accident that occurred in pre-event testing at Monza. The Brazilian stood in with aplomb, arriving late for Saturday practice and yet overcoming a three-month break from test-driving duties with the Williams FW27 to race well enough to finish seventh, right on the tail of Ralf Schumacher's Toyota.

The final point went to Jenson Button. It was a disappointment for the BAR driver as he'd started the race from fourth place on the grid, but a problem with his refuelling rig delayed him and led to him losing several places.

Remarkably, every one of the 20 starters was still circulating at the finish; the first time that this had happened since the Dutch GP in 1961, and only the third time it had happened in the history of F1.

Jordan gave their EJ15B chassis its debut, with Tiago Monteiro winning the toss of a coin with team-mate Narain Karthikeyan for the chance to have the first bite at the apple. However, some of its vital bodywork fell off, thus hampering its handling and increasing its rate of tyre wear as the Portuguese driver finished in 17th place.

MONZA ROUND 15

Date: **4 Sept 2005** Laps: **53** Distance: **190.787 miles/307.028km**
Weather: **Hot and bright**

RACE RESULT

Position	Driver	Team	Result	Stops	Qualifying Time	Grid
1	**Juan Pablo Montoya**	McLaren	1h14m28.659s	2	1m21.054s	1
2	**Fernando Alonso**	Renault	1h14m31.138s	2	1m21.319s	2
3	**Giancarlo Fisichella**	Renault	1h14m46.634s	2	1m22.068s	8
4	**Kimi Raikkonen**	McLaren	1h14m51.434s	2	1m20.878s	11
5	**Jarno Trulli**	Toyota	1h15m02.445s	2	1m21.640s	5
6	**Ralf Schumacher**	Toyota	1h15m12.584s	2	1m22.266s	9
7	**Antonio Pizzonia**	Williams	1h15m13.302s	2	1m23.291s	16
8	**Jenson Button**	BAR	1h15m32.294s	2	1m21.369s	3
9	**Felipe Massa**	Sauber	1h15m44.072s	2	1m23.060s	15
10	**Michael Schumacher**	Ferrari	1h16m04.729s	2	1m21.721s	6
11	**Jacques Villeneuve**	Sauber	52 laps	2	1m22.356s	12
12	**Rubens Barrichello**	Ferrari	52 laps	3	1m21.962s	7
13	**Christian Klien**	Red Bull	52 laps	2	1m22.532s	13
14	**Mark Webber**	Williams	52 laps	3	1m22.560s	14
15	**David Coulthard**	Red Bull	52 laps	2	1m22.304s	10
16	**Takuma Sato**	BAR	52 laps	3	1m21.477s	4
17	**Tiago Monteiro**	Jordan	51 laps	2	1m24.666s	17
18	**Robert Doornbos**	Minardi	51 laps	2	1m24.904s	18
19	**Christijan Albers**	Minardi	51 laps	4	1m26.964s	20
20	**Narain Karthikeyan**	Jordan	50 laps	4	1m25.859s	19

TALKING POINT: FERRARI BOSS SAYS RULES ARE BORING

Following the race, Luca di Montezemolo, the chairman of Ferrari, lashed out at the F1 rules announced for 2006. He claimed that they would make F1 "super boring" and added that the star drivers were being reduced to no more than "taxi drivers" as they had to nurse a set of tyres through an entire grand prix. To him, F1 should be extreme, such as when Michael Schumacher used four sets of tyres to win the French GP in 2004. Di Montezemolo said that the annual rule changes did nothing to help F1. Most of all, though, he said that he despised the one-at-a-time qualifying system.

Ferrari's hierarchy of Jean Todt and Luca di Montezemolo discuss the vexed matter of new regulations

BELGIAN GP

McLaren dominated in wet, damp and dry at Spa, but the team's hopes of a one-two were thwarted when Antonio Pizzonia knocked Juan Pablo Montoya into retirement in the closing laps, leaving the way clear for Fernando Alonso's Renault.

McLaren travelled to Spa-Francorchamps knowing that only a one-two would help their cause. Even then, to keep Kimi Raikkonen in the title chase, they needed runaway points leader Fernando Alonso not to score. This wasn't quite how it worked out, however.

It all started well for McLaren, with Raikkonen setting the pace in the first practice session. But then, as the track is situated high in the Ardennes hills, the rain started, with Red Bull Racing's Vitantonio Liuzzi having a huge accident in streaming conditions in practice session number two. Renault indicated that they might be able to challenge as Alonso topped the final practice session with what was to prove the fastest lap of the meeting. Come qualifying, though, McLaren were back in control, with

Montoya on pole from Raikkonen followed by Toyota's Jarno Trulli in third place on the grid, providing a buffer to Alonso in fourth.

This is how they ran through to the first round of pit stops. All pre-planned tactics were scrapped when Giancarlo Fisichella, who had climbed from 13th on the grid – because of a ten-place penalty – to seventh, crashed at the exit of Eau Rouge on lap 11 and the safety car was brought out. As a result, the entire field elected to pit immediately, with the second car in each team having to wait while the team's lead car was refuelled. There was much changing of tyres, too, as the wet track on which the race had started began to dry. Many opted for dry-weather tyres, but they were soon back in for intermediates again. As all this was going on, the race

order fluctuated like mad. Indeed, Jacques Villeneuve, who had started in 14th and fallen to 16th, rose to second, behind only Montoya. But he had yet to pit and, when he did, dropped away again.

The driver who had made the most realistic gains, though, was Ralf Schumacher, who took over in second place. He then gambled on pitting again shortly after mid-distance, to fit dry-weather tyres, but the gamble didn't come off – the track was still too damp – and he spun, reporting promptly back to the pits to revert to intermediates.

Through all of this, Montoya held sway, but Raikkonen was fuelled for longer, making his second and final stop a few laps later, which was sufficient to put the Finn into the lead he required to claw back his points deficit to

Race-winner Raikkonen manages to raise a smile, but he was less than happy that his team-mate Montoya was knocked out of second place

Alonso. Annoyingly for McLaren, the Spaniard was running third, so Raikkonen would pare only four points from his 27-point lead. With no more stops due, it was Raikkonen, Montoya and Alonso with a clear run to the chequered flag, with Jenson Button coming on strong as the best of the rest.

Yet, this wasn't how they finished, as Antonio Pizzonia, standing in at Williams for Nick Heidfeld again, was to change all that. Running a lap down on Montoya, but outpacing him as the Colombian backed off, he thought that Montoya had waved him through going into the Fagnes esses, but he hadn't and they clashed, taking both of them out on the spot and earning Pizzonia an $8,000 fine. Thus Alonso took second, meaning that his points advantage was 25 with just three races to go.

As a result of Montoya's downfall, Button was elevated to third for his second official podium visit of the season. Mark Webber finished a convincing fourth, and was left cursing his decision to switch to dry-weather tyres, only to have to change back to intermediates again. Rubens Barrichello scored his first points in five grands prix, a state of affairs that we would not have expected from a Ferrari driver at the start of the 2005 season. Villeneuve was a combative sixth, just holding off Ralf Schumacher's fast-closing Toyota.

SPA-FRANCORCHAMPS ROUND 16
Date: **11 Sept 2005** Laps: **44** Distance: **190.787 miles/307.028km**
Weather: **Overcast and damp**

RACE RESULT

Position	Driver	Team	Result	Stops	Qualifying Time	Grid
1	**Kimi Raikkonen**	McLaren	1h30m01.295s	2	1m46.440s	2
2	**Fernando Alonso**	Renault	1h30m29.689s	2	1m46.760s	4
3	**Jenson Button**	BAR	1h30m33.372s	3	1m47.978s	8
4	**Mark Webber**	Williams	1h31m10.462s	4	1m48.071s	9
5	**Rubens Barrichello**	Ferrari	1h31m19.431s	3	1m48.550s	12
6	**Jacques Villeneuve**	Sauber	1h31m28.730s	1	1m48.889s	14
7	**Ralf Schumacher**	Toyota	1h31m28.869s	2	1m47.401s	5
8	**Tiago Monteiro**	Jordan	43 laps	2	1m51.498s	19
9	**Christian Klien**	Red Bull	43 laps	3	1m48.994s	16
10	**Felipe Massa**	Sauber	43 laps	2	1m47.867s	7
11	**Narain Karthikeyan**	Jordan	43 laps	2	1m51.675s	20
12	**Christijan Albers**	Minardi	42 laps	2	1m49.842xs	18
13	**Robert Doornbos**	Minardi	41 laps	3	1m49.779s	17
14	**Juan Pablo Montoya**	McLaren	40 laps/accident	2	1m46.391s	1
15	**Antonio Pizzonia**	Williams	39 laps/accident	4	1m48.898s	15
R	**Jarno Trulli**	Toyota	34 laps/accident	3	1m46.596s	3
R	**David Coulthard**	Red Bull	18 laps/engine	2	1m48.508s	11
R	**Michael Schumacher**	Ferrari	13 laps/accident	2	1m47.476s	6
R	**Takuma Sato**	BAR	13 laps/accident	2	1m48.353s	10
R	**Giancarlo Fisichella**	Renault	10 laps/accident	0	1m46.497s	13*

* DENOTES TEN-PLACE GRID PENALTY

TALKING POINT: MINARDI SOLD TO RED BULL

It had been coming for years and, on the Saturday of the Belgian GP, it finally happened: Minardi was sold. Paul Stoddart always said that he'd sell the team if it meant it would guarantee the future of the personnel. So, when Dietrich Mateschitz's Red Bull cash convinced him, the Australian aviation magnate's four-year tenure came to an end and, in a flash, Red Bull owned 20 per cent of the grid and announced that it planned to run its two teams as separate entities. This wasn't the only deal on the table, though, as Eddie Irvine and Russian backer Roustam Tariko were also keen.

Stoddart had given Formula One his best shot, but the spiralling costs became too much in the end

BRAZILIAN GP

Despite McLaren's best efforts behind McLaren's Juan Pablo Montoya and Kimi Raikkonen, third place was enough for Fernando Alonso to land the crown that had looked his destiny ever since he took the points lead in the second round.

A nightmare sight for owner Sir Frank Williams as his two cars clash near the first corner on the opening lap after clipping David Coulthard's car

It was always going to be an uphill battle for McLaren. After all, Renault's Fernando Alonso arrived at Interlagos with a 25-point lead with only 30 to play for. When he then pulled out all of the stops to qualify on pole position, it seemed as though there was little that the men from Woking could do. Sure, Juan Pablo Montoya lined up second on the grid, 0.157s adrift, but title hopeful Kimi Raikkonen had slipped up, locking up into the very first corner of his flying lap, and started the race only fifth, behind both Alonso's team-mate Giancarlo Fisichella and BAR's Jenson Button.

At least Montoya gave McLaren hope. He may not have prised the lead away from Alonso at the start, although he did a great job in keeping a fast-starting Fisichella behind him on the dash to the first corner, but the Colombian leapt to the front just two

laps later as the safety car withdrew and he got the jump on the Spaniard.

The safety car had been deployed while wreckage following a clash between David Coulthard's Red Bull and Antonio Pizzonia's Williams was cleared. Their contretemps had been triggered when Coulthard went for a gap between Pizzonia and his Williams team-mate Mark Webber as they accelerated away from the line and they clashed as the gap closed. Only Webber continued, albeit after a 25-lap delay in the pits for repairs.

Montoya has always been strong at restarts - something that he learned in his ChampCar career where they are much more common - and this time he hung back through Turn 1 but ensured that he had maximum momentum on the exit and used that to attack and pass Alonso into Subida do Lago.

Once in front, the Colombian pressed as hard as dared and it was enough not only to keep ahead of Alonso but also to keep Raikkonen behind him, despite the fact the Finn had called in later than the Colombian for each of his two pit stops.

Alonso did all he had to, but it was clear when he called in for the first of his two pit stops as early as lap 22 - six laps before Montoya and nine ahead of Raikkonen - that there was no way that he'd be able to match the race pace of the McLarens.

However, despite the best efforts of Michael Schumacher in his improving Ferrari, the Spaniard was safe and sound in third place. This was absolutely fine by him as it would be enough to make him champion. And so it proved, with Alonso - and the whole of Spain - going ballistic as he crossed the finish line.

Fisichella would have been fourth had Schumacher not edged his Ferrari ahead on the opening lap and stayed there. And so McLaren was able to use its first one-two finish for five years to move ahead of Renault in the constructors' championship, something that may have come as some consolation for team boss Ron Dennis but which was of little concern to Raikkonen.

Rubens Barrichello was able to stay on the lead lap, just, in finishing fifth, but it wasn't the sort of result that he desired in his final outing on his home circuit in a Ferrari. Mind you, he'd had the whole season to become accustomed to the fact that his Ferrari was less than the full ticket in 2005.

Even more disappointed, perhaps, was Tiago Monteiro, when the Portuguese Jordan driver's car pulled up with a driveshaft failure to end his run of 16 grands prix without a failure – the best-ever record for a driver in his rookie season.

The final points went to Jenson Button in seventh place and Ralf Schumacher in eighth. The BAR driver had qualified well, but made a poor start from the dirty side of the grid and slipped back further with tyres that were graining. Schumacher, on the other hand, also had tyre problems, but the Toyota driver did enough to overhaul Red Bull's Christian Klien to secure the final point.

INTERLAGOS ROUND 17
Date: 25 Sept 2005 Laps: **71** Distance: **189.357 miles/304.762km**
Weather: **Warm and overcast**

RACE RESULT

Position	Driver	Team	Result	Stops	Qualifying Time	Grid
1	**Juan Pablo Montoya**	McLaren	1h29m20.574s	2	1m12.145s	2
2	**Kimi Raikkonen**	McLaren	1h29m23.101s	2	1m12.781s	5
3	**Fernando Alonso**	Renault	1h29m45.414s	2	1m11.988s	1
4	**Michael Schumacher**	Ferrari	1h29m56.242s	2	1m12.976s	7
5	**Giancarlo Fisichella**	Renault	1h30m00.792s	2	1m12.558s	3
6	**Rubens Barrichello**	Ferrari	1h30m29.747s	2	1m13.183s	9
7	**Jenson Button**	BAR	70 laps	2	1m12.696s	4
8	**Ralf Schumacher**	Toyota	70 laps	2	1m13.285s	10
9	**Christian Klien**	Red Bull	70 laps	2	1m12.889s	6
10	**Takuma Sato**	BAR	70 laps	1	no time	19*
11	**Felipe Massa**	Sauber	70 laps	2	1m13.151s	8
12	**Jacques Villeneuve**	Sauber	70 laps	2	1m13.372s	20*
13	**Jarno Trulli**	Toyota	69 laps/pneumatics	2	1m13.041s	17*
14	**Christijan Albers**	Minardi	69 laps	2	1m14.763s	16
15	**Narain Karthikeyan**	Jordan	68 laps	3	1m14.520s	15
R	**Tiago Monteiro**	Jordan	55 laps/driveshaft	1	1m13.387s	11
NC	**Mark Webber**	Williams	45 laps	2	1m13.538s	12
R	**Robert Doornbos**	Minardi	34 laps/oil pipe	1	no time	18
R	**Antonio Pizzonia**	Williams	0 laps/accident	0	1m13.581s	13
R	**David Coulthard**	Red Bull	0 laps/accident	0	1m13.844s	14

* DENOTES TEN-PLACE GRID PENALTY

TALKING POINT: ALONSO BECOMES YOUNGEST-EVER WORLD CHAMPION

Drivers have been arriving in Formula One at ever-younger ages for the past decade, but Michael Schumacher's title monopoly had prevented any of them from becoming the world champion. However, Emerson Fittipaldi's record – which had stood since 1972 – was finally toppled when Fernando Alonso was crowned on Fittipaldi's home patch at the age of 24 years and 58 days, lopping some 215 days off the Brazilian's long-standing record. Mind you, Lotus driver Fittipaldi claimed his crown just 25 grands prix into his Formula One career, as opposed to the 67 races it took the Spaniard.

Third place for Alonso gave his Renault crew reason to start celebrating the youngest world champion

JAPANESE GP

This was a back-to-front race, with the quickest drivers fighting through from the tail. Kimi Raikkonen judged it to perfection, passing Giancarlo Fisichella for the lead on the final lap with an overtaking manoeuvre that took the breath away.

Every now and then, there's a classic race. This was one, not just for the stunning, around-the-outside manoeuvre that Kimi Raikkonen pulled on Renault's Giancarlo Fisichella to take the lead as well as victory at Turn 1 on the final lap, but also for Raikkonen and Fernando Alonso overtaking the best of the establishment, seven-time World Champion Michael Schumacher.

In truth, there was no way that the German could respond, his Ferrari no match for their McLaren and Renault respectively. Sure, they'd advanced together, tearing through the mid-order from the back of the grid after rain late in qualifying had dashed their hopes of a good grid position.

Indeed, Schumacher, Alonso, Raikkonen and Juan Pablo Montoya who'd been the last ones to come out were all caught out as rain turned heavy. This left them 14th, 16th, 17th and 18th respectively, with Michael's brother Ralf on pole on the debut of the Toyota's TF105B, a car notable for running without a keel and having its suspension mounted higher on the side of the tub than on the TF105.

At the start, Ralf led away, with Fisichella blasting past Jenson Button for third, as the Briton found himself challenged into the opening corner by the fast-starting Red Bull of David Coulthard, up from seventh.

All hell broke out during that first lap and the big guns all benefited, Indeed, Takuma Sato and Rubens Barrichello ran into the gravel at the opening corner. Then several cars over-ran the chicane and Montoya took a wide line to avoid them, only to have his McLaren pushed into the wall hard enough to remove its left-hand wheels. And so, Michael Schumacher found himself up from 14th to seventh by the end of the opening tour, with Alonso and Raikkonen a little more circumspect as they climbed from 16th and 17th to eighth and 12th.

Both then picked off car after car and, by dint of running a long first stint, Raikkonen rose as high as second behind Michael Schumacher, before they both had to pit for fuel. This dropped them back to fourth and fifth, with Raikkonen blasting past the reigning champion. To make matters worse for the German, this embarrassment was turned into humiliation as he did so around the outside at Turn 1 on lap 30.

Knowing that his lack of speed in the by-now recalcitrant Ferrari had already been exposed when Alonso passed him at the tricky 130R corner 10 laps earlier, Schumacher

McLaren boss Ron Dennis shows his delight at Raikkonen's move which took him past Fisichella

was then further embarrassed when Alonso overtook him again, this time around the outside of Turn 1 on lap 33. Had it not been for losing close on 9s in slowing to let Christian Klien past for a second time, Alonso could have finished second or higher.

To talk of these drivers is to ignore Ralf's progress from pole. It was marked and would have been more but for a safety car, which was deployed so that the wreckage of Montoya's first lap shunt could be cleared.

As it was, this delay cost him dear, as did the fact that he'd qualified on pole not only because he'd had the rain stay away until after his run, but because he'd set his time with a light fuel load, so he pitted as early as lap 13, while Michael and Raikkonen lasted twice that long. Fisichella took over at the front. Ralf had to settle for eighth.

The race then boiled down to Raikkonen's pursuit of Fisichella for the lead and ultimate glory, and Alonso's chase of Mark Webber's Williams for third, a position that the Australian had to cede with five laps to go when he was notified that BMW wanted him to turn his engine down to ensure it lasted. And Raikkonen too got his plaudits with his pass of Fisichella on that final lap.

Button was disappointed to slide back to fifth, with fast-starting Coulthard pleased to have scored for the ninth time in 18 races.

SUZUKA ROUND 18
Date: **9 Oct 2005** Laps: **53** Distance: **191.248 miles/307.770km**
Weather: **Warm and bright, but windy**

RACE RESULT

Position	Driver	Team	Result	Stops	Qualifying Time	Grid
1	**Kimi Raikkonen**	McLaren	1h29m02.212s	2	2m02.309s	17
2	**Giancarlo Fisichella**	Renault	1h29m03.845s	2	1m46.276s	3
3	**Fernando Alonso**	Renault	1h29m19.668s	2	1m54.667s	16
4	**Mark Webber**	Williams	1h29m24.486s	2	1m47.233s	7
5	**Jenson Button**	BAR	1h29m31.719s	2	1m46.141s	2
6	**David Coulthard**	Red Bull	1h29m33.813s	2	1m46.892s	6
7	**Michael Schumacher**	Ferrari	1h29m36.091s	2	1m52.676s	14
8	**Ralf Schumacher**	Toyota	1h29m51.760s	3	1m46.106s	1
9	**Christian Klien**	Red Bull	1h29m54.137s	2	1m46.464s	4
10	**Felipe Massa**	Sauber	1h29m59.721s	2	1m48.278s	10
11	**Jacques Villeneuve**	Sauber	1h30m00.433s	2	1m47.440s	8
12	**Rubens Barrichello**	Ferrari	1h30m02.845s	3	1m48.248s	9
DQ	**Takuma Sato**	BAR	52 laps	2	1m46.841s	5
13	**Tiago Monteiro**	Jordan	52 laps	2	no time	20
14	**Robert Doornbos**	Minardi	51 laps	2	1m52.894s	15
15	**Narain Karthikeyan**	Jordan	51 laps	3	1m48.718s	11
16	**Christijan Albers**	Minardi	49 laps	2	1m50.843s	13
R	**Antonio Pizzonia**	Williams	9 laps/spun off	0	1m48.898s	12
R	**Jarno Trulli**	Toyota	9 laps/accident	0	no time	19
R	**Juan Pablo Montoya**	McLaren	0 laps/accident	0	no time	18

TALKING POINT: SATO TAKES SOME STICK

There was a groundswell of support for Takuma Sato when it was announced that he would be dropped by BAR to make way for Rubens Barrichello in 2006. Indeed, tens of thousands of Japanese fans were said to be travelling to the Japanese GP to show their anger at this decision. Cynics said that this was why news was leaked before the race of the formation of a new team for 2006 in which Honda would support an outfit for Sato and Anthony Davidson. Yet still the details remained sketchy. Then, showing how fast opinion can change, Toyota chief Tsutomo Tomita branded Sato wild for taking Jarno Trulli out of the race.

Trulli received support from many quarters when he became the latest driver to be hit by Sato

CHINESE GP

The drivers' title had already been settled, which left Shanghai as the stage on which the constructors' battle would reach its conclusion. McLaren were favourites, but this was Renault's year as they claimed their eighth win of 2005.

He was champion already, but Alonso was determined to exit on a high, with Fisichella in support

Coming just a week after the outstanding Japanese GP, a race which has already been described as one of the sport's best ever, there was always the danger that the finale to the season might disappoint. There was, however, the tussle between Renault and McLaren for the constructors' championship to look forward to, with Renault having edged into a two-point lead over their rivals.

To show just how seriously Renault wanted this crown to add to the drivers' one won by Fernando Alonso, the French manufacturer had the boffins at its Viry-Chatillon engine centre developing their V10 all the way up to this 19th and final round of

the year. This was all the more remarkable, considering that it was the last race before turning to V8s for 2006. Their diligence paid off, too, as Alonso outpaced McLaren rival Kimi Raikkonen to take pole. In fact the Finn would start third, as Giancarlo Fisichella also bested him in the other Renault, with Jenson Button qualifying his BAR fourth ahead of Juan Pablo Montoya's McLaren.

This improved pace was impressive, as the McLaren had been the faster car through the second half of the season. However, no one knew how much fuel they had been carrying. As it transpired, we never will know, since the safety car was called out on lap 18, so that a broken drain cover could be

removed from the track. This meant all the teams scrambled their tactics, with Alonso having his 17s lead annulled.

For McLaren, though, their challenge had already been all but sunk as that drain cover at the final corner had been hit by Montoya when he ran fourth right behind Fisichella and Raikkonen. With his right front tyre punctured, he had to pit and then come in again a lap later for fuel after the safety car had been deployed. This dropped him to 14th. Worse was to follow, as Montoya's engine would fail by mid-distance.

Two against one was hard enough for Raikkonen, but the fact that Fisichella stood between he and Alonso made it harder still.

The race had not long been restarted when the safety car was introduced again as Narain Karthikeyan marked Jordan's final race by destroying his car against the barriers, narrowly missing Jacques Villeneuve's Sauber as he rebounded into his path.

The teams immediately called their drivers in for their second pit stop and McLaren did Raikkonen proud by getting him out ahead of Fisichella. Not everyone pitted, though, and Ralf Schumacher would run second for a while in his Toyota, with Felipe Massa and Christian Klien also staying out behind the safety car, to leave Raikkonen in fifth when the race was restarted on lap 34.

In due course, Massa then Klien and then Ralf came in, moving Raikkonen back up to second. But there was nothing that he could do about Alonso and so the Spaniard equalled the Finn's 2005 tally of seven wins, also claiming the constructors' crown for Renault.

Renault's hopes of having Fisichella on the podium as well were thwarted when the Italian was called in for a drive-through penalty for driving into the pits at an unduly slow speed, thus enabling his team-mate to gain an advantage. This dropped him from third to fourth and elevated Ralf to the final podium position.

SHANGHAI ROUND 19
Date: **16 October 2005** Laps: **56** Distance: **189.68 miles/305.25km**
Weather: **Warm and bright**

RACE RESULT

Position	Driver	Team	Result	Stops	Qualifying Time	Grid
1	**Fernando Alonso**	Renault	1h39m53.618s	2	1m34.080s	1
2	**Kimi Raikkonen**	McLaren	1h39m57.633s	2	1m34.488s	3
3	**Ralf Schumacher**	Toyota	1h40m18.994s	2	1m35.723s	9
4	**Giancarlo Fisichella**	Renault	1h40m19.732s	3	1m34.401s	2
5	**Christian Klien**	Red Bull	1h40m25.457s	2	1m36.472s	14
6	**Felipe Massa**	Sauber	1h40m30.018s	2	1m35.898s	11
7	**Mark Webber**	Williams	1h40m30.460s	2	1m37.739s	10
8	**Jenson Button**	BAR	1h40m34.867s	2	1m34.801s	4
9	**David Coulthard**	Red Bull	1h40m37.865s	2	1m35.428s	7
10	**Jacques Villeneuve**	Sauber	1h40m53.595s	2	1m36.788s	16
11	**Tiago Monteiro**	Jordan	1h41m18.266s	2	1m39.233s	19
12	**Rubens Barrichello**	Ferrari	1h41m26.430s	3	1m35.610s	8
13	**Antonio Pizzonia**	Williams	55 laps/puncture	3	1m36.445s	13
14	**Robert Doornbos**	Minardi	55 laps	2	1m39.460s	20
15	**Jarno Trulli**	Toyota	55 laps	3	1m36.044s	12
16	**Christijan Albers**	Minardi	51 laps/wheelnut	3	1m39.105s	18
R	**Takuma Sato**	BAR	34 laps/gearbox	3	1m37.083s	17*
R	**Narain Karthikeyan**	Jordan	28 laps/accident	1	1m36.707s	15
R	**Juan Pablo Montoya**	McLaren	24 laps/engine	3	1m35.188s	5
R	**Michael Schumacher**	Ferrari	22 laps/spun off	0	1m35.301s	6

*STARTED FROM THE PITLANE AFTER TAKING SPARE CAR BEFORE THE START

TALKING POINT: AND IT'S GOODNIGHT FROM THEM...

Seldom has the final round had so many teams saying goodbye. China was Sauber's finale before its change to BMW. Minardi's Paul Stoddart will also have time on his hands, as this marked his last race in control before the team is renamed Scuderia Toro Rosso by new owner Red Bull. Jordan, bade "over and out" after being run by Midland for a year before the terms of its sale dictated that it would carry the Midland name from 2006. Making it four changes out of ten, BAR too would be no more, although this is more of a simple name change rather than a change of culture following the completion of Honda's buy-out.

There were many sad to see the back of 2005, but Michael Schumacher was not one of them

FINAL RESULTS 2005

	DRIVER	NAT.	ENGINE	R1	R2	R3	R4	R5	R6
1	FERNANDO ALONSO	SPA	RENAULT R25	3F	1P	1P	1	2	4
2	KIMI RAIKKONEN	FIN	McLAREN-MERCEDES MP4-20	8	9F	3	RP	1P	1P
3	MICHAEL SCHUMACHER	GER	FERRARI F2004M	R	7	-	-	-	-
			FERRARI F2005			R	2F	R	7F
4	JUAN PABLO MONTOYA	COL	McLAREN-MERCEDES MP4-20	6	4	-	-	7	5
5	GIANCARLO FISICHELLA	ITA	RENAULT R25	1P	R	R	R	5F	12
6	RALF SCHUMACHER	GER	TOYOTA TF105	12	5	4	9	4	6
7	JARNO TRULLI	ITA	TOYOTA TF105	9	2	2	5	3	10
8	RUBENS BARRICHELLO	BRA	FERRARI F2004M	2	R	-	-	-	
			FERRARI F2005			9	R	9	8
9	JENSON BUTTON	GBR	BAR-HONDA 007	11	R	R	D	-	-
10	MARK WEBBER	AUS	WILLIAMS-BMW FW27	5	R	6	7	6	3
11	NICK HEIDFELD	GER	WILLIAMS-BMW FW27	R	3	R	6	10	2
12	DAVID COULTHARD	GBR	RED BULL-COSWORTH RB1	4	6	8	11	8	R
13	FELIPE MASSA	BRA	SAUBER-PETRONAS C24	10	10	7	10	11	9
14	JACQUES VILLENEUVE	CDN	SAUBER-PETRONAS C24	13	R	11	4	R	11
15	CHRISTIAN KLIEN	AUT	RED BULL-COSWORTH RB1	7	8	R	-	-	-
16	TIAGO MONTEIRO	POR	JORDAN-TOYOTA EJ15	16	12	10	13	12	13
			JORDAN-TOYOTA EJ15B	-	-	-	-	-	-
17	ALEXANDER WURZ	AUT	McLAREN-MERCEDES MP4-20	-	-	-	3	-	-
18	NARAIN KARTHIKEYAN	IND	JORDAN-TOYOTA EJ15	15	11	R	12	13	R
			JORDAN-TOYOTA EJ15B	-	-	-	-	-	-
19	CHRISTIJAN ALBERS	NED	MINARDI-COSWORTH PS04B	R	R	13	-	-	-
			MINARDI-COSWORTH PS05	-	-	-	R	R	14
20	PEDRO DE LA ROSA	SPA	MCLAREN-MERCEDES MP4-20	-	-	5F	-	-	-
21	PATRICK FRIESACHER	AUT	MINARDI-COSWORTH PS04B	17	R	12	-	-	-
			MINARDI-COSWORTH PS05	-	-	-	R	R	R
22	ANTONIO PIZZONIA	ITA	WILLIAMS-BMW FW27	-	-	-	-	-	
23	TAKUMA SATO	JAP	BAR-HONDA 007	14	-	R	D	-	-
24	VITANTONIO LIUZZI	ITA	RED BULL-COSWORTH RB1				8	R	R
	ROBERT DOORNBOS	NED	MINARDI-COSWORTH PS05	-	-	-	-	-	-
	ANTHONY DAVIDSON	GBR	BAR-HONDA 007	-	R	-	-	-	-
	RICARDO ZONTA	BRA	TOYOTA TF105	-	-	-	-	-	-

SCORING

1st	10 Points
2nd	8 Points
3rd	6 Points
4th	5 Points
5th	4 Points
6th	3 Points
7th	2 Points
8th	1 Points

CONSTRUCTOR (RACE RESULT FOR BOTH DRIVERS, i.e. FIRST AND SECOND LISTED AS 1/2, WITH THE TEAM'S BEST RESULT LISTED FIRST)

		R1	R2	R3	R4	R5	R6
1	RENAULT	1/3	1/R	1/R	1/R	2/5	4/12
2	McLAREN-MERCEDES	6/8	4/9	3/6	3/R	1/7	1/5
3	FERRARI	2/R	7/R	9/R	2/R	9/R	7/8
4	TOYOTA	9/12	2/5	2/4	5/9	3/4	6/10
5	WILLIAMS-BMW	5/R	3/R	5/R	6/7	6/10	2/3
6	BAR-HONDA	11/14	R/R	R/R	D/D	-	-
7	RED BULL-COSWORTH	4/7	6/8	8/R	8/11	8/R	R/R
8	SAUBER-PETRONAS	10/13	10/R	7/11	4/10	11/R	9/11
9	JORDAN-TOYOTA	15/16	11/12	10/R	12/13	12/13	13/R
10	MINARDI-COSWORTH	17/R	13/R	12/13	R/R	R/R	14/R

SYMBOLS AND GRAND PRIX KEY

D DISQUALIFIED　**F** FASTEST LAP　**NC** NOT CLASSIFIED　**NQ** NON-QUALIFIER　**NS** NON-STARTER　**P** POLE POSITION　**R** RETIRED　**W** WITHDREW

ROUND 1 AUSTRALIAN GP	**ROUND 5** SPANISH GP	**ROUND 9** UNITED STATES GP	**ROUND 13** HUNGARIAN GP	**ROUND 17** BRAZILIAN GP
ROUND 2 MALAYSIAN GP	**ROUND 6** MONACO GP	**ROUND 10** FRENCH GP	**ROUND 14** TURKISH GP	**ROUND 18** JAPANESE GP
ROUND 3 BAHRAIN GP	**ROUND 7** EUROPEAN GP	**ROUND 11** BRITISH GP	**ROUND 15** ITALIAN GP	**ROUND 19** CHINESE GP
ROUND 4 SAN MARINO GP	**ROUND 8** CANADIAN GP	**ROUND 12** GERMAN GP	**ROUND 16** BELGIAN GP	

R7	R8	R9	R10	R11	R12	R13	R14	R15	R16	R17	R18	R19		TOTAL POINTS
1F	R	W	1P	2P	1	11	2	2	2	3P	3	1P		133
11	1F	W	2F	3F	RPF	1	1P	4F	1	2F	1F	2F		112
-	-	-	-	-	-	-	-	-	-	-	-	-		-
5	2	1	3	6	5	2P	R	10	R	4	7	R		62
7	D	W	R	1	2	R	3F	1P	14P	1	R	R		60
6	R	W	6	4	4	9	4	3	R	5	2	4		58
R	6	NS	7	8	6	3	126	7F	8	8P	3	45		-
8	R	WP	5	9	14	4	6	5	R	13	R	15		43
-	-	-	-	-	-	-	-	-	-	-	-	-		-
3	3	2	9	7	10	10	10	12	5	6	12	12		38-
10	RP	W	4	5	3	5	5	8	3	7	5	8		37
R	5	W	12	11	NC	7	R	14	4	R	4	7		36
2P	R	W	14	12	11	6	R	-	-	-	-	-		28
4	7	W	10	13	7	R	7	15	R	R	6	9		24
14	4	W	R	10	8	14	R	9	10	11	10	6		11
13	9	W	8	14	15	R	11	11	6	12	11	10		9
-	8	W	R	15	9	R	8	13	9	9	9	5		9
15	10	3	13	17	17	13	15	-	-	-	-	-		-
-	-	-	-	-	-	-	-	17	8	R	13	11		7
-	-	-	-	-	-	-	-	-	-	-	-	-		6-
16	R	4	15	R	16	12	14	20	11	-	-	-		-
-	-	-	-	-	-	-	-	-	-	15	15	R		5
-	-	-	-	-	-	-	-	-	-	-	-	-		-
17	11	5	R	18	13	R	R	19	12	14	16	16		4
-	-	-	-	-	-	-	-	-	-	-	-	4		4
-	-	-	-	-	-	-	-	-	-	-	-	-		-
18	R	6	R	19	3	-	-	-	-	-	-	-		3
-	-	-	-	-	-	-	-	7	15	R	R	13		2
12	R	W	11	16	12	8	9	18	R	10	DQ	R		1
9	-	-	-	-	1	-	-	-	-	-	-	-		-
-	-	-	-	18	R	13	18	13	R	15	14	-		-
-	-	-	-	-	-	-	-	-	-	-	-	-		-
-	-	W	-	-	-	-	-	-	-	-	-	-		-

R7	R8	R9	R10	R11	R12	R13	R14	R15	R16	R17	R18	R19		TOTAL POINTS
1/6	R/R	W/W	1/6	2/4	1/4	9/11	2/4	2/3	2/R	3/5	2/3	1/4		191
7/11	1/D	W/W	2/R	1/3	2/R	1/R	1/3	1/4	1/14	1/2	1R	2/R		182
3/5	2/3	1/2	3/9	6/7	5/10	2/10	10/R	10/12	5/R	4/6	7/12	12/R		100
8/R	6/R	W/W	5/7	8/9	6/14	3/4	6/12	5/6	7/R	8/13	8/R	3/15		88
2/R	5/R	W/W	12/14	11/12	11/NC	6/7	R/R	7/14	4/15	R/R	4/R	7/13		66
10/12	R/R	W/W	4/11	5/16	3/12	5/8	5/9	8/16	3/R	7/10	5/DQ	8/R		38
4/9	7/8	W/W	10/R	13/15	7/9	R/R	7/8	13/15	9/R	9/R	6/9	5/9		34
13/14	4/9	W/W	8/R	10/14	8/15	14/R	11/R	9/11	6/10	11/12	10/11	6/10		20
15/16	10/R	3/4	13/15	17/R	16/17	12/13	14/15	17/20	8/11	15/R	13/15	11/R		11
17/18	11/R	5/6	R/R	18/19	13/18	R/R	13/R	18/19	12/13	14/R	14/16	14/16		7

FORMULA 1 RECORDS

GRAND PRIX CHRONOLOGY

1950 The very first FIA World Championship for cars with 1.5-litre supercharged or 4.5-litre normally-aspirated engines. Indianapolis 500 is included as a round, but no F1 teams attend.

1951 BRM and Girling introduce disc brakes.

1952 Championship is run for cars with 2-litre normally aspirated engines, that's to say F2 cars.

1954 Maximum engine capacity increased to 2.5-litres. Supercharged engines are re-admitted if less than 750cc. Minimum race duration of 500km or three hours.

1958 Minimum race duration of 300km or two hours imposed. Vanwall wins first constructors' cup. Moss gets first rear-engined win.

1960 Final win for a rear-engined car. Last year for Indianapolis 500 in championship.

1961 Maximum engine capacity is 1.5-litre normally-aspirated, with a weight limit of 450kg. Commercial fuel becomes mandatory in place of Avgas. Supercharged engines are banned.

1962 Monocoque Lotus revolutionizes F1.

1966 Debut season for 3-litre formula with a 500kg weight limit.

1967 Ford Cosworth DFV, the most successful F1 engine ever, wins on debut. Aerodynamic wings seen for first time above engine.

1968 Wings put on supports to become spoilers, both above front and rear axles. Gold Leaf Lotus heralds age of sponsorship.

1969 Onboard fire extinguishers and roll-hoops made mandatory. Four-wheel drive is toyed with. Moveable aerodynamic devices are banned mid-year.

1970 Bag fuel tanks made mandatory. Minimum weight is 530kg.

1971 Slick tyres are introduced. Lotus tries a gas turbine engine.

1972 Engines with more than 12 cylinders are banned.

1973 Maximum fuel tank size is 250 litres, minimum weight is 575kg. Breathable air driver safety system introduced.

1974 Rear wing overhang limited to 1m behind rear axle.

1975 Hesketh and Hill try carbonfibre aerodynamic parts.

1976 Rear wing overhang cut back to 80cm. Tall air boxes banned from Spanish GP. McLaren introduces Kevlar and Nomex in its structure.

1977 Renault's RS01 brings 1.5-litre turbo engines to F1. Lotus introduces ground effect.

1978 Brabham's "fan car" wins Swedish GP and is banned. Tyrrell tests active suspension.

1979 Renault's Jean-Pierre Jabouille scores first turbo win.

1980 Brabham introduces carbon brake discs.

1981 McLaren's carbonfibre monocoque revolutionizes F1 car construction. Sliding skirts are banned and 6cm ground clearance enforced. Minimum weight now 585kg.

1982 Survival cells made mandatory. Brabham introduces refuelling pit stops.

1983 Brabham's Nelson Piquet and BMW become first turbo world champions. Ground effect is banned and flat bottoms introduced. Michele Alboreto scores last DFV win. Minimum weight cut to 540kg.

1984 Fuel tank cut to 220 litres. Mid-race refuelling banned.

1985 Crash-tested nose box becomes mandatory.

1986 Normally-aspirated engines are banned as F1 goes all-turbo, with maximum fuel capacity of 195 litres.

1987 3.5-litre normally-aspirated engines introduced alongside turbos, with 500kg minimum weight limit against turbos' 540kg. Turbos limited to 4 bar boost.

1988 Pop-off boost limited to 2.5 bar and fuel allowance for turbo cars cut to 150 litres. Drivers' feet must be behind front axle.

1989 Turbo engines banned and fuel tank capacity cut to 150 litres for normally-aspirated engines. Ferrari introduces semi-automatic gearboxes.

1992 Top teams use driver aids such as active suspension, traction control and anti-lock brakes.

1994 Driver aids outlawed. Refuelling pit stops permitted again. Ayrton Senna and Roland Ratzenberger die at Imola, triggering rule changes and introducing more chicanes to slow cars at the faster circuits.

1995 Engine capacity cut. Wing size reduced to cut downforce.

1996 Higher cockpit-side protection made mandatory. Aerodynamic suspension parts banned.

1998 Chassis made narrower. Grooved tyres introduced and slicks banned in order to slow the cars.

1999 Extra groove is added to front and rear tyres.

2001 Traction control is permitted from Spanish GP onwards.

2002 Ferrari dominance spurs FIA to seek solution to make racing more entertaining for 2003.

2003 New 10-8-6-5-4-3-2-1 points system introduced, along with one-at-a-time qualifying procedure and the banning of refuelling between qualifying and the start of the race.

2004 Launch control and fully automatic gearboxes are outlawed. Engines must last an entire grand prix meeting or the driver will be demoted 10 places on the grid.

2005 Engines to last two GPs or penalties incurred if changed. Refuelling only at pit stops, as tyres must last all race.

DRIVERS

1950	GIUSEPPE FARINA **Alfa Romeo**
1951	JUAN MANUEL FANGIO **Alfa Romeo**
1952	ALBERTO ASCARI **Ferrari**
1953	ALBERTO ASCARI **Ferrari**
1954	JUAN MANUEL FANGIO **Maserati & Mercedes**
1955	JUAN MANUEL FANGIO **Mercedes**
1956	JUAN MANUEL FANGIO **Ferrari**
1957	JUAN MANUEL FANGIO **Maserati**
1958	MIKE HAWTHORN **Ferrari**
1959	JACK BRABHAM **Cooper**
1960	JACK BRABHAM **Cooper**
1961	PHIL HILL **Ferrari**
1962	GRAHAM HILL **BRM**
1963	JIM CLARK **Lotus**
1964	JOHN SURTEES **Ferrari**
1965	JIM CLARK **Lotus**
1966	JACK BRABHAM **Brabham**
1967	DENNY HULME **Brabham**
1968	GRAHAM HILL **Lotus**
1969	JACKIE STEWART **Matra**
1970	JOCHEN RINDT **Lotus**
1971	JACKIE STEWART **Tyrrell**
1972	EMERSON FITTIPALDI **Lotus**
1973	JACKIE STEWART **Tyrrell**
1974	EMERSON FITTIPALDI **McLaren**
1975	NIKI LAUDA **Ferrari**
1976	JAMES HUNT **McLaren**
1977	NIKI LAUDA **Ferrari**
1978	MARIO ANDRETTI **Lotus**
1979	JODY SCHECKTER **Ferrari**
1980	ALAN JONES **Williams**
1981	NELSON PIQUET **Brabham**
1982	KEKE ROSBERG **Williams**
1983	NELSON PIQUET **Brabham**
1984	NIKI LAUDA **McLaren**
1985	ALAIN PROST **McLaren**
1986	ALAIN PROST **McLaren**
1987	NELSON PIQUET **Williams**
1988	AYRTON SENNA **McLaren**
1989	ALAIN PROST **McLaren**
1990	AYRTON SENNA **McLaren**
1991	AYRTON SENNA **McLaren**
1992	NIGEL MANSELL **Williams**
1993	ALAIN PROST **Williams**
1994	MICHAEL SCHUMACHER **Benetton**
1995	MICHAEL SCHUMACHER **Benetton**
1996	DAMON HILL **Williams**
1997	JACQUES VILLENEUVE **Williams**
1998	MIKA HAKKINEN **McLaren**
1999	MIKA HAKKINEN **McLaren**
2000	MICHAEL SCHUMACHER **Ferrari**
2001	MICHAEL SCHUMACHER **Ferrari**
2002	MICHAEL SCHUMACHER **Ferrari**
2003	MICHAEL SCHUMACHER **Ferrari**
2004	MICHAEL SCHUMACHER **Ferrari**
2005	FERNANDO ALONSO **Renault**

CONSTRUCTORS

1958	VANWALL
1959	COOPER-CLIMAX
1960	COOPER-CLIMAX
1961	FERRARI
1962	BRM
1963	LOTUS-CLIMAX
1964	FERRARI
1965	LOTUS-CLIMAX
1966	BRABHAM-REPCO
1967	BRABHAM-REPCO
1968	LOTUS-FORD DFV
1969	MATRA-FORD DFV
1970	LOTUS-FORD DFV
1971	TYRRELL-FORD DFV
1972	LOTUS-FORD DFV
1973	LOTUS-FORD DFV
1974	MCLAREN-FORD DFV
1975	FERRARI
1976	FERRARI
1977	FERRARI
1978	LOTUS-FORD DFV
1979	FERRARI
1980	WILLIAMS-FORD DFV
1981	WILLIAMS-FORD DFV
1982	FERRARI
1983	FERRARI
1984	MCLAREN-TAG
1985	MCLAREN-TAG
1986	WILLIAMS-HONDA
1987	WILLIAMS-HONDA
1988	MCLAREN-HONDA
1989	MCLAREN-HONDA
1990	MCLAREN-HONDA
1991	MCLAREN-HONDA
1992	WILLIAMS-RENAULT
1993	WILLIAMS-RENAULT
1994	WILLIAMS-RENAULT
1995	BENETTON-RENAULT
1996	WILLIAMS-RENAULT
1997	WILLIAMS-RENAULT
1998	MCLAREN-MERCEDES
1999	FERRARI
2000	FERRARI
2001	FERRARI
2002	FERRARI
2003	FERRARI
2004	FERRARI
2005	RENAULT

Vanwall was helped to the first constructors' title by Tony Brooks (above) and Stirling Moss

MOST GRAND PRIX STARTS

DRIVERS

256	Riccardo Patrese	(ITA)	162	Mika Hakkinen	(FIN)	143	Giancarlo Fisichella	(ITA)
232	Michael Schumacher	(GER)		Johnny Herbert	(GBR)	135	Jean-Pierre Jarier	(FRA)
217	Rubens Barrichello	(BRA)	161	Ayrton Senna	(BRA)	132	Eddie Cheever	(USA)
210	Gerhard Berger	(AUT)	159	Heinz-Harald Frentzen	(GER)		Clay Regazzoni	(SUI)
208	Andrea de Cesaris	(ITA)	158	Martin Brundle	(GBR)	128	Mario Andretti	(USA)
204	Nelson Piquet	(BRA)		Olivier Panis	(FRA)	126	Jack Brabham	(AUS)
201	Jean Alesi	(FRA)	153	Jacques Villeneuve	(CDN)	123	Ronnie Peterson	(SWE)
199	Alain Prost	(FRA)	152	John Watson	(GBR)	119	Pierluigi Martini	(ITA)
194	Michele Alboreto	(ITA)	149	Rene Arnoux	(FRA)	116	Damon Hill	(GBR)
	David Coulthard	(GBR)		Jarno Trulli	(ITA)		Jacky Ickx	(BEL)
187	Nigel Mansell	(GBR)	147	Eddie Irvine	(GBR)		Alan Jones	(AUS)
176	Graham Hill	(GBR)		Derek Warwick	(GBR)	114	Keke Rosberg	(FIN)
175	Jacques Laffite	(FRA)	146	Carlos Reutemann	(ARG)		Patrick Tambay	(FRA)
171	Niki Lauda	(AUT)	145	Ralf Schumacher	(GER)	112	Denny Hulme	(NZL)
163	Thierry Boutsen	(BEL)	144	Emerson Fittipaldi	(BRA)		Jody Scheckter	(RSA)

CONSTRUCTORS

723	Ferrari	394	Brabham	217	Sauber
596	McLaren	383	Arrows	197	BRM
515	Williams	341	Minardi	193	Renault
490	Lotus	317	Benetton	153	Red Bull
418	Tyrrell	250	Jordan	132	Osella
409	Prost	230	March	129	Cooper

MOST GRAND PRIX WINS

DRIVERS

84	Michael Schumacher	(GER)		Carlos Reutemann	(ARG)		Gilles Villeneuve	(CDN)
51	Alain Prost	(FRA)	11	Jacques Villeneuve	(CDN)			
41	Ayrton Senna	(BRA)	10	Gerhard Berger	(AUT)			
31	Nigel Mansell	(GBR)		James Hunt	(GBR)			
27	Jackie Stewart	(GBR)		Ronnie Peterson	(SWE)			
25	Jim Clark	(GBR)		Jody Scheckter	(RSA)			
	Niki Lauda	(AUT)	9	Rubens Barrichello	(BRA)			
24	Juan Manuel Fangio	(ARG)		Kimi Raikkonen	(FIN)			
23	Nelson Piquet	(BRA)	8	Fernando Alonso	(SPA)			
22	Damon Hill	(GBR)		Denny Hulme	(NZL)			
20	Mika Hakkinen	(FIN)		Jacky Ickx	(BEL)			
16	Stirling Moss	(GBR)	7	Rene Arnoux	(FRA)			
14	Jack Brabham	(AUS)		Juan Pablo Montoya	(COL)			
	Emerson Fittipaldi	(BRA)	6	Tony Brooks	(GBR)			
	Graham Hill	(GBR)		Jacques Laffite	(FRA)			
13	Alberto Ascari	(ITA)		Riccardo Patrese	(FRA)			
	David Coulthard	(GBR)		Jochen Rindt	(AUT)			
12	Mario Andretti	(USA)		Ralf Schumacher	(GER)			
	Alan Jones	(AUS)		John Surtees	(GBR)			

CONSTRUCTORS

183	Ferrari	16	Cooper		Wolf
148	McLaren	10	Alfa Romeo	2	Honda
112	Williams	9	Ligier	1	Eagle
79	Lotus		Maserati		Hesketh
35	Brabham		Matra		Penske
27	Benetton		Mercedes		Porsche
25	Renault		Vanwall		Shadow
23	Tyrrell	4	Jordan		Stewart
17	BRM	3	March		

MOST GRAND PRIX WINS IN ONE SEASON

DRIVERS

13	Michael Schumacher	(GER)	2004
11	Michael Schumacher	(GER)	2002
9	Nigel Mansell	(GBR)	1992
	Michael Schumacher	(GER)	1995
	Michael Schumacher	(GER)	2000
	Michael Schumacher	(GER)	2001
8	Mika Hakkinen	(FIN)	1998
	Damon Hill	(GBR)	1996
	Michael Schumacher	(GER)	1994
	Ayrton Senna	(BRA)	1988
7	Fernando Alonso	(SPA)	2005
	Jim Clark	(GBR)	1963
	Alain Prost	(FRA)	1984
	Alain Prost	(FRA)	1988
	Alain Prost	(FRA)	1993
	Kimi Raikkonen	(FIN)	2005
	Ayrton Senna	(BRA)	1991
	Jacques Villeneuve	(CDN)	1997
6	Mario Andretti	(USA)	1978
	Alberto Ascari	(ITA)	1952
	Jim Clark	(GBR)	1965
	Juan Manuel Fangio	(ARG)	1954
	Damon Hill	(GBR)	1994
	James Hunt	(GBR)	1976
	Nigel Mansell	(GBR)	1987
	Michael Schumacher	(GER)	1998
	Michael Schumacher	(GER)	2003
	Ayrton Senna	(BRA)	1989
	Ayrton Senna	(BRA)	1990

CONSTRUCTORS

15	Ferrari	2004
	Ferrari	2002
	McLaren	1988
12	McLaren	1984
	Williams	1996
11	Benetton	1995
10	Ferrari	2000
	McLaren	2005
	McLaren	1989
	Williams	1992
	Williams	1993
9	Ferrari	2001
	McLaren	1998
	Williams	1986
	Williams	1987
8	Benetton	1994
	Ferrari	2003
	Lotus	1978
	McLaren	1991
	Renault	2005
	Williams	1997
7	Ferrari	1952
	Ferrari	1953
	Lotus	1963
	Lotus	1973
	McLaren	1999
	McLaren	2000
	Tyrrell	1971
	Williams	1991
	Williams	1994
6	Alfa Romeo	1950
	Alfa Romeo	1951
	Cooper	1960
	Ferrari	1975
	Ferrari	1976
	Ferrari	1979
	Ferrari	1990
	Ferrari	1996
	Ferrari	1998
	Ferrari	1999
	Lotus	1965
	Lotus	1970
	Matra	1969
	McLaren	1976
	McLaren	1985
	McLaren	1990
	Vanwall	1958
	Williams	1980

Michael Schumacher shows his delight after scoring his first Formula One win in the 1992 Belgian GP

MOST CONSECUTIVE GRAND PRIX WINS

DRIVERS

9	Alberto Ascari	(ITA) 1952/53		Michael Schumacher	(GER) 2004		Jochen Rindt	(AUT) 1970
7	Michael Schumacher	(GER) 2004	**4**	Jack Brabham	(AUS) 1966		Michael Schumacher	(GER) 1994
6	Michael Schumacher	(GER) 2000/01		Jim Clark	(GBR) 1963		Michael Schumacher	(GER) 2002
5	Jack Brabham	(AUS) 1960		Juan Manuel Fangio	(ARG) 1953/54		Ayrton Senna	(BRA) 1988
	Jim Clark	(GBR) 1965		Damon Hill	(GBR) 1995/96		Ayrton Senna	(BRA) 1991
	Nigel Mansell	(GBR) 1992		Alain Prost	(FRA) 1993			

GRAND PRIX STARTS WITHOUT A WIN

DRIVERS

208	Andrea de Cesaris	(ITA)	**111**	Mika Salo	(FIN)	**97**	Chris Amon	(NZL)
158	Martin Bundle	(GBR)	**109**	Philippe Alliot	(FRA)	**95**	Ukyo Katayama	(JAP)
147	Derek Warwick	(GBR)	**107**	Jos Verstappen	(NED)	**93**	Ivan Capelli	(ITA)
135	Jean-Pierre Jarier	(FRA)	**101**	Jenson Button	(GBR)	**84**	Jonathan Palmer	(GBR)
132	Eddie Cheever	(USA)	**99**	Pedro Diniz	(BRA)	**82**	Marc Surer	(SUI)
119	Pierluigi Martini	(ITA)		Nick Heidfeld	(GER)	**79**	Stefan Johansson	(SWE)

Andrea de Cesaris never won, but his drive for Jordan in the 1991 Belgian Grand Prix looked like giving him second place until his engine failed

MOST POLE POSITIONS

DRIVERS

65	Ayrton Senna	(BRA)	18	Mario Andretti	(USA)		Jacky Ickx	(BEL)
64	Michael Schumacher	(GER)		Rene Arnoux	(FRA)		Juan Pablo Montoya	(COL)
33	Jim Clark	(GBR)	17	Jackie Stewart	(GBR)		Jacques Villeneuve	(CDN)
	Alain Prost	(FRA)	16	Stirling Moss	(GBR)	12	Gerhard Berger	(AUT)
32	Nigel Mansell	(GBR)	14	Alberto Ascari	(ITA)		David Coulthard	(GBR)
29	Juan Manuel Fangio	(ARG)		James Hunt	(GBR)	10	Jochen Rindt	(AUT)
26	Mika Hakkinen	(FIN)		Ronnie Peterson	(SWE)	9	Fernando Alonso	(SPA)
24	Niki Lauda	(AUT)	13	Rubens Barrichello	(BRA)	8	Riccardo Patrese	(ITA)
	Nelson Piquet	(BRA)		Jack Brabham	(AUS)		Kimi Raikkonen	(FIN)
20	Damon Hill	(GBR)		Graham Hill	(GBR)		John Surtees	(GBR)

CONSTRUCTORS

179	Ferrari	12	Alfa Romeo	4	Matra		
125	Williams	11	BRM	3	Shadow		
122	McLaren		Cooper	2	BAR		
107	Lotus	10	Maserati		Jordan		
43	Renault	9	Prost		Lancia		
39	Brabham	8	Mercedes		Toyota		
16	Benetton	7	Vanwall	1	Jaguar		
14	Tyrrell	5	March				

MOST GRAND POLE POSITIONS IN ONE SEASON

DRIVERS

14	Nigel Mansell	(GBR) 1992		Damon Hill	(GBR) 1996		Michael Schumacher	(GER) 2004	
13	Alain Prost	(FRA) 1993		Niki Lauda	(AUT) 1974		Ayrton Senna	(BRA) 1986	
	Ayrton Senna	(BRA) 1988		Niki Lauda	(AUT) 1975		Ayrton Senna	(BRA) 1991	
	Ayrton Senna	(BRA)1989		Ronnie Peterson	(SWE) 1973	7	Mario Andretti	(USA) 1977	
11	Mika Hakkinen	(FIN) 1999		Nelson Piquet	(BRA) 1984		Jim Clark	(GBR) 1963	
	Michael Schumacher	(GER) 2001		Michael Schumacher	(GER) 2000		Damon Hill	(GBR) 1995	
10	Ayrton Senna	(BRA) 1990	8	Mario Andretti	(USA) 1978		Juan Pablo Montoya	(COL) 2002	
	Jacques Villeneuve	(CDN) 1997		James Hunt	(GBR) 1976		Michael Schumacher	(GER) 2002	
9	Mika Hakkinen	(FIN) 1998		Nigel Mansell	(GBR) 1987		Ayrton Senna	(BRA) 1985	

CONSTRUCTORS

15	McLaren	1988	11	Ferrari	2001		
	McLaren	1989		McLaren	1999		
	Williams	1992		Williams	1997		
	Williams	1993	10	Ferrari	1974		
12	Ferrari	2004		Ferrari	2000		
	Lotus	1978		Ferrari	2002		
	McLaren	1990		Lotus	1973		
	McLaren	1998		McLaren	1991		
	Williams	1987		Renault	1982		
	Williams	1995	9	Brabham	1984		
	Williams	1996		Ferrari	1975		

Nigel Mansell was almost unstoppable in 1992, claiming pole for 14 of the 16 GPs

MOST FASTEST LAPS

DRIVERS

68	Michael Schumacher	(GER)	19	Damon Hill	(GBR)	13	Alberto Ascari	(ITA)
41	Alain Prost	(FRA)		Stirling Moss	(GBR)		Alan Jones	(AUS)
30	Nigel Mansell	(GBR)		Ayrton Senna	(BRA)		Riccardo Patrese	(ITA)
28	Jim Clark	(GBR)	18	David Coulthard	(GBR)	12	Rene Arnoux	(FRA)
25	Mika Hakkinen	(FIN)	16	Kimi Raikkonen	(FIN)		Jack Brabham	(AUS)
24	Niki Lauda	(AUT)	15	Rubens Barrichello	(BRA)		Juan Pablo Montoya	(COL)
23	Juan Manuel Fangio	(ARG)		Clay Regazzoni	(SUI)	11	John Surtees	(GBR)
	Nelson Piquet	(BRA)		Jackie Stewart	(GBR)			
21	Gerhard Berger	(AUT)	14	Jacky Ickx	(BEL)			

CONSTRUCTORS

183	Ferrari	22	Renault	12	Matra
128	Williams	20	Tyrrell	11	Prost
126	McLaren	15	BRM	9	Mercedes
71	Lotus		Maserati	7	March
40	Brabham	14	Alfa Romeo	6	Vanwall
35	Benetton	13	Cooper		

MOST POINTS (THIS FIGURE IS GROSS TALLY, IE. INCLUDING SCORES THAT WERE LATER DROPPED)

DRIVERS

1248	Michael Schumacher	(GER)	385	Gerhard Berger	(AUT)		Kimi Raikkonen	(FIN)
798.5	Alain Prost	(FRA)	360	Damon Hill	(GBR)	277.5	Juan Manuel Fangio	(ARG)
614	Ayrton Senna	(BRA)		Jackie Stewart	(GBR)	274	Jim Clark	(GBR)
499	David Coulthard	(GBR)	310	Carlos Reutemann	(ARG)	261	Jack Brabham	(AUS)
489	Rubens Barrichello	(BRA)	304	Ralf Schumacher	(GER)	255	Jody Scheckter	(RSA)
485.5	Nelson Piquet	(BRA)	289	Graham Hill	(GBR)	248	Denny Hulme	(NZL)
482	Nigel Mansell	(GBR)	281	Emerson Fittipaldi	(BRA)	242	Jean Alesi	(FRA)
420.5	Niki Lauda	(AUT)		Juan Pablo Montoya	(COL)			
420	Mika Hakkinen	(FIN)		Riccardo Patrese	(ITA)			

Alain Prost and McLaren were a mighty combination from 1984 (shown) to 1999, when Prost won the world championship four times

CONSTRUCTORS

3444.5	Ferrari	439	BRM	155	Matra
2940.5	McLaren	424	Prost	122	Red Bull
2501.5	Williams	333	Cooper	115	Toyota
1352	Lotus	286	Jordan	79	Wolf
877.5	Benetton	220	BAR	67.5	Shadow
854	Brabham	196	Sauber	57	Vanwall
719	Renault	171.5	March	54	Surtees
617	Tyrrell	167	Arrows		

MOST DRIVERS' TITLES

DRIVERS

7	Michael Schumacher	(GER)		Emerson Fittipaldi	(BRA)		James Hunt	(GBR)
5	Juan Manuel Fangio	(ARG)		Mika Hakkinen	(FIN)		Alan Jones	(AUS)
4	Alain Prost	(FRA)		Graham Hill	(GBR)		Nigel Mansell	(GBR)
3	Jack Brabham	(AUS)	1	Fernando Alonso	(SPA)		Jochen Rindt	(AUT)
	Niki Lauda	(AUT)		Mario Andretti	(USA)		Keke Rosberg	(FIN)
	Nelson Piquet	(BRA)		Giuseppe Farina	(ITA)		Jody Scheckter	(ZA)
	Ayrton Senna	(BRA)		Mike Hawthorn	(GBR)		John Surtees	(GBR)
	Jackie Stewart	(GBR)		Damon Hill	GBR)		Jacques Villeneuve	(CDN)
2	Alberto Ascari	(ITA)		Phil Hill	(USA)			
	Jim Clark	(GBR)		Denis Hulme	(NZL)			

Before Michael Schumacher took over in the 21st century, Juan Manuel Fangio (shown in the 1955 German GP) was the most titled driver

MOST CONTRUCTORS' TITLES

CONSTRUCTORS

14	Ferrari	2	Brabham		Matra
9	Williams		Cooper		Renault
8	McLaren	1	Benetton		Tyrrell
7	Lotus		BRM		Vanwall

DRIVER		TEAM	R1	R2	R3	R4	R5	R6
1	FERNANDO ALONSO	RENAULT	10	8	10	8	8	10
2	GIANCARLO FISICHELLA	RENAULT	R̄	10	5/4	1	3	6
3	KIMI RAIKKONEN	McLAREN	6	R̄	8	4	5	4
4	JUAN PABLO MONTOYA	McLAREN	4	5	R E/F	6	R E/F	R̄
5	MICHAEL SCHUMACHER	FERRARI	8	3	R	10	10	8
6	FELIPE MASSA	FERRARI	–	4	R	5	6	5
7	RALF SCHUMACHER	TOYOTA	–	1	6	–	R	R̄
8	JARNO TRULLI	TOYOTA	–	–	R	R̄	–	–
9	MARK WEBBER	WILLIAMS	3	R E/F	R̄	3	R̄	–
10	NICO ROSBERG	WILLIAMS	2	R E/F	R	–	2	–
11	RUBENS BARRICHELLO	HONDA RACING	–	–	7/3	–	4	2
12	JENSON BUTTON	HONDA RACING	5	6	4	2	R̄	3
13	DAVID COULTHARD	RED BULL RACING	–	R E/F	1	R̄	R̄	–
14	CHRISTIAN KLIEN	RED BULL RACING	1	R	R	R	R	–
15	NICK HEIDFELD	BMW SAUBER	–	E/F	5	–	–	1
16	JACQUES VILLENEUVE	BMW SAUBER	R	2	3	–	1	–
17	TIAGO MONTEIRO	MF1 RACING	–	–	R	–	–	–
18	CHRISTIJAN ALBERS	MF1 RACING	–	–	–	R̄	–	R̄
19	VITANTONIO LIUZZI	SCUDERIA TORO ROSSO	–	–	R̄	–	R̄	–
20	SCOTT SPEED	SCUDERIA TORO ROSSO *	–	R	–	–	–	R
21	TAKUMA SATO	SUPER AGURI RACING	–	–	–	R̄	R̄	–
22	SAKON YAMAMOTO	SUPER AGURI RACING						

de la Rosa   McLAREN

Yuji. IDE   R   R   –   R

WILLIAMS

SCORING AND GP ROUND ORDER

SCORING SYSTEM: 10, 8, 6, 5, 4, 3, 2, 1 POINTS FOR THE FIRST EIGHT FINISHERS IN EACH GRAND PRIX

ROUND 1 12 March BAHRAIN GP	**ROUND 2** 19 March MALAYSIAN GP	**ROUND 3** 2 April AUSTRALIAN GP	**ROUND 4** 23 April SAN MARINO GP
ROUND 5 7 May EUROPEAN GP	**ROUND 6** 14 May SPANISH GP	**ROUND 7** 28 May MONACO GP	**ROUND 8** 11 June BRITISH GP
ROUND 9 25 June CANADIAN GP	**ROUND 10** 2 July UNITED STATES GP	**ROUND 11** 16 July FRENCH GP	**ROUND 12** 30 July GERMAN GP
ROUND 13 6 August HUNGARIAN GP	**ROUND 14** 27 August TURKISH GP	**ROUND 15** 10 September ITALIAN GP	**ROUND 16** 17 September BELGIAN GP
ROUND 17 1 October CHINESE GP	**ROUND 18** 8 October JAPANESE GP	**ROUND 19** 22 October BRAZILIAN GP	

R7	R8	R9	R10	R11	R12	R13	R14	R15	R16	R17	R18	R19		TOTAL POINTS
10	10	10	4	8	4	R	8	R	8	10	8	8		134
3	5	5	6	3	3	R	3	5	6	6	3			72
E/F R	6	6	R	4	6		R	8	R	4	4	4		65 / 80
8	3	R	R		5									
4	8	8	10	10	10	1	6	10	10	R 10	5	5		121
—	4	4	8	6	8	2	10	1	R	8	10	10		80
1	R	R	R	5		3	2	—	R	2	R			20
R	—	3	5	R	2	—		2	R	3	R	R		15
R	R		R	R	R	R		—	1	R	R	R		7
R	—	R	—	—	R	R	R	R	—	—	R	R		4
5	F	R	3	R	R	5	1	3	3	—	2	3		30
—	R	—	R	R	5	10	5	4	5	5	6	6		56
6	—	1	2	—	4	4	—	—	—	R	R	R		14
R	—	—	R	—	R	R	—	—	—	—	—	—		2
2	2	2	R	1	R	6	—	1	2	—	R	R		23
—	1	R	R	—	R									7
—	—	—	R	R	—	R		R	R		—			
—	—	R	R		—		R	—	—	R	F			
—	F	—	1	—	R	R	R	—	—	—	—			
—	R	—	R		—		—	—	R	—				
R	—	—	R	R	R		—	—	—	—				
					R		R	R	—	—	—			
			2	R	R	8	4	R	4	—	—			19

PICTURE CREDITS

The publishers would like to thank the following sources for their kind permission to reproduce the pictures in this book. The page numbers for each of the photographs are listed below, giving the page on which they appear in the book. Location indicator: t-top, b-bottom.

Crash dot net Ltd: 48-49, 76-77, 89.
Empics: /AP/Chuck Robinson: 94; /AP/Dusan Vranic: 87; /James Bearne: 79; /Steve Etherington: 121-2; John Marsh: 6-7; /Ng Han Guan/AP: 115; /Ruben Sprich/AP: 53 t.
Getty Images: /Robert Cianflone: 41t; /Paul Gilham: 41b; /Clive Mason 45 b; /Mark Thompson: 93.
LAT Photographic: 11, 15, 19, 21, 27, 37, 39t, 46-47, 53b, 99, 119, 122, 123, 124, 125; /Batchelor: 43 t; /Lorenzo Bellanca: 14, 23, 29, 38, 78, 90, 100, 103, 108, 111; /Jeff Bloxham: 36, 43 b; /Charles Coates: 2-3, 13, 84, 95, 98, 101, 114; /Michael Cooper: 12, 17, 24, 28, 85, 88, 102, 107, 74-75; /Glenn Dunbar: 40; /Steve Etherington: 4, 8-9, 16, 18, 20, 22, 25, 26, 31, 32, 39b, 42, 48-49, 81, 82, 86, 97, 104, 105, 106, 111, 114, 128; /Yasushi Ishihara: 52; /Lawrence: 35; /Peter Spinney: 10, 33, 34, 109; /Steven Tee: 45 t, 54-55, 80, 91, 92, 96, 112.
Renault Website: 83.

Graphic Illustrations: **Graphic News**

Every effort has been made to acknowledge correctly and contact the source and/or copyright holder of each picture and Carlton Books Limited apologises for any unintentional errors or omissions, which will be corrected in future editions of this book.